OUR
TIME
IS
NOW

OUR
TIME
IS
NOW

Power, Purpose, and the Fight for
a Fair America

STACEY ABRAMS

HENRY HOLT AND COMPANY
NEW YORK

Henry Holt and Company
Publishers since 1866
120 Broadway
New York, NY 10271
www.henryholt.com

Distributed in Canada by Raincoast Book Distribution Limited

Library of Congress Cataloging-in-Publication Data

Names: Abrams, Stacey, author.
Title: Our time is now : power, purpose, and the fight for a fair America /
Stacey Abrams.
Description: First edition. | New York : Henry Holt and Company, 2020. |
Includes bibliographical references and index.
Identifiers: LCCN 2020005940 (print) | LCCN 2020005941 (ebook) |
ISBN 9781250257703 (hardcover) | ISBN 9781250257697 (ebook)
Subjects: LCSH: Elections—Corrupt practices—United States. | Voting—
Corrupt practices—United States. | Voter registration—Corrupt
practices—United States. | Racism—Political aspects—United States. |
Political participation—Social aspects—United States. | Presidents—
United States—Election, 2020. | Abrams, Stacey.
Classification: LCC JK1994 .A37 2020 (print) | LCC JK1994 (ebook) |
DDC 324.60973—dc23
LC record available at https://lccn.loc.gov/2020005940
LC ebook record available at https://lccn.loc.gov/2020005941

Our books may be purchased in bulk for promotional,
educational, or business use. Please contact your local
bookseller or the Macmillan Corporate and Premium Sales
Department at (800) 221-7945, extension 5442, or by email at
MacmillanSpecialMarkets@macmillan.com.

First Edition 2020

Designed by Ellen Cipriano

Printed in the United States of America

1 3 5 7 9 10 8 6 4 2

To my grandparents, Wilter and Walter Abrams, Lillie Bell and James Hall, who gave me a legacy; to my parents, Robert and Carolyn, who gave me life; to my siblings, Andrea, Leslie, Richard, Walter, and Jeanine, who keep me grounded, and their spouses, Brandon, Nakia, and Jimmie, who stand with me; and to my nephews and nieces, Jorden, Faith, Cameron, Riyan, Ayren, and Devin, who give me hope.

We will stay and stand up for what belongs to us as American citizens, because they can't say that we haven't had patience.

—FANNIE LOU HAMER

Contents

Introduction

Who Is Stealing America's Future?

In January 2019, my grandmother passed away. Wilter Abrams, known as Bill to family and friends, was a formidable woman. She gave birth to six children in a span of four years—two daughters and then two sets of twin boys, born in 1946, 1948, 1949, and 1950. She and my grandfather, Walter Abrams or Jim, raised five of their kids into adulthood in the crippling poverty of Mississippi and segregation, losing my father's twin brother in his infancy. Neither of my grandparents had unexpressed opinions, and they brought their children up to also hold strong convictions. Both of my grandparents were cooks at the local state university, serving students at a school their own children could not attend.

My grandfather, a slender bantam of a man, served in World War II as a navy cook and fought as a boxer during his tour. When he got drafted into the Korean War, he did his duty again, knowing the entire time that he was returning to the segregation and racial venom of the Deep South. Bitterness fought with practicality as he returned twice to a country that denied him basic civil rights. In 2011, in the weeks before he passed, I left the special legislative session where we were drawing new political districts. I shared my frustration about the ways black and brown voters were being stripped of power. A man of colorful language, he basically warned me not to let the bastards get me down.

Just before the 2018 election, I traveled to my parents' home in Hattiesburg, Mississippi. The detour from the campaign trail was unusual, but both a fundraising opportunity and a deep call to see my family brought me there. One evening, I went to the master bedroom my parents had ceded to my grandmother when she could no longer live alone. She sat in her favorite recliner, watching the news on MSNBC, cell phone in her lap. I perched on the edge of her bed. Grandma turned down the volume and she asked about my election. By then, national attention had been fixed on the voter suppression allegations against Brian Kemp and on the tight numbers in our contest. I explained the latest developments to her and vented about the worries I had carried from Georgia.

When I finished, she patted my hand. Then she told me about the first time she'd ever voted. Like my grandfather, she had been incensed at the strictures of Jim Crow since childhood. Smart and quick, she had seen lesser minds advance because of racial discrimination. But she understood how the systems worked, and when her children became agitators in the civil rights movement, she warily supported their activism. Both she and my grandfather had been quieter in the movement because they understood the consequences if they got caught. Putting food on the table and keeping their house kept both of them primarily on the sidelines. But Grandma had faced the menacing growls of the massive dogs used to control protesting crowds, and she had been violently sprayed by the water hoses used to remind blacks of their place. She'd gathered up the bail money to free her teenage son from jail when he got arrested registering voters. At one point, the local police were calling her regularly to interrogate her about the protest actions of her children. By the time the Voting Rights Act passed in 1965, she understood its significance. But she also knew not to expect immediate change, and she was right. Across much of the South, the implementation came very slowly; thus her first real opportunity to vote didn't arrive until 1968.

That night, I listened to her talk and, suddenly, her voice grew tremulous. I worried that I had worn her out. But I quickly realized that the soft trembling came not from exhaustion but from shame. Quietly, she recounted the day of the election, how Granddaddy, his brother L.P., and others got ready to go and cast their first ballots in Mississippi. My dad would still be two years too young to vote, but she had the opportunity. Yet, she told me, she refused to leave her bedroom, where she sat para-lyzed by fear. The laws had changed, but they had changed before. There was the promise of an emancipation that still left her great-grandparents enslaved, and the school desegregation that took nearly a decade to arrive. But the right to vote carried the most significant victory—and she did not believe this promise was real. She explained how my grandfather called for her to meet them at the front door, but she wouldn't budge. Finally, he stormed down the hall and into the shadowed room. Impatiently, he demanded to know what was taking her so long, when history awaited their arrival.

Grandma squeezed my hand as she remembered the explana-tion she gave to her husband: "I'm afraid, Jim. I'm afraid of the dogs and the police. I don't want to vote." She covered my hand, and her eyes held mine. "Stacey, your grandfather got so angry.

He reminded me about your daddy and your aunts and uncles. All those young black children who fought so hard to get these rights. And there I was, afraid to use them. I was ashamed of myself." Instead of cowering in the bedroom, fearing the worst, she followed the example of her children, the call of her conscience. She screwed up her courage, gathered her purse and coat, and told my grandfather she was ready to go. Together, they traveled to the precinct to cast their very first ballots. By her side, she clutched my hand again, the paper-thin skin stretched tight. She leaned in to me and rasped, "I'm so proud of you, Stacey. I know I can't vote for you, but I'm so very proud that my granddaughter is on the ballot and our people can be heard."

When I tell this story, it's not because of my grandmother's pride in my campaign, although that means a lot to me. I use this story as a warning of the fear that even the most stalwart can feel about their exercising the power of the vote. A woman who had braved economic hardship and rabid racism recoiled not at the theft of power but the possibility of taking it. That perversion of democracy continues to play out across our country every day. Voter suppression works its might by first tripping and causing to stumble the unwanted voter, then by convincing those who see the obstacle course to forfeit the race without even starting to run.

A few months ago, my youngest sister, Jeanine, met some friends at a local restaurant for margaritas at the end of a long workweek. One of the women sitting around her table made a point of telling Jeanine that she had voted for me for governor. Jeanine started to thank her for the support, but the young woman wasn't done. She then told my sister she had no intention of voting again. Recounting stories she'd heard about voters who had been sent to the wrong polling place or suddenly had their registration vanish, she said the entire process seemed too suspicious and, in the end, her vote didn't matter. She told Jeanine she saw malicious intent in the treatment of folks who couldn't afford gas for a second round-trip to the polls or had no available time off to fix problems. Disillusionment hit her that much harder because she'd believed that the outcome could be different if she tried.

Across America, would-be voters continue to turn away like my grandmother did, or opt out of the system like my sister's friend. Their fear is again and again made real by stories of neighbors denied provisional ballots or lines that wind around city blocks because voting machines lack electrical cords. By undermining confidence in the system, modern-day suppression has swapped rabid dogs and cops with billy clubs for restrictive voter ID and tangled rules for participation. And those who are most vulnerable to suppression become the most susceptible to passing on that reluctance to others.

THE MECHANISMS OF voter suppression have transformed access to democracy in ways that continue to reshape not only our partisan politics but the way we live our daily lives. In 2020, a poor woman in South Georgia, miles away from a doctor or a hospital, may discover her pregnancy too late to make a choice. If she makes more than $6,000 per year, she is too rich to qualify for Medicaid and too impoverished to afford anything else because the governor refuses to expand the program.[1] If she is black in Georgia, she is three times more likely to die of complications during or after her pregnancy than a white woman in the same position.[2] Her child is more likely to attend underfunded schools, face a return to "tough on crime" policies that target black and brown people, and live in a state with a minimum wage of $5.15 an hour. All because her vote didn't count in 2018.

In 2018, I ran for governor of Georgia, with the goal of building a new coalition of voters to change the electorate. In response, Donald Trump tweeted nasty words at me. Tucker Carlson ranted about me. Breitbart and Fox News called me a liar. My cardinal sin is that I have refused to concede the outcome of the 2018 gubernatorial contest, and I have made a crusade of calling out and defeating voter suppression. I do so as a private citizen, and this reality greets me every day. As I have traveled the country in the months since the election, I typically begin my speeches the same way. "I am not the governor of Georgia," I tell the assembled crowds, to boos and hisses of support. Then I declare with equal conviction a truth I hold deep in my heart: "We won."

In our campaign, we increased turnout to record numbers, engaged voters who never wanted to before, and forced the closest election in Georgia since 1966. As I traveled the state for eighteen months, running for governor, I met skeptical Americans who neither trusted government nor believed their votes counted. But 1.9 million voters showed up for me on Election Day, the highest number of Democratic votes in Georgia history. We won because people trusted, if only for a single election, that it was worth a leap of faith. In political circles, what we accomplished would be dismissed as a moral victory. To that, I say, absolutely. Because I learned long ago that winning doesn't always mean you get the prize. Sometimes you get progress, and that counts. This lesson has been drummed into me for most of my waking life. When it comes to voting in America, I certainly believe.

Civil rights icon Congressman John Lewis often refers to

the right to vote as "almost sacred." As the child of ministers, I understand his hesitation to label a simple, secular act as sacred. Voting is an act of faith. It is profound. In a democracy, it is the ultimate power. Through the vote, the poor can access financial means, the infirm can find health care supports, and the burdened and heavy-laden can receive a measure of relief from a social safety net that serves all. And we are willing to go to war to defend the sacred.

I am not calling for violent revolt here. We've done that twice in our nation's history—to claim our freedom from tyranny and when we fought a civil war to recognize (at least a little) the humanity of blacks held in bondage. Yet, as millions are stripped of their rights, we live out the policy consequences, from lethal pollution running through poor communities to kindergartners practicing active shooter drills taught with nursery rhymes. I question what remedy remains. The questions that confront me every day are how to defend this sacred right and our democracy, and who will do so. As it stands now, on one side, we have a Republican Party in power that believes that it has complied with the letter of the law, having twisted the rules to barely reflect its spirit. On the other hand, the Democrats—the party to which I hold allegiance—talk about full civic engagement but take inconsistent steps to meaningfully expand the electorate and build infrastructure. Embedded in this duality is a fundamental concern: Who is entitled to full citizenship? Based on our national story, and from where we stand now, the list is far shorter than it should be.

Full citizenship rights are the bare minimum one should expect from the government. Yet, for two-thirds of our history, full citizenship was denied to those who built this country from theory to life. African slaves and Chinese workers and Native American environmentalists and Latino gauchos and Irish farmers—and half the population: women.

Over the course of our history, these men and women, these patriots and defenders of liberty, have been denied the most profound currency of citizenship: power. Because, let's be honest, that is the core of this fight. The right to be seen, the right to be heard, the right to direct the course of history are markers of power. In the United States, democracy makes politics one of the key levers to exercising power. So, it should shock none of us that the struggle for dominion over our nation's future and who will participate is simply a battle for American power.

Right now, we are experiencing a massive cultural change, spurred by a demographic transition sweeping the nation. According to the U.S. Census Bureau, people of color comprise nearly 40 percent of the U.S. population; and millennials and Gen Z are the largest combined age cohort in the country. When added to socially moderate and progressive-leaning whites, this population is a New American Majority, and their impact on American life can be felt in nearly every corner. Diversity, which we can admit is an incomplete descriptor of this transformation, has altered how we engage and interact, from the Black Lives Matter movement to marriage equality to Dreamers pressing for action on immigration to women challenging the silence of sexual harassment and assault.

We can also trace a darker, angrier politics to this evolution, including a resurgence of neo-Nazi rhetoric in the open, domestic terrorism against black, Jewish, Latino, and LGBTQ+ groups, a xenophobic response to immigration, rising religious intolerance, and a retrenchment of hyperconservative ideology. Those who see their relative influence shrinking are using every tool possible to limit access to political power. For those who cling to the days of monochromatic American identity, the sweep of change strikes a fundamental fear of not being a part of an America that is multicultural and multicolored. In their minds, the way of life that has sustained them faces an existential crisis, and the response has been vicious, calculated, and effective.

However, they are not using new tools. At its inception, our nation served as a refuge to those whose difference placed them in danger; but the same newcomers stole land from and murdered the original inhabitants, enslaved blacks and stripped them of their humanity, and denied basic rights to women and nonwhites from abroad. This history means we understand what is at stake, how our opponents will try to block change, and, most important, our obligation to realize our destiny. At its core, America's challenge is a question of who we are. Some on the right will dismiss this as absurd identity politics, but identity is politics. I will make a case for that fact here. Choices are based on personal needs—end of story. Yet so much of today's politics require mollifying people terrified of this basic fact. A multiracial, multiethnic, youth-driven majority has grown over the last twenty years; and as a result, we've seen nothing less than a sea change toward progress.

There's a famous psychology test of situational awareness, where the subject is told to count how many times a certain action is performed. The viewer instinctively focuses on the task so intently, he invariably misses a glaring oddity: a person in a gorilla suit crossing through his field of vision. As Americans, we have become accustomed to a fundamental belief in the inevitability that we'll get it right in time: that from bigotry to poverty to the planet's very sustainability, eventually, we will make the right choice. This confidence in the American experiment has welded together a disparate group of folks, driven by conflicting desires and intersectional needs. But our belief in the resilience of our national narrative has been so complete that we've missed the Invisible Gorilla in our existing political system: those at risk of losing power—that powerful minority—have changed the rules of the game. Again.

As the first black woman ever to win a primary for governor for a major political party in American history, one who ran against one of the worst purveyors of voter suppression and xenophobia since George Wallace, I watched in real time as the conflicts in our evolving nation became fodder for racist commercials, horrific suppression—and the largest turnout of voters of color in Georgia's history. Because, despite the final tally of the election, our campaign energized this New American Majority in tremendous ways, proving the resilience and possibility of our national destiny. What excites me about this book is not the litany of challenges to our body politic—although they must be explored and exposed—but the potential I saw in the tired eyes of an African American shift worker waiting in a four-hour line to cast a ballot of hope.

This is not a behind-the-scenes campaign book but a narrative that describes the urgency that compels me and millions more to push for a different American story than the one being told today. It's a story that is one part danger, one part action, and all true. It's a story about how and why we fight for our democracy and win. Using stories from my own life, those of others I've met as I've traveled through Georgia's rural towns and cities, interviews with candidates on the same path I am on, as well as political insights I've gained along the way, this book will be a primer on how we can guarantee our right to choose the vision we want for our country—and how we make it so.

REAL ACCESS TO THE RIGHT TO VOTE ISN'T A
GUARANTEE—AND THAT'S A PROBLEM

Most of us can recite the preamble to the Constitution (or sing it if we learned the words from *Schoolhouse Rock!*). The promises of justice and liberty come with the responsibility for electing leaders to protect and make them real. Yet, from limiting original voting rights to white men, to the elitist and racist origins of the Electoral College, American democracy has always left people out of participation, by design. Any lasting solutions come solely from the U.S. Constitution, the highest legal bar imaginable; and over the centuries, we clawed out access to the ballot for people of color through the Fifteenth Amendment, women in the Nineteenth Amendment, and young voters in the Twenty-Sixth Amendment. But each of those amendments contained a loophole for suppression: leaving implementation to the states, particularly the ones most hostile to inclusion. Add to that the generational underfunding of the basic mechanics of elections, where incompetence and malfeasance operate in tandem, and the sheer complexity of the national voting apparatus smooths suppression into a nearly seamless operation.

Since 2008's election of the first black president, we have achieved extraordinary victories. Millions of Americans, too used to seeing themselves only on the margins or not at all, have participated in historic and hopeful wins in the House and hard-fought victories for the U.S. Senate and gubernatorial races. However, across the country, we witnessed a "power grab" from the minority desperate to hold on to power. The examples of this abound: Native Americans living on reservations in North Dakota were told that in order to vote, they had to have street addresses—where none existed. In Mississippi, impoverished elderly folks who needed an absentee ballot had to pay for a notary public to submit the ballot—resulting in a new-fashioned poll tax. In Georgia, tens of thousands of people of color had their applications for registration held up because of typographical errors in government databases and a failed system called "exact match." Of the 53,000 applications blocked by this process, 80 percent were from people of color.

Voter suppression—from getting on the rolls to being allowed to vote to having those votes count—is real. But Americans need a robust understanding of what suppression looks like today. Today, the ones barring access have shifted from using billy clubs and hoses to using convoluted rules to make it harder to register and stay on the rolls, cast a ballot, or have that ballot counted. To move forward, we must understand the extent to which the shrinking conservative minority will go to create barriers to democracy. Citing voting rights experts and my own work in expansion of voting access for the past twenty-five years, here I will not only explain the problem but offer concrete solutions to fix it.

WHO WE ARE MATTERS: IDENTITY POLITICS AND THE CENSUS

The United States has always fumbled in its pursuit of social equality, but we face a new round of concerns that are particularly damning. Whether it's the stories of police brutality against blacks or the invisibility of the disabled community, who we say we are as a country is not currently held up by how our systems behave. For the New American Majority—that coalition of people of color, young people, and moderate to progressive whites—to be successful, we have to stop letting them tell us who we are and how to succeed. That begins when we reject the false choice of "identity" versus "universality."

We are strongest when we see the most vulnerable in our society, bear witness to their struggles, and then work to create systems to make it better. Whether it's the civil rights acts of the early '60s or the advance of women's rights or marriage equality, we are a better country when we defend the weakest among us and then empower them to choose their own futures. In these pages, I will dissect how identity has been weaponized against the very communities that need its power. Through stories of how identity politics have shaped and changed the fabric of our nation, and with ideas for how we can reclaim the power of identity via the U.S. census, this book will detail a path forward where identity is celebrated, not feared.

Voting by identity works. Just look at how the right's power has been apportioned. Now, it's time for the New American Majority to leverage the same tools to achieve the goals of expanded access to opportunity. In theory, this should work too. Our numbers are bigger. Our successes, from the New Deal to the Affordable Care Act, are more durable. Our coalition is energized. We have the ability to permanently affect policies and shape the delivery of justice, but we have to pay attention to what's been accomplished under our noses and own the identities that made it possible.

DEFEATING POPULISM AND WINNING ELECTIONS TO SAVE DEMOCRACY

My experience in 2018 was pretty straightforward. I ran for office, dogged by a racist demagogue who carefully disenfranchised hundreds of thousands of Georgians and who controlled the levers of the election. I watched him be rewarded for joining a growing pool of political leaders who revel in a pervasive, systemic process of stripping the right to vote from some and building obstacles to access for others.

But the threat is also coming from inside the coalition itself: citizens grappling with racism, sexism, homophobia, and poverty are the *least* likely to vote. They have come to expect suppression from the opposition and inaction from the winners. Worse, the candidates who should engage them are afraid to reach out. We need active and relentless participation in our elections and government. Unfortunately, candidates and their consultants tend to view these groups as the hardest and most expensive to reach, so campaigns typically decide to hunt elsewhere for votes. Or political leaders fear that visible engagement with these marginalized groups will cost them votes from white traditional voters, and they deliberately ignore their communities.

True progress can only happen if we knit together the "who" of identity with the "how" of voting into effective, inclusive campaigns and movements. We must dispel myths that give primacy to the archetype of a working-class white man in Ohio who voted for Reagan in 1980, and instead expand our polity to recognize that his daughter might be married to a Kenyan woman who is waiting for permanent residence and their first child in Arkansas. The blue wave election of 2018, which included victories and close losses in unexpectedly competitive territories, demonstrates that demographic changes have come to fruition and are ready to become a political road map to sustained progress. But to do so, we must understand the hard work of civic engagement. We can't wait for election time to come around.

Candidates and the campaigns they run matter now more than ever. I ran a campaign different from anything that preceded it and, by doing so, proved that what happened with Obama was not a fluke but a foreshadowing of how we can win even more. In our campaign, and in campaigns around the country, new people were able to step forward and win—and they did so by recognizing the intersection of identity and voting rights.

Beyond Congress, there are the unmentioned corridors of power we too often cede: state and local elections, from school boards and county commissions to boards of elections and secretaries of state. These elections matter because the architecture of our rights begins closest to home. The attention to national politics makes sense for those who have been denied access. States' rights—the idea that each state should be allowed to set its own rules—controls much of how life is lived in America. The practical reality is that where you live determines your ability to marry, buy a house, get an abortion, or start a business, and creating equality in these areas has usually required federal action to guarantee basic rights. Thus, by recognizing and harnessing the power of nonfederal offices, those who long for a more homogenous, segregated bygone era have grown stronger and more resilient.

The Trump administration has amplified weaknesses in our democracy, but he and his enablers in Congress and the judiciary have shone a spotlight on the dangers of populism here and abroad. Americans must understand the compelling nihilism of authoritarian populism to avoid a permanent breakdown in democracy. Across the globe, former democracies are slipping into autocracy, and the United States is not immune. To restore our country, we have to deconstruct what got us here and how to repair our nation before it's too late.

Whether it's the looming 2020 election or the first congressional election post-redistricting in 2022, or a post-Trump era, we must do the same long-term planning of those who work to

deny us agency. Our obligation is to fortify democracy's infrastructure and to train those who have been isolated from power
to use this formidable weapon of demographic supremacy.
Demography is not destiny; it is opportunity. We have internal-
ized the worst lessons of our opponents and hamstrung our own
progress by catering to the backbiting, loathing, and timidity of
fear. At its core, I hope this book will be a manual of action
where readers know how to protect the right to vote, champion
the diversity of who we are today, and demand political leadership that does both from now on.

I have two siblings who missed out on most of my campaign
for governor: a brother who watched my race from a television
in a state prison and a sister who is forbidden to engage in partisan politics as a federal judge. My vision for America isn't one
where Leslie is the star and Walter is simply a cautionary tale.
My America sees my brother and my sister as the promise of
what our nation can and must become—a place of extraordinary success that transcends barriers and a place of redemption
that defies the cynicism of our politics. This is a vision that only
comes into being when everyone has a true voice in our futures.
America, for all its faults, has always been a place of promise and
renewal, of mistakes made and the constant pursuit of atone-
ment. This is a new manifesto for our progressive future, one
emboldened by understanding that our time of waiting is over.
The fight for our future has already begun.

And guess what? We won.

CHAPTER 1

Everything Old Is New Again

On November 15, 2018, I sat frozen on my living-room sofa, the earbuds to my phone still dangling from my ears, but I heard nothing. I'd just hung up from a call with my campaign manager, Lauren Groh-Wargo, and I was numb. The final numbers from the court-mandated count of recovered absentee and provisional ballots had finally come in. In order to force a run-off, we needed nearly 17,000 more votes, but they had not materialized. This call was like several I'd received in the nine-day interim between Election Day and that evening, but bitter in its finality. Four lawsuits had been filed, and the chance for victory hung in the balance for every decision. But now the numbers had been tallied.

We'd run an extraordinary campaign that proved our theory that increasingly diverse Georgia had become a Democratic-leaning state. *Early investments in infrequent voters?* Check. *Consistent, authentic progressive messaging?* Check. *Outreach in multiple languages?* Check. *Centering the issues of communities of color and marginalized groups typically exiled to the fringes of statewide elections?* Check. The results of these efforts on the Democratic side of the ballot had been incredible: We had tripled the turnout rates of Latino and Asian American Pacific Islander (AAPI) voters. We increased youth participation rates by 139 percent. Black voters, who had reached a peak in voting strength in 2008 in the Obama election, had settled back down, and the 2014 election for governor yielded roughly 1.1 million voters total. But in 2018, more than 1.2 million black voters turned out to cast ballots for me. And the fear that, by engaging these groups, my efforts would cost me white votes also proved false. Our election increased white participation for Democrats to 25 percent overall, higher among suburban white women and college-educated whites of either gender. In contrast to previous recent elections, I received the highest percentage of white votes *in a generation*.

Yet, the final tally fell 54,723 votes shy of victory or even that legally mandated runoff. My conversation with Lauren was perfunctory. We discussed the hard truth of the likely outcome and made preparations for the next day. I would announce an end to the campaign. Talk turned to venues for the event and my upcoming speech, but neither of us mentioned the savage edge of sorrow of the result. We had both been preparing ourselves for the outcome since election night. Our strategy had gamed out what could happen, from Scenario A all the way to Scenario Z. We'd landed squarely in Z, our shorthand for absolute chaos.

As more than fifty thousand phone calls poured in to our voter hotline from around the state over the ten days between Election Day and our call, Lauren and I debriefed each night. The routine had become painfully familiar: first, the decision of the day from one of the several suits in process. Then the conversation transitioned into the updated vote count: sometimes in the teens and, on exciting days, thousands of reclaimed votes. Our campaign had sent volunteers and staff across Georgia to chase provisional ballots from voters who'd stood in lines for hours, only to be told that they had insufficient identification or some other grievous error or that, more troubling, the precinct had run out of real ballots. Lauren and I would strategize about the ongoing fundraising necessary to keep the hundreds of folks in the field and to keep our public service announcements on the air, reminding voters of their rights. Finally, she would alert me to news of the vile: updated stories about how the system had been undermined by its overseer, the secretary of state and my opponent, Brian Kemp; ballots rejected for simple mistakes like transposed dates or refusal to put identifying information like birthdates on the outside of the absentee envelope.

Or, like the catastrophe in Pooler, Georgia, where the morning of the election, the line stretched out of the parking lot and into the dark street at Rothwell Baptist Church. While cars drove past them, voters stood in the fitful rain, in the gutter, waiting in line to cast their ballots. One voter came back to the church three times throughout the day, but the line remained prohibitively long. Another voter, who arrived at 5:00 p.m. with his six-year-old daughter, turned back without voting when told that the line would take three hours. There were still sixty people in line at Rothwell at 10:30 p.m. election night. Across town, the under-resourced election workers had no better luck. Voters in Pooler were denied their right to vote when their polling location ran out of provisional ballots. At Pooler Church, one poll watcher witnessed four voters leave without voting because there were no provisional ballots left, despite the federal requirement that all eligible voters be given the option. Another Pooler voter stood in line for three hours only to find out that, after years of voting at the same polling place, he had been moved to another location. He was not able to vote at the new location either, because it had taken him so long to get to the check-in station that his correct location had already closed.

On the evening of the fifteenth, Lauren's voice, typically a rapid-fire volley of information and strategy, held a careful, solemn tempo. We both knew what was coming, but we still had to say the truth aloud: our hope had run out. Too many ballots had been trashed or rejected or blocked long before Election Day, and some county election officials failed to maintain a record of these lost votes.[1] When these potential votes were added to those turned away from the polls or forced away because of long lines and under-resourced precincts, our outrage at the conduct of the election mounted. The bottom line, though, was that the numbers simply did not add up to the 17,000 we'd need to formally force a runoff.

As I digested the update, I understood the next decision to be made. Per my request, our attorneys had prepped two memos for me in the event that we didn't reach the runoff threshold: The first one laid out how to contest the election results based on the evidence we had amassed. The other memo took a more radical approach, born on the morning after the election as my key advisers sat with me around a hotel table. Rather than litigate the election results, a potential lawsuit would focus instead on the voting infrastructure itself. This approach would do nothing to advance my cause of becoming the eighty-third governor of Georgia, but it could transform the election's process forever; and our lead attorneys, Allegra Lawrence-Hardy and Dara Lindenbaum, together with Lauren, had dived deep into the possibility.

On the call that day, Lauren and I quickly discarded the contest idea without much discussion. The moment I lodged the challenge, the stories of thousands of individual disenfranchised voters would be overshadowed by one politician's crusade for redemption. But a lawsuit to invalidate the system of laws that permitted a ninety-two-year-old woman to be erased from the rolls or that blocked a college freshman from casting her first ballot—that would be an unprecedented case in the twenty-first century, one worth fighting.

The next night, I acknowledged the legal sufficiency of the election results—and honestly, the system worked as manipulated. However, I refused to offer the typical concession to my opponent, not because I intended to subvert the democratic system, as some allege with false comparisons to Richard Nixon's apocryphal decision in 1960 or Trump's wholly manufactured claims in 2016. My choice came from the lessons learned from my parents and grandparents and a host of civil rights advocates whose lives stood as a testament to the struggle of suffrage. In conceding the election, I would validate the system that slashed voters from the rolls, ensured thousands could not cast ballots, and blocked thousands more from being counted. By making the election about one candidate's fight, I would mask the war that has been waged against millions of voters in Georgia and across the country for centuries. The contours and tactics of voter suppression have changed since the days of Jim Crow, Black Codes, or suffragettes, but the mission remains steady and immovable: keep power concentrated in the hands of the few by disenfranchising the votes of the undesirable.

My non-concession speech on November 16, 2018, served as a declaration of intent. We have been taught to expect concessions not only to the outcome of an electoral contest but to the system that undergirds it. But we forget that the system is not simply constructed for picking politicians. The vast, invasive, and complex electoral system controls everything—from determining the quality of our drinking water to the lawfulness of abortion rights to the wages stolen from a domestic worker. The voting system is not just political; it is economic and social and educational. It is omnipresent and omniscient. And it is fallible. Yet, when a structure is broken, we are fools if we simply ignore the defect in favor of pretending that our democracy isn't cracking at the seams. Our obligation is to understand where the problem is, find a solution, and make the broken whole again.

Voter suppression is not a new phenomenon, and, truth be told, it isn't entirely partisan. Suppression began before the advent of political parties and became a favored tool of the party in power. Democratic-Republicans, Know-Nothings, Democrats, and Republicans have all leveraged the power of suppression to win elections and deny votes to the other side. The stripping away of rights comes through racial and sexist animus, incompetence, willful ignorance, and malfeasance. Sometimes, these occur all in the same action. Since our nation's inception, the brokers of power have sought to aggregate authority to themselves. At first, that meant old white men who denied a political voice to their wives, their slaves, their indentured servants, and the native landholders. These white men—and they were all white men—relied upon women, slaves, servants, and Native Americans to build the commerce and physical structures of the colonies, and then all were conscripted in some fashion into the Revolutionary War. They wrote the Constitution with a grandiose and seductive ideal of freedom at its core, one that embedded hypocrisy in its three-fifths compromise for slavery and the omission of women altogether. But the appeal of freedom and the moments of courage and valor that have made up the American story means we still hold that aspiration today. But we sell the story to other nations without fully confronting the internal conflict our actions demonstrate to those who look to America as a model of behavior. In order to tell the whole truth—which we must do if we have any chance of moving forward—we must understand how the story of America's democracy yielded so many terrible examples of its complicated promise.

DENY AND DELAY: THE FIGHT FOR VOTING RIGHTS NEVER ENDED

My father lives to tell stories. Like any good Southern man, his tales begin with the truth and quickly turn fuzzy on the details, weaving the kind of color commentary that holds an audience enraptured. He played football in high school and, with each telling, the players he faced grow more mammoth in size and meaner in temperament. Over the years, a young Robert Abrams has grown faster and more agile, solidified in his version of events as a wunderkind of the gridiron stopped only by foul weather, bad calls, or injuries so serious he's still nursing them today. For most of my life, I have heard and memorized his tales, tall and otherwise. I've learned to read between the stories and understand how my dad confronted challenges, laughed off pain, or simply admitted defeat.

On the other hand, when my mother is asked about her experiences growing up, she agonizes over the exactitude of her memories, reluctant to share an anecdote without careful parsing of the truth. The emotions of the moment matter to her, as well as the contours of time and place and mood. A librarian by training and a pastor by calling, Mom revels in the atmospherics as much as the moral lesson to be drawn. And there is always a moral lesson to be drawn.

Both of my parents are ministers, and their differences in storytelling have shaped how I understand the nature of communication. Daddy's tendency toward broad anecdotes and elaborate description demands the attention of the listener and shoves them directly into the center of the action. Mom, in contrast, invites the audience inside, tangling their minds and hearts as we discover the truth of the matter together. On the issue of voting rights, understanding where we are now has required me to hear their recollections separately and together, their contrasting styles offering the truest illustration of how justice and democracy actually became real in the Deep South. More important, from them, I finally understood how to separate myth from reality, to recognize the painful contours of a history that has, for too many of us, become fuzzy on the details.

In 1964, my dad was a skinny, black fifteen-year-old growing up in Hattiesburg, Mississippi. Like most boys his age, he loved football and girls, but he wasn't the greatest fan of school. The county school he attended, Earl Travillion High School, remained segregated a decade after *Brown v. Board of Education* (1954) demanded the dismantling of the inherently unequal educational system pervasive throughout the South and around the country. Across town, my mother, Carolyn Abrams, née Hall, matriculated at Rowan High School, the segregated city school. Despite the passage of a bevy of civil rights laws and the supposed end of Jim Crow, my father and mother graduated from deeply segregated high schools in 1967 and 1968, respectively.

By the end of summer 1967, Hattiesburg had grudgingly adopted a "freedom of choice" model, which permitted students to opt for an integrated experience. As my mom explains the process, my dad snorts in derision. He had been merged into Rowan High School due to the annexation of his community into the city of Hattiesburg. But the change of school names did not mean a true change of color composition. Black students previously separated only by district lines now attended the same black segregated school, still devoid of resources and access years later.

So my father transferred the civil rights activism he had started at Travillion to this new high school. He and his siblings held protests and marched against the racist divisions that blocked them from full participation in American life. Though he was too young to vote himself, he was arrested in 1964 for fighting to guarantee suffrage for blacks in town. As Daddy recounts the marches to me, perched on the edge of his seat, he peppers the story with anecdotes about who protested with them—about the fears of the battering blast of water hoses and vicious, snarling dogs that kept grown men and women from exercising a fundamental right. Though the Voting Rights Act would come the next year, like *Brown v. Board of Education*, the act of Congress would be slow to penetrate and create real change. We often see these historical moments as flash points with instant gratification; however, with most movements, the new laws, the new rules, only herald possibility. More must be done to make it so.

My dad's telling is boisterous and excited. In contrast, my mother's telling is full of compassion. She explained the worries of the domestic workers whose employers threatened to cast them out if they dared register to vote, the factory employees held hostage by a company-town boss who promised retribution for any who defied the rules of Southern hegemony. *Brown*, like the freedom promised in the Thirteenth, Fourteenth, and Fifteenth Amendments, meant little in real life. Blacks did not have the right to desegregated schools or integrated voting. They could only recite the myth of civil rights progress that they read about in the newspapers or saw on television. Without a state system forced to accept the federal edicts, racial oppression continued for years after change had supposedly come. This is one of the persistent problems of our ideal of democracy: grand, sweeping national laws or legal decisions announce a new way of behavior. Yet, our fifty separate states have little reason to fully adhere to the rules without being compelled to by threats from those higher powers in the federal system. Without the ability to demand obedience to the moral victories, what my parents and others experienced in the wake of civil rights victories was often just more of the same, executed quietly and without consequence.

What made the Voting Rights Act real, what forced desegregation, were the local political leaders who made it so. They were often normal men and women who saw modest progress as less harmful than obstinacy. The school boards afraid of lawsuits began to experiment with integration, and the county elections boards eventually caved in to the demands of the federal Department of Justice. But the most compelling reason for change was often the desire to garner the additional ballots represented by a new cadre of eligible voters: blacks who could finally influence elections.

As my parents recalled their activism and the role of voting in forcing change, I thought about the times they'd taken us to vote. I remember entering the booth with them, but I never saw a political sign in our yard or a politician at our door. My parents are best described as "super-voters," those folks who never miss an election, be it county clerk or president of the United States. In political speak, they are the most coveted voters. At the other end of the spectrum are the infrequent voters, the ones who vote in presidential elections only, when they vote at all. In between, most voters are scored based on how likely they are to vote and how much work a campaign will need to do to get them to the polls. The higher the score, the more likely you are to agree with the political party doing the scoring, and you show up at the polls regularly—a very coveted *super-voter*. Various campaigns assign other titles as a voter score decreases: regular voter, low-propensity voter, and nonvoter. The lowest score signals that you support the other side. No consultant would advise a candidate to trouble my parents with multiple calls. They vote rain or shine, in every election. They believe that more than protest, a true activist must put people in office who share their values. Likewise, they raised us to believe our voices would be heard if we too attended to every election as though our lives depended on casting that ballot. In telling their stories, they wanted us to understand the complexity of progress, how what is written on paper has to be made real by engagement and attention. Yet, I wondered if they knew how they raised us in the veil of mythology too. Securing the right to register did not mean someone had the right to vote. Casting a ballot sometimes bore no relationship to whether that vote got counted. As my election experience proved, the vestiges of Jim Crow laws to legally block access to the right to vote have been replaced by voter purges, shuttered precincts, and broken voting machines in black neighborhoods.

SUPPRESSION STARTS WITH WHO BELONGS HERE

Our nation's core narrative can be summed up in the disconnect between the Constitution's pledge of equality and the rampant disregard for that ambition that has plagued the United States of America ever since. Though the Founding Fathers gave a nod to universal equality in the Declaration of Independence, they abandoned the aspiration by the time they penned the country's organizing documents. Let me be clear here: the codification of racism and disenfranchisement is a feature of our lawmaking— not an oversight. And the original sin of the U.S. Constitution began by identifying blacks in America as three-fifths human: counting black bodies as property and their souls as nonexistent.

Voting rights are the most basic tenet of our democracy, and the bare minimum one should expect from the government. Our presidents can send our neighbors to war. Local elected officials decide the mundane questions of trash pickup and the weightier issues of hospital closures. At every level of our lives in this republic, we choose men and women to speak for us, yes, but also to determine the direction of our daily lives. And all it takes is a teachers' strike or a government shutdown to remind us how vital elections can be to the daily rhythms of life.

Over the course of our history, the right to vote had to be purchased by blood and protest in each generation. The Revolutionary War included enslaved patriots and Native Americans who would be denied citizenship once the nation became official. The savagery of the Civil War had no clearer argument than whether blacks were property or human beings capable of self-governance. Even the suffrage movement tangled with complex issues of gender and race, where white women would benefit from obtaining suffrage while working to deny the same to the black women who helped power the movement.

But the right to vote is not simply a request for voice in the conduct of the affairs of state. People have sacrificed their lives in pursuit of the most profound currency of citizenship: power. Because, let's be honest, that is the core of this fight. Power is the right to be seen, the right to be heard, the right to direct the course of history and benefit from the future. In the United States, democracy makes politics one of the key levers to exercising power. Simply put, the struggle for dominion over our nation's future and who will participate is a battle royal for America's power, full stop.

However, the battle has long targeted the marginalized and the dispossessed, cordoning off the right to vote for a select group, from the beginning. In the first full year of our nation's founding, the Naturalization Act of 1790 passed to prevent anyone except former slaves and "free white persons" from becoming citizens. This targeted the Native Americans who had occupied the nation long before the *Mayflower* reached American shores. Having dispatched with the potential of too many freed slaves by enshrining slavery into the founding documents, the U.S. Supreme Court cemented this position in *Dred Scott v. Sanford* (1857), deciding that blacks could not be considered American citizens and had no standing to challenge slavery. Chief Justice Roger Taney wrote, "A negro, whose ancestors were imported into this country, and sold as slaves" was permanently disenfranchised because a black person inherently was "[not] a member of the political community formed and brought into existence by the Constitution."

The notion of "political community" lay at the heart of this denunciation of black participation in American democracy, creating a private club where the only accepted members had to look and act the part. At the country's inception, the Founding Fathers decided who would be deemed worthy of citizenship; and they used, as a measuring stick, the ability to maintain the class and power structure that had laid the foundation for their wealth and political dominance. Not surprisingly, only white men were granted such esteemed status. Dred Scott, in contrast, was an enslaved man who had been moved along with his wife and children into first Illinois and then the Wisconsin Territory. Under the laws of the time, Scott and his family were due to be freed because the slave owner had remained too long in a territory that did not allow slavery. Scott sued for his family's emancipation; but Justice Taney, rather than reviewing the law, went to the fundamental question of whether Scott had the right to sue in a court of law, a perquisite of citizenship. Justice Taney rejected Scott's bid for freedom because he did not see in Dred Scott the markers of privilege that would entitle him to redress. That is to say that because Scott was not a white male, one whom the Founding Fathers had deemed worthy of citizenship when the Constitution was written, Justice Taney and the majority of the Supreme Court held that Scott and all descendants of African slavery were permanently barred from citizenship. Despite later decisions overturning Dred Scott's case, Justice Taney set a course for the intervening centuries to test our battle for voting rights. For Justice Taney and his ilk, only privileged white men had the constitutional rights of citizenship and the right to chart the course of the nation. From the mundane decision of taxation to the sale of human chattel, the Constitution envisioned the narrowest class of power brokers, and constraints on citizenship are the most effective means to filter out the interlopers.

What is so damning about *Dred Scott* is the absolute denial of citizenship—of participation in power—to an American who had every reason to believe he was entitled to the protection of membership. With the decision in Scott's case, states continued to deny the rights to citizenship. Slavery flourished until the Civil War, and even in the free states, blacks were allowed to be state citizens but had no say in federal laws or decision making. Each time the most effective marker of citizenship—the right to vote—is suppressed, there are echoes of Justice Taney's edict. Those who cannot vote have no say in the operation of government, which creates a permanent state of powerlessness.

A MOMENT'S GRACE: RECONSTRUCTION TO A FALSE REDEMPTION

After the Civil War, from 1865 to 1877, the United States made a brief, aborted attempt at meeting the basic premise of democracy by enforcing, for the first time, the rights of black Americans. This period was known as Reconstruction. The opening salvo came in the form of the Thirteenth Amendment, ratified in 1865, which abolished slavery and involuntary servitude, a critical prerequisite for expanded black participation in the decisions of their communities. However, even the abolition of slavery carried a wicked reprisal, allowing for involuntary servitude as punishment for the commission of a crime, a feature exploited eagerly by not only former Confederates but their Northern and Western white compatriots in power. With newly freed slaves mostly living in the South (there were more than four million enslaved at the time of the Civil War), the fight to prevent full citizenship was waged for more than a decade. The Black Codes, formalized by Southern states in the 1860s, had counterparts in Northern states, some dating back to the colonial era.

In the South, a newly freed black man had no right to vote. In the lawless towns that existed after the war, blacks could not own weapons to defend themselves, even though organized law enforcement might not exist. Even the act of walking down a city street carried peril. Vagrancy laws made it illegal for blacks to move about without proof of a job. A black man waiting on a street corner to meet his wife could be arrested and jailed for nothing more than standing still. Once this happened and the man was convicted, the Thirteenth Amendment allowed him to be subjected to involuntary servitude. Taken together, these laws and rules established the limits of black lives regardless of where they dwelled. The passage of these state laws enraged more liberal Republicans in Congress, and new federal rules were proposed to enforce fairer participation for black Americans.

During Reconstruction, the Civil Rights Act of 1866, as well as the Fourteenth and Fifteenth Amendments, began the painful reassertion of our nation's core principles of equal protection under the law. The little-known Civil Rights Act of 1866 followed the end of slavery, and it transformed the lives of blacks in America. For the first time, federal law guaranteed legal rights, allowed for labor rights, and permitted access to education and freedom of religion. Black churches, often maintained in secret, flourished. Historically black colleges and universities educated teachers, doctors, and businessmen, and other black students gained acceptance to historically white institutions. Economic opportunity opened up for hundreds of thousands grappling with the terrible transition from slavery into the putative free market economy. But the act had its fiercest opponent in Democrat Andrew Johnson, serving his turn as president in the wake of Lincoln's assassination. Johnson vetoed the act, but a Republican Congress overrode his veto. In 1868, three years after the end of the Civil War and the end of slavery, the Fourteenth Amendment granted citizenship to anyone born in the United States, which overturned the Supreme Court's decision in *Dred Scott*. Black men and women finally held a status they had been historically denied—but Native Americans did not benefit from this change. No persons considered visitors to the United States, or Native Americans living on reservations, as most laws required them to do, could lay claim to citizenship or its benefits. Two years later, the states ratified the Fifteenth Amendment as a guarantee of a right to vote for citizens regardless of race or color; however, women still could not vote for decades to come.

During Reconstruction, black men rose to power in the former Confederate states, serving in both chambers of Congress and as governors. The veneer of inclusion tarnished quickly, despite constitutional changes and new laws. While the Fifteenth Amendment guaranteed the right to vote, it left it to the states to decide the administration of voter registration and the whole panoply of election laws, from polling locations to candidacy to date and timing of elections. So, even if blacks had the right to vote in their state, the polling place might be located ten miles away. With no means of transportation, many could not physically reach the location.

Literacy tests were a favored tool borrowed from the Northeast, and they were particularly popular because both immigrants and freed black Americans often had limited education. Connecticut pioneered literacy tests in 1855 to limit access to the ballot and exclude Irish immigrants. Under these tests, voters would have to prove their command of language by reading a passage aloud and then answering questions showing their reading comprehension to the satisfaction of the examiner. Of course, the tests were administered in a fashion that made it harder for those whom the establishment wanted to disenfranchise. In Alabama, for example, white voters would be asked to read and discuss an eight-word passage from Section 20 of the state's constitution, which simply states, "That no person shall be imprisoned for debt." The black voter, however, would be asked to read and explain the entirety of Section 260, 187 words of convoluted language that established laws of taxation and state bonds.[2] For most of us born after the end of literacy tests, we have a vague grasp on what hurdles our parents and grandparents faced to vote, let alone their grandparents. Black voters had to unravel complex laws that trained lawyers would have trouble deciphering. All in a bid to cast a vote.

Similarly, Southern states levied poll taxes, a requirement of payment for the right to cast a ballot. But these also existed in the North, including in Connecticut, Maine, Massachusetts, and Pennsylvania, where the goal was to price immigrants, the poor, and people of color out of the vote. These taxes, fees paid simply for the opportunity to vote, might equal a day's pay or a week's wages. They had their intended effect, winnowing out the poor and dispossessed from any say in how they might better their station in life. In the South, grandfather clauses accompanied poll taxes in order to exempt poor whites in the Southern states from their effect: if a potential voter's father or grandfather had previously cast a ballot, they didn't have to pay the tax.

The hope that the Civil War amendments carried—that the states would enact the same principles of freedom that the federal laws demanded—proved to be a fiction. When the Democrats regained power in Congress and the Republicans lost interest, the former Confederate states set upon a scheme of permanent disenfranchisement for blacks, reversing the gains of Reconstruction and punishing those who dared treat black citizenship as whole and real. At the core of this seizure and denial of rights lay a devious scheme of passing the buck. Federal laws granted rights in theory but left to the states the responsibility of implementation. States took full advantage of this, perfecting their craft by invoking the Tenth Amendment, the last addition to the Bill of Rights, which granted to the states an independence from responsibility to those who lived within its borders. Heralded as "states' rights" to all who would listen, the Tenth Amendment became an unscalable barrier against civil rights for millions.

In the former Confederate and sympathizing states, slavery may have ended, but nothing bound the white men in charge from imposing new forms of degradation on the black Americans who continued to live there, in the areas they'd known their entire lives. At the onset of the Post-Reconstruction era in 1877, the infamous Jim Crow laws took hold when rights granted by Reconstruction were swiftly taken away. The eleven Confederate states plus two sympathizer states that formed the core of the Jim Crow region were: Alabama, Arkansas, Georgia, Florida, Kentucky, Louisiana, Mississippi, Missouri, North Carolina, South Carolina, Tennessee, Texas, and Virginia. We've all heard of the stark inequities in access at one time in these states, from segregated bathrooms to no-admittance hospitals to isolated burial plots. Despite the fact that black Americans now held nominal citizenship after the Thirteenth Amendment, the courts refused to enforce the privileges of belonging for them, deferring instead to the right of states to inculcate their racist dogmas into the laws that governed the most basic actions.

Former slaves faced the most sustained brutality, but the humiliations and very real harms of not belonging affected other communities of color too. In *Botiller v. Dominguez*, the federal government turned a blind eye when Mexican Americans, who had their land seized in California, faced the misery of losing not only their land but also the gold on it because a Supreme Court decision had stripped them of property rights. On top of that, they had no right to vote in an effort to overturn the decision. The California Alien Land Law of 1913 prohibited "aliens ineligible for citizenship" from owning property, a turn of phrase that targeted Asians brought here by the Gold Rush and by the building of our nation's transportation infrastructure. Classified as visitors, despite their tenure in the country, the lack of full citizenship prevented them from seeking redress at the ballot box. En masse, nonwhites were denied the right to own land, the right to education, the right to free and full enjoyment of their lives in America—by virtue of not having a right to vote to gain the representation to create change.

A DIM LIGHT GROWS: THE RISE AND FALL OF THE VOTING RIGHTS ACT

Blacks and others chafed under the loss of freedoms that had been briefly won during Reconstruction. Over time, they began to organize protests and agitate elected officials to restore what the Thirteenth, Fourteenth, and Fifteenth Amendments promised in the Constitution. In 1948, with Executive Order 9981, Truman integrated the armed forces. Though heralded for its progress, the act simply enshrined that which should have been instinctive: that those who risked their lives for our democracy shouldn't be discriminated against while doing so. In 1951, the civil rights movement began in earnest. Under the leadership of a newly emboldened Supreme Court and determined jurists like Thurgood Marshall, a litany of cases and new laws began to construct our modern understanding of civil rights.

The Civil Rights Act of 1957, weakened by the actions of then Senate majority leader Lyndon B. Johnson, held that the federal government has the right to enforce laws prohibiting the denial of voting rights and establishes the Civil Rights Division of the Justice Department. Three years later, the Civil Rights Act of 1960 restored key portions of the 1957 proposal, including empowering the federal government to enforce court orders regarding desegregation and other civil rights legislation, along with the ability to file civil rights lawsuits on behalf of the public. Prior to this provision, an aggrieved black citizen had to personally file, and few had the resources or capacity to seek redress. Among the most famous is the Civil Rights Act of 1964, which banned discrimination based on "race, color, religion, or national origin" in employment practices and public accommodations.

Despite glacial gains, the crowning achievement for bedrock democracy came in the form of the Voting Rights Act of 1965, which restored and protected voting rights at the federal level and held certain states and jurisdictions, referred to as "covered jurisdictions," accountable for discrimination. The most effective provision of the law would be found in the preclearance mechanism of Section 5, which mandated that any time a covered jurisdiction—be it city, county, or state—attempted to change any election law, practice, or procedure, the U.S. Justice Department had to agree that it did not have a discriminatory purpose or effect.

Thus, where Jim Crow had flourished, the Voting Rights Act served as the arsenal to quash the Tenth Amendment's escape clause for voter suppression. Years passed before the act reached full force and effect, but where it did, lives changed forever. Black voters were able to coalition with other people of color and sympathetic white voters to elect representation that looked like them and shared their histories. Precincts opened in neglected neighborhoods and poll taxes, literacy tests, and other obstacles to voting died. Although doing so took another decade, eventually non-English speakers were able to get the Act amended to require multilingual ballots and protection for translators to enter the booths with non-English speakers. Under Republican president Richard Nixon and his GOP successor, Gerald Ford,

Congress agreed to extend the protections of Section 5 for five years in 1970 and then added a second extension for seven years in 1975, including protections for Hispanic, Asian, and Native American citizens. The Voting Rights Act got a twenty-five-year extension in 1982 under President Ronald Reagan; however, this version added a process for covered jurisdictions to "bail out" or be removed from the oversight of the act. Even as late as 2006, the renewal of the Voting Rights Act enjoyed bipartisan support. Then, in 2008, the Voting Rights Act ushered in the most diverse voting electorate in American history, and a coalition convened to elect the nation's first black president, Barack Obama.

The backlash to the sudden participation of long-dormant groups came immediately, with conservatives chafing at the reordered power structure and new voters brimming with the confidence of electoral might. From talk radio to speeches in state legislatures, right-wing pundits began to offer conspiracy theories about the legitimacy of President Obama's election, and they privately began to worry about how active these new voters might be in state and local elections. The combination of young voters, voters of color, and moderate and progressive whites roundly rejected Republican talking points and rarely voted for their candidates. But so many had not been active voters before Obama, the worry had been academic until the 2008 election.

In response, the GOP undertook a yearslong effort to win state legislatures and gubernatorial contests in 2010, in order to control the 2011 redistricting process—how state legislatures outline the geographic boundaries of voting districts at the congressional, state, and local levels. By sweeping in the largest contingent of Republican legislators and leaders in history, state laws protecting voters began to face challenges from their own leaders in places like Wisconsin and Ohio, where the Voting

Rights Act preclearance provision had no reach because they had not been included among the states with the worst histories. The only barrier to wholesale decimation of the rights and protections won through the Voting Rights Act, though, were the states and jurisdictions subject to federal oversight. Enter *Shelby County v. Holder*, an Alabama case that argued that racial animus in voting rights had been vanquished and preclearance was no longer necessary.

In 2013, the U.S. Supreme Court issued its *Shelby County v. Holder* decision, finding agreement with Alabama. The results have dramatically undermined access to full participation in our democracy. By effectively negating the core mechanism for preventing voter suppression, Section 5 of the 1965 Voting Rights Act, the court asserted a premise that racism had ended in election practices and so too must federal oversight. In so doing, the *Shelby* decision effectively eliminated the requirements that states with long histories of discrimination preclear voting changes. Rather than seeking permission for restrictions on voting, states could do whatever could pass their legislatures and their courts. This created a new channel for the practice of voter suppression, during a time of dramatic demographic change. However, no assault on democracy will ever be limited to its targets. As the franchise is weakened, all citizens feel the effects and even the perpetrators eventually face the consequences of collateral damage—an erosion of our democracy writ large. Without *Shelby*, politicians are free to restrict the right to vote virtually anywhere, and while they may start a few neighborhoods away, there's no telling who is next.

Jurisdictions formerly covered under Section 5 have raced to reinstate or create new hurdles to voter registration, access to the ballot box, and ballot counting, Immediately after *Shelby*, election officials in covered jurisdictions immediately began picking at the low-hanging fruit and moving to close polling places in minority communities and to limit early voting opportunities that allowed working-class citizens to vote without missing work. The long game included actions ranging from voter purges to restrictive voter ID requirements to polling place closures. States facing more voters of color or younger voters have changed the rules so that, while facially neutral, the new laws result in a disturbingly predictable adverse effect: it's harder to vote. Among the states, my home state of Georgia has been one of the most aggressive in leveraging the lack of federal oversight to use both law and policy to suppress the votes of people of color.

The core value of the Voting Rights Act was to create equal access to the ballot, regardless of race, class, or partisanship. Yet, the *Shelby* decision and its aftermath deny the real and present danger posed by those who see voters of color as a threat to be neutralized rather than as fellow citizens to be engaged. Justice Taney refused to see Dred Scott as a citizen and, in the process, stripped him of his right to participate in the direction of his future and that of his progeny. Without a Voting Rights Act–style oversight, voters of color once again face the specter of being outside the protections of our Constitution. Without a protected right to vote, the *Shelby* decision and the proliferation of anti-voting laws have destabilized the whole of our democratic experiment. Rather than a Justice Department that prevents discriminatory voting policies from taking effect in the first place, the Supreme Court created a system of disproportionate impact, one in which justice could prevail in select instances and only after multiple federal courts intervened.

To fight voter suppression, we must understand what things look like post-*Shelby*. Voter suppression no longer announces itself with a document clearly labeled LITERACY TEST or POLL TAX. Instead, the attacks on voting rights feel like user error— and that's intentional. When the system fails us, we can rail and try to force change. But if the problem is individual, we are trained to hide our mistakes and ignore the concerns. The fight to defend the right to vote begins with understanding where we've been and knowing where we are now. Only then can we demand a fair fight and make it so.

CHAPTER 2

A License to Be Heard
(Voter Registration)

My favorite speech by Dr. Martin Luther King is not his extraordinary "I Have a Dream" delivered at the 1963 March on Washington. I actually prefer his lesser-known 1966 speech delivered in Kingstree, South Carolina, where his audience gathered in folding chairs and he addressed listeners from a makeshift podium, asking them to "March on Ballot Boxes." On a damp Mother's Day morning, the almost entirely black gathering heard him lay out his case, arguing that the ability to change the legislative agenda—and by extension their very lives—began with registering to vote. Like a golden ticket, the act of voter registration opens the process of democracy, and without it, citizens are just aspirants at the gate. His rhetorical flourish hammered home an essential truth: regardless of the constitutional amendments ratified and the electoral laws passed, the point of entry into the process of participation rests solely on being among those allowed to write their names on the rolls. Dr. King understood this and he challenged the audience to register at least ten other people before the upcoming primary.

Growing up, my parents ensured that my siblings and I understood the critical nature of registration. Beyond my father's own arrest for encouraging eligible black men and women to sign up, I had my own personal experiences with the issue of registration. In 1991, I enrolled at Spelman College, part of the Atlanta University Center. The AUC, as it is known, contained four historically black colleges and universities, as well as a medical school and a school of theology, also historically black. I was a freshman in college there when I turned eighteen, and my greatest excitement came from being able to register to vote. By the fall of 1992, I spearheaded a voter registration drive at the AUC to sign up black students across the campuses. That summer, Democrats had nominated Arkansas governor Bill Clinton, and his running mate was the senator from Tennessee, Al Gore. The Gulf War had ended in early 1991, but the incumbent Republican president grappled with a failing economy, rising health care costs, and the angst of young voters and voters of color who felt unseen and unheard. I eagerly canvassed dorms and stood in Manley Plaza on Spelman's campus, begging my fellow students to sign up.

The national excitement of the election eased the process, but getting students to sign up still proved to be a slog. I remember more than one conversation about why someone should care or why they thought the game was rigged. In response, I would often invoke the Rodney King decision, arguing how things might have been different if the jury looked more like the community where he lived. I talked about the violence and the poverty that existed in the housing projects just outside our college gates. Sometimes it worked, but usually it did not. Still, I kept begging for sign-ups and thus began my voting rights fight that has never ended.

While it has been at the forefront of my mind for most of my life, for most Americans, the issue of voter registration—the point of entry into our electoral process—rarely crosses their minds. Communities with a history of easy participation often take for granted the civic system's accessibility and relative ease. In seventeen states plus the District of Columbia, voter registration occurs automatically, typically through the state's Department of Motor Vehicles (DMV). In almost every other state, registration when you get your license is an option because of the Voter Registration Act. More commonly referred to as the Motor Voter Act, Congress passed this law in 1993, as my efforts to register voters in the AUC were under way. The Motor Voter Act required states to offer eligible citizens the option to register to vote when applying for or renewing a license at the DMV or when interacting with other state agencies.

But, as was clear to me on a college campus in the middle of an economically depressed area of Atlanta, what seemed like a catchall for voter registration suffered from some major flaws. First, while most states use the DMV process, not every eligible citizen drives or has a driver's license. This is even more true now than it was in the early 1990s: in the past few decades, the percentage of licensed drivers has dropped, particularly among the younger generations. Those who live in densely urbanized areas with public transit have less reason to drive, and then there are those areas where the residents simply can't afford to own a car. These populations, which often intersect with the hardest-to-register groups—poor people, rural populations, or people of color—do not universally benefit from motor-voter sign-ups. They may also be from communities where access to the DMV or a voter registration agency is simply more difficult. Take, for example, the brief skirmish in Alabama in 2015, when the state proposed the closure of thirty-one driver's license offices across the state. As a result of the proposed closures, eight out of the fourteen counties in the only majority-minority district in the state would not have had a DMV location.

Overall, the Motor Voter Act continues to fall short of its aims because it targets only a select clientele for registration. Organizations like Demos and the Lawyers' Committee for Civil Rights Under Law have been litigating compliance cases for years, with good reason.[1] In the United States, groups with historical disenfranchisement either have limited access to the voter registration process or do not trust the process. In other nations, voter registration is automatic and the responsibility of the government, a system followed by most European democracies as well as countries like Peru and Indonesia. The United States is one of the few democratized, industrialized nations that uses the piecemeal, inconsistent, state-by-state method of registration— and that puts the onus on the citizen to get on the rolls. With the management of elections left to individual states, the fractured, disjointed process is key to voter suppression. Where registration is easier, voters are more likely to participate.[2]

When I ran for the Georgia House of Representatives in 2006, voter registration was a part of our campaign strategy. Then, in 2010, I became Georgia House Democratic Leader following an election where Democrats lost big at every level of government. I spent my first few years in my post trying to block Republicans from controlling a two-thirds majority in the House, which they already held in the Senate, in addition to their absolute control of the executive branch. I gave almost as much time to traveling the state, getting to know the members of my caucus and the people they served. As my attention focused on the insular world of political fisticuffs, voter registration receded as a goal. I left that work to others, my eyes focused narrowly on turning out the voters already on the rolls. *Get them to vote at full strength and the rest would follow,* I thought.

The danger of my shifting attention would become clear in 2013, during the implementation of the Affordable Care Act, President Obama's long-awaited health care plan to cover the uninsured. As we worked to ensure that Georgia's most vulnerable citizens had access to affordable health care, Dr. King's lessons about the importance of voter registration became more salient than ever. For as poor Georgians would soon see, regardless of the passage of the Affordable Care Act, the point of entry for Georgians in need of health care rested heavily on the ability to sign up and be counted as voters.

As part of the rollout, states received generous allocations of dollars to fund *navigators*, trained personnel deployed to neighborhoods to explain how to traverse the complex system of health insurance that would now require mandatory compliance. In Georgia, the issue was particularly acute: the state had one of the highest uninsured rates in the nation. Every state participates in Medicaid, the low-income health care program that shares costs between the states and the federal government. Because the program is primarily administered by the states, qualification differs based on where you live. In Georgia, Medicaid does not cover low-income childless adults, regardless of their poverty level; and it only covers working parents who make less than 50 percent of the federal poverty level or approximately $9,765 a year for a family of three in 2013.[3] With one of the most restrictive policies in the nation, those of us who had been agitating for better health policy cheered when the Affordable Care Act plans included coverage for the working poor through the Medicaid expansion program.

However, the governor of Georgia rejected the funds for Medicaid expansion, like many other Republican governors. Health care advocates had braced ourselves for this decision. Then the state took a step few of us anticipated: it joined with a handful of states to make becoming a navigator nearly impossible beyond the limited federal program by imposing additional costs and licensure requirements few could meet. Despite the governor's animosity to the Affordable Care Act, I had not imagined he would also object to *educating* citizens about a way to gain health insurance and possibly save their lives. I'd been to Hancock County, where the loss of their hospital meant folks who had strokes there were more likely to die than in towns with their own hospitals.[4] More than once, I had traveled to Stewart and Calhoun Counties where the loss of the local hospitals had cost jobs in areas where more than half the population would be eligible for Medicaid expansion or the Affordable Care Act. We'd run candidates in the most impoverished swath of Georgia, where the population was mostly black and the hospitals and doctors had disappeared. Without navigators or Medicaid expansion, the Affordable Care Act functionally did not exist.

In response, I launched a program called the New Georgia Project, my attempt to correct for the governor's decision to block access to vital information in our most desperate areas. The New Georgia Project (referred to as the New Georgia Project–Affordable Care Act) would step into the gap and help poor Georgians learn about health insurance. We would train teams of low-income rural South Georgia community members to explain the new health insurance enrollment opportunities available through the Affordable Care Act. The New Georgia Project–Affordable Care

Act existed to explain health insurance to families who'd never had the option before. We hired local community members to knock on more than twenty thousand doors and make more than 180,000 phone calls.

It worked. The Obama administration had estimated how many Georgians would sign up for health care through the Affordable Care Act, based on the size and poverty of our state's population. Through our work, we increased anticipated sign-up rates and received recognition from President Obama's administration for our efforts. But beneath our success lurked a darker reality. Nearly 600,000 Georgians were ineligible for the Affordable Care Act marketplace; they could only receive health care via the expansion of Medicaid. That meant that even in places like Calhoun County, where the poverty rate hovered at around 30 percent, health care remained out of reach. I met a middle-aged man who worked in a chicken processing plant. He'd heard about the new health care law and was eager to sign up. But his salary fell below the threshold to participate in the Affordable Care Act marketplace. The federal law anticipated this and, instead of ignoring him, made provisions for people like him to gain coverage under the existing Medicaid program. In theory, Medicaid expansion would guarantee him coverage as well. But not in Georgia.

As our teams made contact, we heard a constant question: why didn't President Obama want Georgians to have Medicaid? The canvassers had been trained to answer that Medicaid expansion was a state decision, not federal. The governor and conservative state legislators had refused the funding, not President Obama. Then came the blank stares or silence on the phone. Most of those we contacted had no idea who their state representatives were—these men and some women who had argued against health insurance for the poor and vital investment in hospitals and clinics were strangers to them.

As the Democratic Leader of the House, my instinct was to explain whose fault it was, to direct these underserved populations to the wrongdoers who denied them health care. I wanted to help them vote these ne'er-do-wells out of office. But, as I did the all-important work of educating and engaging, the fundamental problem became clear. It wasn't that the affected populations needed to vote to throw the scoundrels out, they needed to register to vote to even be considered. In Georgia in 2013, more than 800,000 eligible people of color were *not* registered to vote, thousands of them in the most economically depressed parts of the state. So they could never elect legislators and executives to put their needs first. The words of Dr. King once again spoke loudly to me, and my focus once again centered on the fight that birthed my political career: the march on the ballot boxes.

The ability of these desperate and forgotten communities to elect legislators and a governor who would put their needs first— to seize this a priori power of democracy—rested on their ability to effectively sign up, be processed, and stay on the rolls. In the '90s, my efforts faced only the apathy of college students. However, in the fall of 2013, the demise of the heart of the Voting Rights Act manifested itself as a series of hurdles I faced in pursuit of voter registration. Though my experience centered on Georgia's aggressive attempts to block access to the rolls, other states had already been hard at work with the same intentions. Former Confederate states, joined by states facing a changing demographic and potential loss of power, together and separately pursued policies to weaken the Fifteenth Amendment's guarantee of the right to vote for everyone. The toolbox for effective disenfranchisement includes demonizing and blocking third-party registration of new voters. Major monkey wrenches are obstructing the ability to process the applications of new voters in a timely manner and creating a system that is opaque and confusing. Disenfranchisement based on status is a key tool to impede the rights of certain classes of people—primarily the disabled and ex-felons. And for the boldest, there is the increasingly used tactic of the voter purge. Recognizing these ingredients are key to comprehending and fighting the scourge and efficacy of voter suppression.

NO NEW VOICES

When the *Shelby* legal decision removed states from automatic compliance with the Voting Rights Act, one of its victims was a young black woman named Diamond. I met Diamond in 2014, after I converted the New Georgia Project from an Affordable Care Act sign-up program to one of the largest voter registration efforts in Georgia since the civil rights movement. At the time, she was a freshman at Columbus State University, a college a few hours west of Fayetteville, Georgia, where she'd been born and raised. She celebrated her eighteenth birthday while in high school, and she registered to vote at a high school registration drive. Once she got to college, she realized that getting home for her first election presented a logistical challenge. Diamond, like so many young people, didn't have a car at school, so getting back to Fayetteville to vote would be nearly impossible. Worse, she'd have to miss class to try to make it work. Instead, she opted to change her address from Fayetteville to her new college domicile. Like a conscientious citizen, she updated her registration with a New Georgia Project canvasser in late August, her neat handwriting clear and easy to read.

Months later, though, NGP reached out to her because, as

of October 2, she had not appeared on the voter file. When we spoke to her, she still hadn't heard from Muscogee County confirming her registration or noting a deficiency in her application. NGP kept a copy of her application—as we did for nearly every applicant—and we confirmed that her application was complete and legible. We also looked her up using the state's online system. She wasn't on the list and she wasn't alone. The New Georgia Project collected more than 86,000 registration forms during our first foray in 2014. For each applicant, we went a step further and secured their permission to retain a copy of their form. In the end, nearly 40,000 of our applications—including Diamond's—disappeared from the process of registration in 2014.

We had a copy of Diamond's registration as well as the records of our numerous calls to the state and county officials who stridently denied she had registered. Finally, when our lawyers (and several statewide news articles about the missing registrations) pushed hard enough, Diamond learned she had been processed, which the county's lawyers confirmed to our lawyers in court. With excitement, she headed to the polls in Columbus to cast her very first ballot. In Georgia, the first stop is the form table, where a prospective voter writes in information about the election and their identity. Next, the voter takes the form to a poll worker who verifies the form, checks for valid photo identification, and compares both to the voter rolls. Finally, the voter is directed to a desk where they are issued an electronic card for casting a ballot. But not for Diamond. On November 4, 2014, Election Day, a poll worker checked her information against the database and told her she didn't exist as a valid Georgia voter.

Distraught but well armed, she called our lawyer, who told her how to proceed. She returned to the worker and demanded they look for her on a supplemental list created for the thousands who had not been properly processed despite their best efforts. The poll worker found her name on a paper list along with a few other names, but then the standoff renewed. Despite proof that she had duly registered, the worker told Diamond she could not access a regular ballot. Instead, she would have to vote a provisional ballot. (We'll explore the dangers of provisional ballots later on, but suffice it to say, sometimes a provisional is a guarantee your vote won't count.) Once again, Diamond reached out to NGP, and our team asked the poll worker why Diamond had been denied a regular ballot. The poll worker couldn't explain her reasoning, and she refused to let the staffer speak with a manager. When we escalated the issue to an attorney and the head of elections, suddenly Diamond was free to vote using a regular ballot.

Despite her gauntlet, Diamond's saga had a happy ending, one too many others do not have because they haven't bothered to learn the intricacies of electoral law, between their day jobs and family obligations. The average American facing voter suppression likely cannot be as diligent and persistent as Diamond, and even she required the help of New Georgia Project more than once. The convoluted rules of voting access—and the beating heart of voter suppression—begin with the hazards of voter registration. Diamond's story is just one example of how insidious Georgia's post-*Shelby* obstacles to voter registration had become. Our organization conducted voter registration across 159 counties, well aware that for low-propensity voters (people unlikely to vote regularly)—people of color and students—this type of in-person registration is most effective. Third-party voter registration is a critical path to engaging citizens of color in the democratic process, and minorities are twice as likely to register through a voter registration drive as are whites.

The data speaks for itself. In one of its studies, *State Restrictions on Voter Registration Drives*, which focuses on the challenges posed across the country, the Brennan Center for Justice, a renowned organization that researches voting rights, highlights research about the importance of third-party voter registration for racial and ethnic minorities—namely that our type of effort has doubled the likelihood of registration. Where only 7.4 percent of non-Hispanic white voters will rely on these registration efforts, 12.7 percent of blacks and 12.9 percent of Hispanics used them in 2004. In 2008 and 2010, the disparity continued, with black and Hispanic voters using third-party registration at twice the rate of white voters. These registration efforts not only create new registrants but also serve to create new and active voters. Research completed by Dr. David Nickerson at the University of Notre Dame sought to understand the impact of drives on voting. The researchers conducted experiments in Detroit and Kalamazoo, Michigan, and Tampa, Florida, the results of which demonstrate that 20 percent of low-income citizens who register in a door-to-door drive actually go out and vote.[5]

There is no doubt a direct correlation between the effectiveness of such efforts and the post-*Shelby* legislation and efforts in states like Georgia, Tennessee, North Carolina, Texas, and Florida to impede these activities. The difference being, after the Supreme Court gutted the Voting Rights Act, states no longer had to hold back on their attacks on these groups. In Georgia, the secretary of state, Brian Kemp, accused me and New Georgia Project of committing fraud due to the sheer volume of people of color who registered through our statewide effort. As proof, his team cited the number of applications with false or inaccurate information. However, as a protection against actual fraud or cherry-picking voters, Georgia law requires the submission of all collected forms, even if Mickey Mouse filled it out. His team refused to explain why nearly half our applications were never processed.

Rather, he announced to a GOP gathering about New Georgia Project and other groups, "Democrats are working hard, and all these stories about them, you know, registering all these minority voters that are out there and others that are sitting on the sidelines, if they can do that, they can win these elections in November."[6] Our ambitious project began the tough work of bringing hundreds of thousands out of the shadows and into the electorate. In response, we faced attacks from the secretary of state, who refused to put our eligible applicants on the rolls by Election Day 2014.

New Georgia Project wasn't the first group targeted by this secretary of state. Helen Kim Ho, the founder of the Asian American Legal Advocacy Center (AALAC), had hit upon the ingenious idea of coordinating with naturalization services to register newly sworn-in citizens. As an attorney, she'd carefully developed the process, and she communicated with the appropriate bureaucracies to ensure that these new Americans got to exercise their most fundamental right. But during the 2012 election cycle, Helen began receiving troubling calls. New voters registered by her group had been turned away from polling places, their right to vote challenged by election officials. She reached out to the secretary of state's office to find out why so many of those she'd signed up hadn't made it onto voting rolls, even though early voting had started in Georgia. Rather than address the issue of eligible voters not being added to the rolls by Election Day, Secretary Kemp opened an investigation into AALAC and its work, creating a cloud of suspicion over the group. The accusations included a failure to properly secure permission from registrants for their information or other technical issues. Kemp investigated AALAC for two years, then closed the investigation without a single finding of wrongdoing.

This is not just a Georgia phenomenon. In Florida, Wisconsin, Texas, and Tennessee, groups that know that third-party registration is the gateway to participation for certain voters are finding it harder and harder to operate. Following the 2008 election, Florida Republicans targeted the process of voter registration, creating one of the nation's strictest laws for third-party registration. The law, which set tight restrictions, including a forty-eight-hour clock for turning in forms and a $50 penalty per form, had the desired effect of blunting registration efforts. After seventy-two years of operation in Florida, the League of Women Voters halted its efforts, saying the new law would require them to have a lawyer and a secretary on hand at every event. Rock the Vote stopped reaching out to high school students, fearing teachers would face fines and penalties for their participation.

A volunteer organization registering new voters on a Sunday found out the hard way what the law intended. The Sunday drive occurred during a three-day weekend, when government offices were closed on the following Monday. The group turned in their forms on Tuesday but received a chilling warning of the potential for fines because the applications were late—even though the office could not have accepted the forms. The *New York Times* analyzed that 81,471 fewer voters registered in the period following the law's adoption than in the same period four years earlier. Given that Florida statewide elections are often decided by fewer than 25,000 votes, the narrowing of the electorate matters.

In 2019, Tennessee upped the ante on targeting effective third-party registration. After 10,000 voters registered through the Black Voter Project in 2018, the GOP passed a law that also fined groups for delays in turning in forms. In addition, Tennessee lawmakers added a criminal penalty for incentivizing registrars to sign up voters. The proponents of the law argued that these registration efforts increased the likelihood of voter fraud, without any evidence. They also cited potential errors in forms, which are more likely made by the person completing the form rather than the person accepting the form. But with organizations facing up to $10,000 fines and jail time, civil rights organizations challenged the law in federal court. In September 2019, a federal judge enjoined the new law from taking effect; however, as has happened with other rulings, the law may eventually take effect and voters of color are likely to suffer the consequences.

NO TRANSPARENCY IS THE POINT

Criminalizing and fining third-party registration proved to be an effective quiver in the arsenal of voter registration suppression. Several states play hide-and-go-seek with the administrative voter registration process and in how voters actually get on the rolls by creating a maze of bureaucratic hurdles. In 2014, New Georgia Project learned about how those in charge of the system of registration complicated the process and hid their behaviors, to the detriment of potential voters. Through our project and in cooperation with other organizations that worked to increase registration among communities of color, we tracked the processing of forms, all 86,419 of them. We knew a substantial number might be duplicates because some voters are targeted by multiple groups, and occasionally, when a voter hasn't voted recently, they sign up again. Other forms were invalid because of pranks or simply bad information. Then there were those rendered ineligible due to felony disenfranchisement or other restrictions. In anticipation of these errors, we proactively attempted to collaborate with the office of the secretary of state.

However, when we submitted thousands of verified forms, then Georgia secretary of state Brian Kemp, and those he oversaw as the state's election superintendent, refused to add these names to the rolls, leaving voters like Diamond without the right to vote. Quietly, our teams reached out to county officials and the secretary of state to determine what happened. Here, we encountered the first of the transparency issues: tracking registrations. In response to our queries about where voters were in the process, Secretary Kemp publicly accused me of voter fraud, a claim he walked back a few days later. But he still failed to account for the missing 40,000 voters. We entered a tense standoff of dueling press conferences, including one where we delivered photocopies of the missing forms to his office.

Kemp's response—and those of the counties he oversaw as secretary of state—claimed that the forms didn't exist, despite our evidence to the contrary. With Election Day 2014 fast approaching, we filed suit as a last-ditch effort to understand the missing 40,000 forms. The state judge denied our writ of mandamus (a legal demand that the elected official do his job). The court found that we had not proven that Kemp et al. failed; they just hadn't moved fast enough for our taste, a defect the court did not find compelling. Worse, state law in Georgia *does not require* timely processing of applications before an election. In fact, it set no deadline at all. Potential voters had to register twenty-nine days before an election, but the state had no legal obligation to get the name on the rolls in time for an election. According to the judge, state law set deadlines for voters but not for the people in charge of the election, even if their delay meant a person would be prohibited from voting or not receive confirmation that their registration was accepted and the address of their polling location. Thus, with the election looming, the refusal to compel action was a damning blow. Our 40,000 voters hung in limbo.

Election Day passed without resolution; however, we refused to let the mistreatment of our registrants go unavenged. This continued investigation led to our second discovery: secret agency rules. With our legal counsel from the invaluable Lawyers' Committee for Civil Rights Under Law, in 2015, we uncovered unpublished internal rules such as the ninety-day blackout period during which no voter registration forms were processed. Most government agencies have a process where they write rules to determine how their workers should follow the law. As a former deputy city attorney, I certainly understood the process, as would anyone who has tried to read a statute or an ordinance. Often, agency rules act as guidelines to explain how a worker is supposed to meet the obligations of the laws. But in this case, the rules written went beyond the law. Georgia is a state with runoff elections if no one receives 50 percent + 1 on the first round. The May primary of 2014 spilled over into a July runoff.

In years past, the timing between the primary and the runoff had been shorter, but due to a federal lawsuit, the delay had increased. The goal of the rule, we were told, was to make sure voters who hadn't registered by the primary didn't vote in the general election. But a ninety-day delay failed to simply weed out new applicants in that waiting period. We discovered that this had contributed to the untimely delays in processing the forms submitted both before and during the runoff period: three full months of inaction on thousands of forms, without notice to the applicants about what was taking so long. Our attorneys secured a promise to halt the practice in 2016, but it returned with a vengeance during the special election for a congressional race in 2017, the first of the Trump presidency. Once again, eligible citizens eager to participate in the election's process had their applications held hostage by the state's secret rule. However, because of our experience and that of others, attorneys filed a federal lawsuit. The federal court agreed with concerns about the delay, and the judge ruled that the policy violated the law. While we were grateful for the federal fix after three years, citizens lost their right to vote. In the end, 18,000 of New Georgia Project "missing" applications were processed in early 2015, *after* the 2014 election.

The delays in processing had served to keep voters of color off the rolls, but Kemp had another strategy he had deployed without notice to the public. Kemp had revived a discredited policy of "exact match." The exact match system requires perfect data entry by state employees to secure a proper registration in Georgia. Why? Because that entry is then matched against the Social Security Administration database or Georgia's Department of Driver Services database. Neither database is designed for this purpose, and the risk of a mismatch is highest for people of color and women.

Take a female voter with a newly hyphenated last name. Her application will be flagged if the hyphen is not properly entered. So, if the county registrar's staffer types in Tanisha Hagen-Thomas rather than Tanisha Hagen Thomas, the entries do not match and the application is rejected. For communities of color, the danger grows where names including punctuation such as hyphens or apostrophes are cultural norms, like La'Tasha or Pai-Ling. Add last names with spaces or common conjunctive use of first and middle name, and the error rate grows. The exact match system rejects the application, but the applicant is never told why. Therefore, an unsuspecting Joaquin de Mero submits his form, and when compared to the driver's license database that prohibits spaces in last names, the application is tossed out.

Before Kemp installed the exact match system, he knew that the process would disproportionately affect voters of color. Back in 2009, his predecessor Karen Handel sought permission to use the system. In response, the Obama Justice Department summarily rejected exact match as presenting "real," "substantial," and "retrogressive" burdens on voters of color—warning that it would have a racially discriminatory effect. With the *Shelby* decision eliminating the need for the state to get permission to use exact match, Kemp resurrected the discredited policy. Between 2013 and 2016, more than 34,000 applications were suspended under the system, including thousands of New Georgia Project applications submitted in 2014—and most of the applications suspended were from voters of color, just as the Justice Department predicted. A coalition of groups uncovered the use of this system and sued Kemp. At the end of 2016, Kemp agreed to a settlement and to process the applications. However, in the following state legislative session in early 2017, Kemp asked for and received a state-sanctioned version of exact match in defiance of his 2016 federal court settlement. This use of exact match this time led to 53,000 voter registrations being held hostage in 2018, 80 percent of whom were people of color and 70 percent of whom were black voters, who comprise roughly 30 percent of Georgia's eligible voters. In 2018, Georgia officials lost another lawsuit pertaining to exact match.

Between 2015 and 2018, federal courts admonished both black-out periods and multiple iterations of the exact match process; however, these remedies came too late for Georgia's would-be voters in the 2014, 2016, and 2018 state and federal elections. In 2014, those 18,000 voters who had fully completed their applications before the 2014 election never received permission to cast a ballot. The 34,000 applicants restored by a federal court, some of whom had been in limbo since 2013, missed out on state elections in 2014, local elections in 2015, and presidential primaries in 2016. In 2018, thousands of the exact match voters likely received provisional ballots—if they tried to vote, which means they had to take extra steps to ensure their votes counted. The reality, though, is that too many of these eligible Americans simply gave up, finding the system too obdurate and opaque to fight. Again and again, in Georgia and across the country, schemes like this block citizens from being part of the body politic, a fundamental violation of their right to vote.

"VOTING IS A privilege," declared Republican governor Ron DeSantis of Florida on January 16, 2020.[7] He issued the statement in celebration of a state court victory that partially reversed a 2018 state ballot initiative restoring voting rights to felons. A few days later, he attempted to walk back the statement, but his sentiments were crystal clear. And wholly wrong. Voting is a constitutional right in the United States, a right that has been reiterated three separate times via constitutional amendment. For the incarcerated and those returning to their communities, the right to vote varies substantially from state to state. Only two states—Maine and Vermont—do not restrict the right of citizens to vote, even during incarceration. Felons in sixteen states and the District of Columbia lose the right to vote during their incarceration; however, upon release, their rights are automatically restored.

In the rest of the United States, laws left over from Jim Crow and other restrictive codes add more obligations. Twenty-one states strip felons of their voting rights during incarceration and the prohibition remains after release for as long as the returning citizen is on probation or parole. In addition, those who wish to vote may also be obligated to pay any outstanding fines, fees, or court-ordered restitution prior to being allowed to vote.

Georgia is one of the states that use felonies to rescind voting rights, a law born out of Jim Crow and exacerbated by the state's unique history of incarceration. This type of disenfranchisement was added to Georgia's constitution in 1868, and its inclusion reinforced the "Black Codes" and poll taxes intended to suppress black votes after the Thirteenth, Fourteenth, and Fifteenth Amendments were ratified. Today, nearly 60 percent of Georgians disqualified because of a felony conviction are black. Georgia has the tenth-highest rate of felony disenfranchisement in the country[8] and the state has removed more people from the voter list (nearly 147,000) because of a felony conviction than any other state in the country.[9] Under a joint effort by the previous governor and legislators like myself, Georgia attempted to tackle our legacy as a state of mass incarceration, but two-strikes laws (mandatory sentencing after two convictions) and aggressive use of post-release conditions like parole and probation continue to affect potential voters who served time. As of 2016, Georgia had 410,964 people on probation, more than any other state. Although California is the most populous state, with nearly forty million residents, and four times the population of Georgia, the probation numbers are reversed. In 2016,

California had 288,911 probationers, half the number of those in Georgia.[10]

The most restrictive states (Alabama, Arizona, Delaware, Florida, Iowa, Kentucky, Mississippi, Nebraska, Tennessee, Virginia, and Wyoming) strip felons of their voting rights indefinitely for certain offenses, mandate a pardon from the governor, require a waiting period after the end of the sentence—including after the conclusion of probation or parole—and may also tack on additional requirements. Former army pilot Desmond Meade wanted to vote for his wife, Sheena, when she ran for the state legislature in Florida in 2016, but he could not. As a former felon convicted of drug charges and illegal possession of a firearm, he served his time. I met Desmond in 2017, as he traveled the country raising money for Amendment 4, a ballot initiative to restore voting rights to felons in his state. Desmond served his sentence and earned a law degree; however, state law did not allow him to sit for a bar license or to vote in any election. Undeterred, he launched the Florida Rights Restoration Coalition, secured more than 760,000 signatures, and got the amendment placed on the ballot. Amendment 4 passed by an overwhelming majority in 2018, and it should have placed Florida in the category of automatic restoration after completion of a sentence.

In 2019, however, a hyper-partisan GOP-led state legislature passed and DeSantis signed SB 7066.[11] The bill reverses the amendment's language, using the "completion of sentence" clause to undermine the clear intent of the 64.5 percent of voters who approved the change.[12] Under the new law, completing a sentence means not only release, but the completion of probation, parole, the fulfillment of any terms ordered by the courts, the termination of any ordered supervision, and full payment of any ordered fines, fees, costs, or restitution.

Desmond's response has been to lead an effort to raise funds to pay down those obligations for anyone who wants to regain the right to vote. Felon disenfranchisement denies a fundamental right, but it also harms their reintegration into society. Research shows that when people released from correctional control are able to vote, they are more invested in community and are less likely to commit new crimes and return to prison.[13]

YOU'RE OUTTA HERE: EXCESSIVE VOTER PURGES

For people of color, young people, and the marginalized, getting on the rolls can be difficult, if not impossible. Yet the ability to remain on the voter rolls has become a greater challenge for millions across the country. Like so much with voting rights, the Voting Rights Act compelled states to act carefully before removing voters. Federal law has long required states to maintain accurate lists of eligible voters, and states adopted a range of bipartisan legislation to meet the obligation. However, in states like Ohio, Florida, and Georgia, voter purges have become an effective tool to strip eligible voters of their rights. Under the guise of fighting virtually nonexistent voter fraud, Republican secretaries of state have systematically leveraged seemingly neutral rules for removing voters who have died or left the state and executed vast removals of eligible voters.

Imagine a working-class voter who has just finished a second shift at work. She races home to check on her kids, then hurries over to her polling location. The last time she voted was a while ago, probably for president. No one reached out to her to vote in local elections, whenever they were—she can't quite recall, given her jobs as a pre-K teacher and a cashier at the local pharmacy.

But she tries to vote when she can. After waiting in line for nearly two hours, she reaches the front desk, identification in hand. Only, the poll worker tells her she is not on the list. Confused, she explains that she still lives at the same address and hasn't changed anything about her circumstances. She hasn't committed a felony, and she cares about this race because the candidate seems to have a plan for increased access to childcare. However, she sheepishly admits that she hasn't voted since Obama won the first time. The kindly poll worker explains that the woman has probably been purged. She's lost her right to vote because she didn't use it often enough. For a purged voter, the hours in line and frustration of being invisible cannot be recovered. In order to vote, she'll have to start the process of registering and getting on the rolls all over again—when she can find the time.

Most states have adopted best practices that tracked voter behavior to determine if a voter needed to be removed from the database. Typically, the rules held that if a voter didn't vote after a certain number of elections, this should trigger an investigation to assess if the voter is deceased or no longer in state. However, in states with a history of voting discrimination, the process of making contact with the voter is often ineffective and typically consists of mainly sending flimsy postcards that resemble junk mail. Instead of improving the quality of the voting lists, long-time voters often find themselves cut from the rolls, forced to prove their rights against an indifferent bureaucracy. According to the Brennan Center, "Between 2014 and 2016, states removed almost 16 million voters from the rolls—a 33 percent increase over the period between 2006 and 2008. The increase was highest in states with a history of voting discrimination."[14]

Many of those removed are neither dead nor gone; they

simply opted not to cast a vote in recent elections. This excuse for removal, known as "use it or lose it" among election experts, presumes that the failure to exercise a right justifies taking it away. The National Association of Secretaries of State officially cites Alaska, Florida, Georgia, Oklahoma, Maine, Montana, Pennsylvania, South Dakota, and Wisconsin as "use-it or lose-it" states,[15] but other election experts place the number much higher than these nine. According to various congressional reports on voting rights, NAACP briefings, and expert studies, nearly all states have a version of this rule. A 2017 National Association of Secretaries of State report found that "in forty-four states, voters who fail to respond to a notice will be removed from the registration list if they do not vote, update their registration, or take some other action specified by law from the time of the notice through two federal general elections." No other right guaranteed by our constitution permits the loss of a right for failure to use it—to wit, I don't lose my Second Amendment right if I choose not to go hunting and I still have freedom of religion if I skip church now and then.

Georgia secretary of state Brian Kemp strongly favored the "use it or lose it" power in Georgia, where he removed over 1.4 million voters in a state with 6 million registered users. In July 2017, he removed more than half a million voters in a single day, reducing the number of registered voters in Georgia by 8 percent. An estimated 107,000 of these voters were removed through "use it or lose it."

The removal process captures not only those who have not voted; the inefficient approach taken by a number of states often removes voters who could demonstrate regular voting patterns. One of these voters was Ms. Christine Jordan, a ninety-two-year-old resident of Atlanta, Georgia, and cousin of Dr. Martin Luther King Jr. She arrived at the polls on November 6, 2018, prepared to vote as she had for the past fifty years, in the same neighborhood. Since 1968, when the Voting Rights Act finally compelled the state to grant her access to the franchise, she never missed an election. Yet, on that day, the poll workers told Ms. Jordan that she did not exist on the voter rolls. She'd been purged. For hours, her granddaughter argued with staff, perplexed as to how a voting legacy that had stretched through the civil rights era, Watergate, and Obama had suddenly disappeared. The answer: an emboldened and incompetent process that swept out the dead and the living with equal disregard.

In 2018, in the aftermath of the gubernatorial election, I launched Fair Fight Action and a political action committee known as Fair Fight PAC. We immediately filed suit against the state of Georgia for its incompetence and malfeasance in running Georgia's elections system. Our goal was and is to hold the state accountable for its actions, including its troubling history of voter purges. In October 2019, the newly elected secretary of state announced a new round of voter purging for Georgia, this time targeting 313,000 voters—roughly 4 percent of the state's list of voters. Fair Fight Action set up phone banks and text banks to reach out to the voters slated for removal. Due to our efforts, 4,500 voters learned that they were likely to lose their right to vote months before the presidential primary. But we didn't stop there. Fair Fight Action also filed for an injunction against the purge, citing the state's failure to follow its own laws. On the day of the purge, due to our efforts, another 22,000 voters were restored to the rolls. That's nearly 10 percent of the targeted purge population—and enough votes to affect an election.

Once again, though, Georgia is not alone. It is one of nine states that will remove voters for not voting. From April to August 2019, at the urging of its Republican governor, the state of Kentucky purged 175,000 voters from its rolls, including thousands flagged for failure to vote.[16] The Democratic secretary of state cried foul, but the GOP appointees on the state's election board ignored her objections. In response, a coalition of groups brought suit against the purge, and a federal judge agreed that the state failed to follow its own protocols. A month later, the Republican governor lost by just over 5,000 votes, an outcome that might have been vastly different if the illegal purge had stood.

Around the same time, the Republican secretary of state in Ohio tagged more than 235,000 voters for a fall purge. Jen Miller, an Ohio voter and the head of the League of Women Voters in the state, began reviewing the list for issues. She knew what to look for because she spent every day helping voters register and become engaged. As she combed through the list, she discovered that among those slated to be removed was one Jen Miller—despite voting in three elections the previous years. Ms. Miller, in cooperation with other organizations reviewing the list, found more than 40,000 errors on the lists—nearly 20 percent of those flagged had not forfeited their right to vote under the strictest application of the rules.

As the 2020 election nears, conservative groups are filing lawsuits demanding the purging of rolls, including in the swing states of Wisconsin and Michigan, where approximately 35,000 votes between them helped decide the 2016 election. Fair Fight 2020 is working with leaders in these states as part of our initiative to protect the right to vote in the battleground states for the presidency, the U.S. Senate, and down-ballot races like secretaries of state, attorneys general, and state legislative chambers. Our system of participatory democracy begins with the license to vote, and without it, a citizen will not be heard. But assuming a voter makes it onto the list of eligible voters, the next question is: will they be allowed to cast their vote?

CHAPTER 3

Getting Beyond the Gates
(Access to the Ballot)

"They thought they could make an example out of me."[1]
Talking to a reporter in 2019, Mayor Nancy Dennard
described how then secretary of state Brian Kemp justified why
she and eleven others faced 120 felony charges for winning an
election in Southwest Georgia less than a decade earlier. Back
then, Dr. Dennard was an African American speech pathologist
who had run twice for the school board in Quitman, Georgia,
to no avail. In white-majority Brooks County, where Quitman
is the largest city, the public schools were predominantly black.
Dr. Dennard worried that too few blacks held positions of leadership within the school system, and she ran for school board. First
in 2004 and again in 2008, she ran and lost. But when a special
election came up in 2009, she was ready.

After her first campaign, from hundreds of miles away, a
Republican-controlled state government in Atlanta had eased
the rules for absentee ballots—the ability to vote from home
and mail in your choices. Historically, Republicans had utilized

absentee ballots far more frequently than Democrats, so the decision made sense. But Dr. Dennard studied the rules and put them to use. She ran a stealth campaign to increase absentee ballots among black voters, and it worked. Dr. Dennard won a special election to the board, drawing the attention of local leaders and voters alike.

For the 2010 primary for other available school board seats, she recruited more black women to run, and she trained them and a committed group of organizers on the laws of absentee ballots. Once again, the strategy succeeded. A handful of black women got elected to the Brooks County School Board, and control of the board flipped from white majority to black majority. In a town described by some residents as Mayberry of *The Andy Griffith Show*, the Technicolor victories were hard to take.

Angered by the unexpected wins, a vanquished school board member, a suspicious postmaster, and the school board's attorney banded together to challenge the legitimacy of the new slate's electoral wins. First, they simply tried to undo the election. Dr. Dennard's allies had run for office during the Democratic primary because almost everyone in town ran as a Democrat. That should have ended the matter. In Georgia, candidates can run for office in a primary, but if they lose, they can't try to get on the ballot in the general election that same cycle. The prohibition is commonly referred to as the "sore loser" law. But the candidates who lost decided to go around the law and get a second shot in November. To Dennard's surprise, a local judge allowed the losing candidates to run again as independents. But the team was ready, and black turnout tripled—exceeding white turnout 1,461 to 1,259, and absentee ballots made the difference. The losers lost a second time.

Confounded by the success of the absentee ballot strategy and the second routing in a year, the rejected incumbents and their cronies reached out to Secretary Kemp. He responded aggressively to the false accusations of voter fraud, the only excuse opponents could come up with to explain their defeat. Black voters didn't vote absentee, and certainly not in Brooks County. Kemp, newly installed in his office, took up the cause of the losers and the conspiracy theories. He authorized the Georgia Bureau of Investigation—the state's version of the FBI—to pursue the matter on the department's behalf. Agents raided their homes and offices and arrested the duly elected school board members and their supporters. The governor removed them from office, and several lost their regular employment, their reputations smeared.

Years passed before their criminal trials commenced; and in the end, not a single person was convicted. No voter fraud had occurred, just clever use of a process rarely leveraged by black voters. But the damage was done, the goal accomplished: black voters had been punished for utilizing rules white voters had enjoyed for years. Access to the ballot had severe limits; and despite doing nothing wrong, the consequences of full engagement could be devastating.[2]

The horrible tale of the Quitman 10 + 2 (so named due to the original ten organizers plus two additional supporters included in the indictments) illustrates a truism that extends far beyond Georgia. If a voter has survived the gauntlet of challenges to staying on the rolls, the next issue is the ability to access a ballot and vote. While Kemp's attack on the black voters of Quitman occurred before the gutting of the Voting Rights Act, his actions simply previewed what would follow. State legislators, secretaries of state, and governors—almost entirely Republican—returned to their greatest hits in voter suppression. Limits on absentee ballots and restrictive voter ID laws came first, followed by an increase in closed or consolidated precincts, reductions in early voting, vulnerable or inadequate equipment, and lax oversight of county application of state laws. Separately and together, these actions block voters from accessing the ballots that make voting real. In state after state, incompetence and malfeasance operates in tandem, and the sheer complexity of the nation's voting apparatus transforms voter suppression into a nearly seamless system.

These hurdles have had their desired effect of hampering voters, making it harder to cast a ballot. Federal court systems have aided bad state actors by allowing more and more rules to limit access or stop voters from getting a remedy. Where President Obama harnessed unlikely voters into an electoral phenomenon, states responded by slashing when and how voting occurred and who could participate. Voting lines for black voters in the nation grew longer. Native Americans faced a nightmarish return to second-class citizenship in states where their votes could tip the balance of elections. Naturalized citizens had to sue for their newly secured rights, and organizations continue to fight for ballots and access in multiple languages. The disabled community found itself pitted against black voters in an attempt to justify limits to access. Moreover, across the country, where states neglected their elections infrastructure, the result has been vulnerable, sometimes inoperable machines that were inadequately distributed to communities.

In isolation, each of these examples is troubling, as it represents a voter who could not fully participate in the body politic. Combined, they demonstrate the disenfranchisement of American voters in general and the targeting of communities of color and other marginalized groups in particular. Ballot access is the second line of attack on our voting rights, and to defeat its malicious affect, we must understand how it operates.

THE FALSE SEDUCTION OF VOTER ID

Whenever I raise the issue of voter suppression, I can be certain proponents of more restrictive rules will respond with two standard retorts. The first is the specter of voter fraud, the rationale frequently used by conservatives to justify the implementation of several forms of suppression. As the argument goes, the rules are required to stop a horde from skewing the outcomes of elections. However, voter fraud has been debunked as exceptionally rare by multiple reputable organizations, not to mention the ersatz voting commission established by Donald Trump.

Nevertheless, for the record, let's review. Voter fraud refers typically to one of two occurrences: (1) impersonating another voter or (2) a noncitizen, nonresident, or ineligible voter effectively casting a ballot. The former almost never happens; in fact, an American is more likely to be struck by lightning than to impersonate a voter.[3] To be more specific, according to analysis, out of 1 billion votes cast between 2000 and 2014, only 31 instances of voter impersonation occurred.[4] As to noncitizen or nonresident voting, the almost universal explanation is voter *confusion*. In the United States, we have fifty-one different democracies in operation between individual state laws and federal laws. For example, if a person moves from Maine to Oklahoma, the rules change dramatically with regard to registration timing, eligibility, and remedies. National experts barely understand the complexity of local voting laws—how would the average person?

Fraud is a crime of intent. Most accusations of voter fraud are best described as misunderstandings.[5]

Restrictive voter identification is the main weapon to fight the nonexistent wave of voter fraud, but this is not the same as basic voter ID. Basic voter ID has been a part of voting since the beginning, and both Democrats and Republicans agree that people should provide proof of who they are before casting ballots. Thirty-five states require a form of identification and the remaining fifteen states typically accept identifying information based on what has been previously provided by a voter, such as a signature on file.[6] What has changed in recent years is the type of identification required and the difficulty or expense of securing the necessary documents. Restrictive voter ID severely narrows the list of permitted documents that serve as proof, and these laws typically exclude previously permissible documents. Due to the success of this narrowing filter of acceptable documents, restrictive voter ID laws have become a key tool in the suppression toolbox.

In 2008, the U.S. Supreme Court authorized the first restrictive voter identification laws proffered by Georgia and Indiana, based on a case from Indiana.[7] In 2005, Georgia Republicans controlled both the governor's office and the state legislature for the first time in modern history. Their victories were slim: the state's first GOP governor since Reconstruction won his election in 2002 by 104,000 votes over his Democratic opponent. The state legislature soon flipped to Republican; in 2005, the state legislature adopted a voter identification scheme designed to prevent voter fraud, despite no evidence that fraud had occurred in recent elections. The law removed a number of previously permissible forms of identification and instead required either a driver's license, certain government IDs, or a special card. For example, student IDs issued by state colleges and universities would no longer be allowed, even though they were from a government agency. In Indiana, the new laws were similar. Lower courts struck down the provisions as a poll tax, due to the costs associated with securing these IDs. However, the conservative-leaning Supreme Court ruled that the restrictive IDs were okay as long as states made a free form of ID available.

Additional states have also tightened rules to limit the types of identification eligible for use.[8] Supporters argue for these laws by citing that identification is de rigueur in America, that is, one must have an ID to go to the bank, to board a plane, or to operate a car. Voter identification, they exhort, is a logical extension, and no right-minded person could reasonably object. But the reality of life in America is that even access to identification can be fraught with bureaucratic mistakes, legal impossibilities, and our nation's continued struggle with race and class. By limiting forms of identification that almost anyone can provide or, worse, by requiring proof that is nearly impossible to secure, restrictive identification blocks access to the right to vote.

In 2012, Heidi Heitkamp won election to the United States Senate from the state of North Dakota. As a Democrat, her election stunned many, including the Republicans who controlled most of the power in her home state. Her victory had been the result of several factors, not the least of which was the strong support from Native American citizens who cast their ballots on her behalf. Their turnout rates carried Senator Heitkamp to a narrow victory, and she praised their engagement. A few years later, in 2016, members of the Standing Rock Sioux banded together to block the construction of a pipeline across their lands. Their activism drew international attention, particularly from those angered by their audacity to protect their own territory.

With the amplified presence of Native American voices in both electoral politics and in civic engagement, the Republican power base sought to reassert their control over the operation of the state. Muting Native American voices at the ballot box gave the Republicans a clear course of action. The upcoming 2018 election would determine if Heitkamp, the state's sole Democratic senator and only statewide elected Democrat, remained in office. She'd won in 2012 by the slimmest of margins: 2,936 votes, a victory attributed in large part to Native American voters.[9] In response, Republicans looked to a tool they'd tried to use before, a policy of restrictive voter identification: the requirement that lawful voters in North Dakota must have residential street addresses on their IDs. The law had passed years before, but federal courts had enjoined the state from imposing the obligation due to the specific effect it would have on Native Americans in North Dakota.

For most Americans, providing a valid street address would hardly be an issue. After all, we must use that address for pizza delivery, Amazon Prime packages, and emergencies. But for the several tribes who inhabit the vast lands of North Dakota, a verifiable residential address is a luxury and, for thousands, an impossibility. Among of the casualties of the law were Leslie and Clark Peltier, members of the Turtle Mountain Band of Chippewa Indians. A professor, Leslie taught at the local college, and Clark served as foreman for the maintenance department at the local housing authority. For more than a decade, they lived in their house on the reservation, a family home surrounded by gravel roads and no street signs. The absence never struck them as unusual. Native American reservations rarely have residential addresses, as the state or local governments often fail to assign them. So life on reservations has adapted to use a combination of P.O. boxes, cluster boxes, and approximated street addresses to direct emergency vehicles. In 2012, when the Peltiers went to vote, the registrar notified them of the updated residential address that would now be used for 911 calls.

The Peltiers dutifully recorded the address and updated their drivers' licenses to reflect the new information. However, when they went to vote in 2013, the poll worker told them that the new residential address meant they had to vote in a different city, off the reservation. They hadn't moved their home or changed anything else in twelve years, except their licenses, based on governmental information. The change in address now meant they'd have to vote in one place for races like U.S. Senate, governor, or local leaders, and in a completely different place for tribal elections, even if elections occurred on the same day. They adapted as best they could, as did thousands of others facing similar outlandish requirements.

Then, just before the pivotal reelection of Heidi Heitkamp, the U.S. senator swept into office six years before, Republican leaders in the state started to strictly apply the residential address requirement. For the Peltiers, compliance was impossible. They discovered that the residential address they'd dutifully updated onto their IDs did not match the assigned 911 address for their home. No one could explain the conflict or seem to resolve it; therefore, they could be denied the right to vote. Because of the resurgence of this impossible standard, a coalition of Native American plaintiffs filed suit against the state of North Dakota, and in their complaint, they detailed several examples of this flawed process: a young couple from the Spirit Lake Sioux who had been issued a residential address by the government, only to be told the same address was deemed invalid by the *same* bureaucracy; a sixty-nine-year-old member of the Standing Rock

Sioux told that his government-issued address corresponded not to his house but to a liquor store; and the Peltiers.

The irony of the lawsuit glared from the complaint: the North Dakota GOP secretary of state sought to apply a standard that the state and local governments had made it *impossible* to meet. In the last days of the 2018 election, the U.S. Supreme Court sided with the state of North Dakota and refused to intervene in blocking the enforcement of the irrational requirement. Almost everyone else would be fine, went the justification, so if this minority group of Native Americans faced harm, it paled in comparison to the rationality of the overall system.

What the North Dakota tribes faced in 2018 simply followed the trail of voter ID restrictions in Georgia, Indiana, Kansas, Mississippi, Tennessee, Virginia, and Wisconsin. In Wisconsin, Donald Trump's narrow victory by fewer than 23,000 votes (or 0.77 percent) in 2016 has been attributed in part to the state's controversial voter ID law. Nationally, researchers differ on the effects of voter ID on election outcomes, as part of the issue is proving a negative—that a voter did not vote because of ID versus another plausible reason. In the case of Wisconsin, researchers at the *Election Law Journal* found that at least one percentage point of nonvoting occurred based on a combination of factors, including both an absence of valid identification and confusion about how to meet the new law's parameters.[10]

For those who seek to comply, gaining access can prove prohibitively difficult. In the town of Sauk City, Wisconsin, those in need of free voter ID cards could secure them at the local DMV; however, the nearest office was open only four times in 2016—on the fifth Wednesday of every month.[11] Another barrier is securing the appropriate documents themselves. Mrs. Smith, a native of Missouri, had lived and voted in Milwaukee since

2003. After Wisconsin adopted its restrictive voter ID laws, Mrs. Smith attempted to get the required photo identification. To do so, she had to produce a birth certificate that would prove her date and place of birth. But Mrs. Smith, an African American woman born during segregation in 1916, does not have a birth certificate because, like many blacks of her era, she was born at home due to lack of access to a hospital. She attempted to use the ID Petition Process at the Wisconsin Department of Motor Vehicles, ostensibly designed to help citizens like her get an ID. Although they found a record of Mrs. Smith in the 1930 census, they could not connect her to a qualified Missouri birth record. Denied a restricted voter ID, Mrs. Smith could not vote in the 2016 election because, at the age of one hundred, she could not prove her identity to the state of Wisconsin.[12]

Even the federal Government Accountability Office (GAO) has taken notice of the effects of restrictive voter ID. In 2014, after reviewing research on how these policies alter voter behavior, the GAO conducted its own study using the states of Kansas and Tennessee as models, and comparing general elections from 2008 and 2012 to turnout in the control states of Alabama, Arkansas, Delaware, and Maine, all states without strict photo ID laws.[13] The GAO found evidence that the new ID requirements in both Kansas and Tennessee had demonstrable effects on turnout, decreasing it by 1.9 to 2.2 percentage points in Kansas and 2.2 to 3.2 percentage points in Tennessee. In both cases, the declines were greater in these two states than in the comparison states. Specifically, the highest declines were noted among young voters and African Americans, and, as the GAO noted, "the results were consistent across the different data sources and voter populations used in the analysis."[14] For the elderly, those with limited financial resources, people of color, the transgender community, and others, restrictive ID has the direct effect of limiting access to the ballot, not making voting more secure.

THERE'S NO VOTING AT A CLOSED POLL

Voter identification is directly connected to suppression because the ID *is* a voter's access card to the polls. Yet, for millions who have to navigate the labyrinth of voter ID laws, the next hurdle awaits: the challenge of physically getting inside the voting booth. One of the favored schemes during Jim Crow was making polling places so difficult to reach that voters simply gave up.

When she came down to campaign with me, Oprah Winfrey told the story of Otis Moss Sr., father of famed pastor Otis Moss II and grandfather to my Morehouse classmate Otis Moss III, himself a gifted minister. Mr. Moss, a sharecropper in Troup County, Georgia, attempted to vote in 1946 in the first election where blacks would have a chance to speak to the future of the state. Eugene Talmadge, an avowed segregationist, stood for reelection, and Mr. Moss intended to hoist him out of office. As Oprah recounted to the enrapt crowd, "Otis Moss Sr., who, right here in Georgia's Troup County, got up in the morning and put on his only suit and his best tie. And he walked six miles to the voting poll location he was told to go to in LaGrange. When he got there after walking six miles in his good suit and tie, they said, 'Boy, you at the wrong place. You need to go over to Mountville.' So he walked another six miles to Mountville, and when he got there, they said, 'Boy, you in the wrong place. You need to go to the Rosemont School.'

"I picture him walking from dawn to dusk in his suit, his feet tired, getting to the Rosemont School. And they said, 'Boy, you too late. The polls are closed.' And he never had a chance to vote. By the time the next election came around, he had died."

Twenty years later, the Voting Rights Act included protection of polling places as a central feature. The ability to actually reach the assigned location for voting has been a long-standing hurdle for millions. As sanctioned by the Fifteenth Amendment, states have the authority to govern electoral laws, and where a person is permitted to cast a ballot is key. If the location is too far away from public transit, those who have no access to vehicles may be unable to vote. If the location is non-ADA compliant, those with physical disabilities cannot reach the polls. When the polling place isn't in a neutral location like a school but rather a police station or judicial complex, the atmosphere can threaten a voter's confidence. However, under the VRA, states with a history of manipulating polling locations as a means to restrict voter participation had to get permission before they could change a single voting location. During my tenure as deputy city attorney for Atlanta, part of my portfolio included helping the city clerk prepare her submission to the federal Department of Justice outlining any precinct location changes.

Changes were inevitable. Schools and churches required maintenance that put them out of commission for a cycle. Libraries became too small as populations grew, and fire stations shifted as neighborhoods evolved. The VRA acknowledged that locations would move over time, but the rule mandated that the voter's needs always came first. But the gutting of the VRA in 2013 reversed nearly fifty years of protection and voter promotion. By removing the requirement of preclearance—the requirement that jurisdictions get permission before changing local voting rules—states raced to take advantage of the lack of oversight. For example, according to analysis by the *Atlanta Journal-Constitution*, officials closed 8 percent of Georgia's polling places and nearly 40 percent were relocated, all between 2012 and 2018, with the bulk occurring after 2013's court decision.[15] They tell the story of Maggie Coleman, 71, who has knee and back pain. She used to live within a mile of her polling place in Clay County, but local officials moved it ten miles away. Ms. Coleman has access to a car and can drive herself the distance, but Clay County's 43 percent poverty rate means that many of her neighbors likely have no access to vehicles, and Clay County does not operate a public transit system.

Georgia is not alone. In the five years since *Shelby*, 1,688 polling places closed in states subject to preclearance. Between the 2012 and 2016 elections, states closed nearly 3,000 physical polling places, according to the Election Assistance Commission, a decline from 119,968 locations in 2012 to 116,990 in 2016. Around the country, the closure or consolidation of precincts unfairly punishes those who have challenges with transportation or who have other issues, like a physical disability. Particularly for those with physical disabilities, location matters because when buildings are inaccessible or inconvenient, these voters face limited options or none at all.[16] Poll closures that shift voters from one location to another often fail to account for physical barriers like steps, steep entryways, or ungraded pathways. For example, churches are often used as polling locations, but under the Americans with Disabilities Act, religious facilities are exempt from compliance.[17] Once inside, not all polling locations are created alike. When a location has fewer outlets, the special voting machines disabled voters rely on may not be supported or available. Or, if the location is cramped, wheelchairs or other equipment can be difficult to maneuver.

While some closures can be attributed to expanding voting options like early voting, absentee balloting, or mail-in ballots, the broader implications remain. Certain marginalized or historically disenfranchised communities face a complex web of challenges to physical access to polling locations. Like many public policy decisions, the connections between actions seem innocuous to the casual observer. Yet, put together, the combination of factors becomes a permanent impediment to voters, preventing them from reaching the polls.

For example, a public transit authority removes a bus stop in a low-income neighborhood due to an increase in ridership in a nearby community and budget constraints. A year later, the county defunds a precinct location and moves it to a location on the edge of the county, again citing budget issues. Transit dollars are squeezed, so routes become less frequent. For the elderly or non-driving voters in that neighborhood, their ability to reach their new polling location is now *absolutely* more difficult. If they live in a state without other voting options, then their right to vote is null and void. Consider the state of Missouri, which does not allow early voting; instead, a voter must be out of the jurisdiction, be incapacitated, or fall under a narrow list of exceptions to not come to the precinct on Election Day. If a polling place moves miles from a person's home, and there is no transit or someone willing to drive, the voter cannot cast a ballot.

Like the saga of Mr. Moss and Troup County's polling places, Georgia once again surged into the spotlight of suppression under then secretary of state Brian Kemp. Once *Shelby* lifted the shield of protection for precincts, Kemp's office circulated a training guide that emphasized how and why counties should close or move polling locations. In Georgia, as in most states, local governments like counties make the ultimate decision about polling locations. However, these elections officials take their cues from the secretary of state, particularly if he emphasizes how local governments can now *legally* close locations without the pesky oversight of the Department of Justice. Over and over, Kemp's guide reminded the stewards of elections that they no longer had to meet the stringent requirements of the VRA. Instead, they could shut down locations by following laxer state laws.

In 2015, the New Georgia Project, now led by Nse Ufot, hired a law student to begin tracking precinct closures in the state of Georgia. One of the shifts we identified occurred in predominantly black Macon-Bibb County, where the board of elections attempted to move a long-standing polling place from a community gymnasium to the sheriff's office. Instead of going into a safe space where neighbors regularly gathered, would-be voters would have to go through the process of voting under the watchful eye of law enforcement. Until 2014, Georgia had the fourth-highest incarceration rate in the nation, with one of the largest black populations behind bars. Today, Georgia remains the number one state for having people on probation or parole. The state's carceral reputation, as well as citizens' understandable sense of intimidation, led to protests about the decision. Luckily, action by the New Georgia Project and a group of community organizations, utilizing a petition option buried in the Georgia code, reversed the decision, and the precinct moved to a local church annex. In 2018, a consultant recommended by Kemp suggested the closure of two polling locations in Randolph County that served majority black voters, while leaving untouched the ones serving white voters. National outrage led the board of elections to reverse its decision. Yet, the effects in Georgia reverberated through the 2018 contest. Again, according to the AJC analysis, "Precinct closures and longer distances likely prevented an estimated 54,000 to 85,000 voters from casting ballots on Election Day last year, according to the AJC's findings. And the impact was greater on black voters than white ones, the AJC found. Black voters were 20% more likely to miss elections because of long distances."

African Americans tend to be the victims of voter suppression efforts like those in Georgia, but growing populations like Latinos face familiar hurdles from precinct closures. In predominantly white Ford County, Kansas, the 28,000 voters in Dodge City lost their sole polling location in the city's civic arena. The decision by the white county elections official had a direct effect on the majority Latino town. Voters in the community received notice that they would have to find their way to the outskirts of town to a new polling location, despite the lack of public transportation. Any voter who used the bus would have to walk a full mile to reach the location. For a community comprised largely of workers at local meatpacking plants, the issue of transportation had serious consequences. Worse, Dodge City already experienced a disproportionate voter load at its one precinct: 13,000 voters as compared to the average of 1,200 for other Kansas precincts.

When the ACLU warned the Ford County clerk, Deborah Cox, about the potential harms and asked her to publicize a local hotline to aid stranded voters, she forwarded the email to Secretary of State Kris Kobach with the message, "LOL." Kobach, a disgraced elections superintendent dedicated to voter suppression, has himself been sued and cited for acts of malice toward voters of color. Like Brian Kemp of Georgia, Kobach and other

Republican secretaries of state have waged war on voter access, their targets uniformly being people of color, naturalized citizens, and students—all populations more likely to vote Democratic.

WHEN VOTING ISN'T EASY, IT CAN BE IMPOSSIBLE

Thirty-nine states currently permit early voting, a designated period before an election when any voter can show up in person and cast a ballot.[18] Absentee ballots, which allow the voter to receive theirs at home, are available in all fifty states—and there are two challenges: getting them and having them counted. The first challenge of being able to vote from home is a core issue of access to the ballot. Thirty-three states and the District of Columbia place no restrictions on who can utilize this convenient and effective method of voting; however, seventeen states require the voter to have a valid excuse, ranging from permanent disability to proof the voter will be out of town. The theory behind early voting and absentee balloting is simple: voters should also be able to fully participate in elections, regardless of circumstances. For senior citizens, the physically disabled, and workers, particularly those with erratic shifts, the flexibility provided by these methods can be their sole method of participation.

My home state of Georgia allows both early voting and absentee balloting, as do several of the more aggressive voter suppression states like Ohio, North Carolina, Wisconsin, and Florida. In fact, when accused of bad action, these states often point out early and absentee voting as methods of voting as defense. However, the contention faces a fundamental flaw. States may put the best array of options on the menu, but if they are always unavailable to a certain clientele, the option isn't real. In 2018, Florida and Georgia both faced issues with absentee ballots actually reaching voters. Tony Doris, a reporter in Florida, detailed the issues his older son experienced with receiving his ballot.[19] Despite applying for it earlier, the ballot only reached him in Boston a few days before the election. Florida law requires that a request for an absentee ballot be received by the tenth day before an election, and the completed ballots must be received by 7:00 p.m. on Election Day. Mr. Doris's son was not alone in facing delays. During the 2018 general election, Doris reported that 174,649 absentee ballots mailed out to Democrats were not returned to election supervisors, which is 91,038 more than those not returned by Republicans.[20] While a number of unreturned absentee ballots signal a voter's decision to not reply, for thousands, the primary culprit was late arrival of ballots due to the state's flawed system or a complete failure to send the absentee ballots out at all. However, Florida county election supervisors failed to send out more than 20,000 requested absentee ballots by the legal deadline of October 31. Reports of late ballots plagued Georgia as well, prompting affidavits in Fair Fight Action's lawsuit against the state. Ofodile Anachuna and Lorene Bell never received their requested ballots,[21] and one county is under investigation for failing to send out 4,700 requested ballots.[22] County election supervisors oversee the daily operations of elections, but the state's obligation cannot be minimized or ignored.

Much like the issues with absentee ballot access, Republicans have targeted early voting operations that have helped increase voter participation, to their apparent dismay. In North Carolina, following President Barack Obama's successful 2008 campaign, Republicans slashed early voting from seventeen to ten days and curbed or eliminated Sunday voting due to the popularity of "souls to the polls" campaigns that encouraged black voters to turn out en masse after church services. Florida Republicans responded to the wide use of early voting by cutting the days from fourteen to eight for the 2012 presidential election and beyond, no doubt in reaction to Floridians' votes for Obama in 2008. Wisconsin, for decades regarded as a leader in voting rights, responded to the wave of Democratic voters by eliminating early voting hours at night and on weekends: the precise times most used by low-income and minority voters. For Ohio's GOP majority, the cuts to access included chopping off six days of in-person early voting, jettisoning Sundays and evenings, and eliminating voting the day before the election.

Policymakers who propose these cuts have a standard playbook.[23] First, point to the costs of early voting and then appeal to the fear of voter fraud. As a state legislator for eleven years, I heard the pitch for limits to early voting, and I gave each proposal due consideration. In 2011, I cosponsored legislation to eliminate twenty-four days of early voting in Georgia, reducing time allowed from forty-five days to twenty-one days, the gold standard for early voting periods. In states with early voting, the goal is to offer long enough for voters to take full advantage but to not cause a cost-prohibitive burden to the local government operating elections. Small towns and rural counties reported facing cuts to law enforcement or human services to fund the full elections period, even though very few voters used the first twenty-four days. In a state like ours, with 159 counties and more than 500 local jurisdictions, the standardized costs for small towns proved prohibitive. Whether a town has a population of 500 or 500,000, the rules for staffing and operating an election remained the same: keeping staff on duty even when no one used the facility, funding the security of the machines, and paying the overhead for the locations. The request had been made by Democrats and Republicans, and the financial evidence

was compelling. The Obama Justice Department agreed and pre-
cleared the reduction, which still allowed three solid weeks of
early access. Then, after the VRA decision, the Republicans in
Georgia noted two trends. One: in 2014, 44 percent of voters
in Georgia, with a hefty number of nonwhite voters in the mix,
used early voting. Two: the margin of victory for Republicans
shrank from 8 percent in 2008 to just over 5 percent in 2014.
That time, I fought against newly proposed restrictions, as not
one of the proponents would provide a fiscal analysis to show
how reducing the days from twenty-one to twelve would help
communities.

Research from North Carolina and Ohio painted a clear picture of the trend the GOP was anxious to avoid. In the presidential elections of 2008 and 2012, 70 percent of black voters cast
their ballots early. In Ohio, black voters used early voting twice
as much as white voters in 2012. Even today, the issue of early
access has become a weapon of choice for voter suppression. Both
Texas and Florida have attempted to limit early voting on college campuses, where the voting trends show increased participation and a decidedly Democratic lean to young voting patterns.
Watching the surge in college-age voting with trepidation, the
GOP-dominated Texas legislature banned early voting sites on
college campuses that did not stay open for the full twelve days
of early voting.[24] Because colleges must bear the brunt of costs,
the new regulations proved cost prohibitive, and sites—some that
served more than 14,000 voters—have all been shuttered. Florida
has attempted the same quashing of student participation by prohibiting any early voting site on campus with inadequate parking,
despite the residential nature of most of the colleges.

Restrictive ID prevents citizens limited by means or access
from voting in elections in one state, while identical voters with

basic identification or none at all vote annually in another state. The disparity is not only stark, it is unnecessary; and the disparate treatment undermines confidence in our democracy. Likewise, when polling places are closed, early voting is cut, or absentee ballots never arrive or come too late, vulnerable voters cannot cast a ballot. This is not a coincidence. Young people and people of color typically benefit from the expanded access, due to their unpredictable schedules, limited resources, and greater suspicion of the electoral system. In 2018, the share of college students voting doubled from just four years before, mostly to the benefit of Democrats. Likewise, black voting patterns have been on the rise since 2008, even accounting for non-presidential years.[25] Among AAPI and Latino voters, increases in participation have affected state and federal elections, adding to Democratic gains at every level of government.[26] In response, the illusion of voter fraud has been trotted out to justify purges and barriers to access, but the reality of voter theft stands out much more clearly. Whether the right erects new hurdles to voting or shuts off clear avenues of engagement, Republicans have hewed to their mission of stopping the vote. The knotted web of rules and bureaucratic puzzles stifle participation in voting, and therefore in democracy. Voter suppression begins with barriers to registration, and it continues by limiting access to the ballot. But beyond these measures, the enemies of fully participatory democracy have a final weapon to get their way: making sure certain votes never count.

CHAPTER 4

When the Numbers Lie (Ballot Counting)

O n October 22, 2018, I went to South DeKalb Mall to vote early. Traditionally, I cast my ballot on Election Day, like millions of others, and I'd grown up with it as a sort of civic holiday—a day where you show up, do your part, and, before midnight, a winner is declared. I voted for the first time in 1992, in the presidential primary, and then in nearly every election since. When I ran for the state legislature in 2006, I voted on July 18, in person at my designated precinct. But the 2018 general election was different.

In early October, the Associated Press had broken a story declaring that Secretary of State Kemp suspended the voter registrations for more than 53,000 Georgians.[1] As he was also my opponent for governor, the media swarmed over the story's details, at last asking the question of how the person in charge of the election could also be a candidate. Our campaign office fielded queries from terrified voters who worried that they would be denied access because of his history of suppression.

Our campaign, which had been agitating for better coverage of his conflict of interest, now had to thread a very fine needle. One of the most pernicious and salient effects of voter suppression is that it not only blocks a voter from casting a ballot but convinces others to not bother trying. Why play a rigged game? Experts on voter suppression often caution against amplifying the issue because calling out the problem may convince low-propensity voters to not risk disappointment. That is to say, if unlikely voters believe their votes won't count, they may opt not to participate in the first place.

This is perfectly illustrated by what occurred in Hancock County, Georgia, when the Board of Elections and Registration dispatched deputy sheriffs to challenge the voting rights of black voters in the county ahead of a key municipal election in 2015. Hancock sits in central Georgia, where law enforcement arrested blacks at 3.3 times the rate of nonblacks.[2] In the weeks ahead of the vote, deputies pulled up alongside black men as they walked on public streets or knocked on their doors to demand proof of residency. Barry Fleming, a Republican state representative and author of several bills to restrict access to voting, serves as the county attorney for Hancock. In an interview with the *New York Times* about the challenges to black voters, he dismissed the process as "more about politics and power than race."

Yet, in Georgia and around the country, race and politics are intimately entwined with the struggle for power. And both have the effect of chilling participation. As news spread of the unwanted calls and visits from law enforcement, reluctant voters became scared of participating in local elections. Facing the possibility of law enforcement knocking on their doors or coming to their jobs, the risk of being a voting citizen seemed too high.

Life in rural communities may create more space, but it also limits privacy and options for avoiding detection. Small towns tend to have fewer employers, so people know who works where, and less housing stock, so they know where everyone lives. This means the line between familiar and intrusive is slim, and in the wrong hands, the line can become invisible. Once, I visited my parents in Wiggins, Mississippi, and I needed to cash a check. I drove over to the local bank, only to realize that I didn't have my wallet with me. As I apologized to the teller for the inconvenience, she smiled and took the endorsed check from me. "You are the spitting image of Rev. Carolyn. I trust you." In towns where everybody knows your name and where you live, a paycheck every two weeks or the rent on a house might come at the cost of not getting into trouble at the polls. When the decision to vote puts a person's livelihood and family on the line, the safest option can be deciding not to participate at all, which is what happened in Hancock County after law enforcement began challenging black electors. According to the *New York Times* article, "'A lot of voters are actually calling to say they no longer wish to be on the list, so now we have people coming off the list who no longer want to vote,' Tiffany Medlock, the elections supervisor for the Hancock County elections board, told a Macon television reporter in late September." And so in a tight election for mayor of the county seat, the white candidate won.

Despite its troubled past, Georgia actually has some gold-standard laws on the books about voting access, meeting the best practices promoted by voting rights advocates like the Brennan Center. Here, a voter has three options for casting a ballot rather than just one: vote from home using a no-excuses absentee ballot, use an early voting location in their county of residence, or— as is the baseline—show up at their designated polling place on Election Day. The goal in states with multiple options for voting is to recognize the complexity of life today in America. When our nation began, in an agrarian economy, national elections were set to a time that allowed the harvests to be completed before winter weather interfered. With the advent of the telegraph, new worries emerged about early voting states affecting the outcomes in later states. Congress shrank the time available for voting and set the first Tuesday after the first Monday in November as the date of federal elections. The states soon adopted the nineteenth-century practice.

In the modern era, however, states began to liberalize their voting methods. Variations in employment, recognition of issues like disability and extended travel, and the increasing volume of participation have led to a range of options for how the vote is cast. The greater the number of options, the higher the number of people who can find a way into the process. Consider domestic workers who cannot leave their employers' homes to cast a ballot or rural voters who lack transportation to get from a job site back to a local precinct in the middle of the day. College students often have the option of voting at their schools or in their hometowns, and distance workers like truck drivers and offshore drilling crews require a flexibility that the first Tuesday in November cannot provide. However, when those well-intentioned laws can be manipulated by people in power, the consequences reach beyond a single election. Worse, because the rules differ from state to state, and the implementation changes from county to county, access to democracy becomes a lottery of location. With more than 116,000 polling locations across the country, each election is filtered through the best practices and worst impulses of poll workers who may use individual prejudices to determine the eligibility and access of voters.

We premised our 2018 gubernatorial campaign on reaching different types of voters, including ones who'd voted before but stopped participating due to fear or disinterest. We sent out more than a million applications for absentee ballots, the most ever deployed by a Democratic candidate in the state's history. But on the ground, we heard worry from voters about whether it was worth the effort. Those who lived in places where polling places had closed or who'd followed the news about Kemp's record with exact match doubted that a secretary of state could be fair and act as both referee and contestant. National broadcasts led with the controversies over unprocessed registrations. Local news reported problems with rejected absentee ballots or ridiculously long lines due to equipment shortages.

Across the state, we had to quickly quell the anxiety of our target voters. We had to demonstrate that we could only fight voter suppression through overwhelming participation. So, to combat the potential drop-off due to the nearly constant stories about these voting irregularities, we decided that instead of my habitual Election Day ritual, I would take advantage of Georgia's three-week in-person early voting option, never imagining what I would confront.

I arrived at the polling location a few miles from my house, with family and supporters in tow. Local, national, and international broadcasts had cameras following my every step, from the check-in at the front desk to the array of tables where I'd receive my voting card. However, when I smiled at the young woman who had greeted me, she gave me a wobbly response. "Ms. Abrams," she told me quietly, "it says you've already voted by absentee ballot." She offered me the date when my ballot had been cast, which came as a great surprise to me. "I've never requested an absentee ballot," I explained politely and in an equally low tone, aware of the reporters hovering nearby. Indeed, my practice had been to vote in whichever state I lived in during college and grad school: Georgia, Texas, and Connecticut. I liked voting in person—never absentee.

The poll worker's eyes widened in dismay, and she tapped the screen in front of her. "But it says . . ." she repeated. "But I didn't request a ballot," I assured her. "Can you get your manager?" She quickly scurried off to find someone else to deal with my issue. Around me, in the cavernous room filled with early voters and harried poll workers, my presence had created a stir. This was home for me, a place where I'd canvassed for voters in previous elections; delivered pizzas during a prolonged wait time in the primary. Most of the voters called out greetings and wished me well, a room filled mostly with African Americans determined to be heard in this pivotal election. The young worker returned with her supervisor, who quickly repeated the news to me about my phantom vote. Rather than grow annoyed, I teased, "I would remember voting for me, I promise."

Seeing my desire to resolve our issues quickly, the manager and I huddled about options, both pretending to ignore the camera crews at my back and the quizzical looks from voters waiting to be processed. She tapped on the computer, muttering a few times. After a few minutes, she lifted her head and nodded. She'd sorted out the error and, with little fanfare, issued my voting card. Trailed by reporters, I made my way to a polling station and quickly ran through the pages on the screen, beginning with my selection of STACEY ABRAMS FOR GOVERNOR. Once I'd voted on legislators, constitutional amendments, and county officials, the yellow card popped out, confirming my selection. Relieved, I exchanged it for a peach sticker from a poll worker declaring, I VOTED. Outside, in the mall parking lot, joined by dozens of well-wishers, I answered a range of questions about the experience. I reminded the viewers on the other end of the cameras, "In a time when people are concerned about whether their ballots are counted, if we vote early, we can guarantee that people have time to correct any mistakes, to deal with any concerns—and we'll know by Election Day where we stand."[3]

Yet, as I encouraged others to take advantage of early voting, I remained deeply troubled by my experience. As an attorney, a former legislator, and a candidate, my privilege inside that voting location was nearly unparalleled. I knew the rules, the process for filing a grievance, and I had the ability to throw a tantrum that would be broadcast from Georgia to Australia. But what of the first-time voter who could not fight back? Or the voter afraid of being followed home by a deputy sheriff? That is the danger of voter suppression at the ballot box. A voter can get close, but even at the finish line, the effects might still deny power to the voter, which is the ultimate act of suppression.

Early voting, absentee ballots, mail-in ballots, and provisional voting exist to ease the burdens of voting on a single day between 7:00 a.m. and 7:00 p.m. In our current economy, millions work for companies that grudgingly acknowledge the federal mandate to permit voting, though many only superficially. The federal law does not require that an employee receive pay for the missed time used to vote, particularly when long lines and inadequate machinery slow the pace of elections. For those who work on on-demand schedules, the best-laid plans can be disrupted by a call from a boss changing not just a work shift but also child care arrangements, transportation options, and second jobs. Worse, when a voter does take full advantage of the limited time allotted for voting, no federal law protects workers from retaliation if they must go back to the elections board to prove they had the right to vote.

To fully understand how voter suppression occurs at the ballot box, we must expand our understanding of what actually constitutes the "ballot box" in America today. The majority of Americans now live in states that permit early voting (thirty-nine states and the District of Columbia).[4] These are states where any qualified voter can visit a location and cast a ballot in person prior to Election Day. For those who cannot do so in person, all states provide an option, but the limits on who can use it vary from state to state. There are basically two types of absentee ballots: excused and no-excuses. The seventeen states that require excuses limit who can use this voting method. However, thirty-three states and the District of Columbia give anyone the right to request an absentee ballot, without providing a reason. In a handful of states, voters receive a ballot automatically mailed to them, in every election. These states—Colorado, Hawaii, Oregon, Utah, and Washington—also permit voters to visit the polling locations. Another variation on absentee ballots is known as Uniformed and Overseas Citizens Absentee Voting Act ballots or UOCAVA. These voters, typically military voters or expats living abroad, have a separate process for requesting and submitting their mailed ballots. Yet, across the board, with the exception of the military-heavy UOCAVA mailed ballots, these processes have also been hijacked by those intent on suppressing the right to vote. Because it works.

SIGNATURES, REJECTIONS, CURING, OH MY!: ABSENTEE BALLOTS

Marcus Soori-Arachi moved to Georgia in 2017, and he immediately applied for a driver's license. Unfortunately, the license misspelled his last name, leaving out a letter. A recent law graduate, Mr. Soori-Arachi corrected the mistake because he understood how critical accuracy was. Like thousands in Georgia, after living first in DeKalb County, he and his wife moved to Gwinnett

County, an adjacent county. Georgia law requires a change of address be submitted to the state after a move. Mr. Soori-Arachi is a "belt and suspenders" guy, so he checked the box on his updated license application to simultaneously update his voter registration on September 27, 2018. When he failed to receive a new voter registration card, he took the initiative to go online and make a second request, but the new card contained the old misspelling.

Because he thought it important for him to vote in the upcoming election, he requested a name change on his voter registration card to match the identification the state would require from him. But the correction never arrived. Stymied, he opted to cast an absentee ballot, which would not require him to show the mismatched card and license. However, his requested ballot never arrived. Not one to give up, he abandoned the state's system for a third-party website called Vote.org, where he could apply using his smartphone and provide his signature. Finally, the ballot arrived via Vote.org, but the notice warned that the county office would not accept his submission because his signature did not match what the state had on file. Instead, he was instructed to email a copy of his driver's license in order for his ballot to count. Marcus submitted the license and mailed the ballot, even adding two stamps just in case. He delivered it to the main post office in town, in an attempt to cut down on the lag time for delivery. And yet, when he checked his status on November 7, the day after the election, his ballot had not been received. He called our hotline for help, then reached out to the county to figure how what happened to his ballot.

Marcus was told it had never been received, then that his email with his license had also not arrived. After being pressed, someone advised him that the email went to the "wrong area," never explaining what the "right area" might be. In the end, having jumped every conceivable hurdle and followed the letter and spirit of the law, Mr. Soori-Arachi attested in an affidavit, "I really cared about voting, and I felt that there was a new and unexpected obstacle for me to vote at every step of the process. I was very committed to voting, so I did everything I could to jump every hurdle that was put in my path. At the end of the day, though, my vote still was not accepted and counted. *I can only imagine what happened to people who are less committed to voting, who are less educated, who are not as savvy with technology as I am, or who simply do not have the time.*"

Intended as a way to ease the process of voting, absentee ballots ostensibly allow people to vote from home, without having to stand in line on Election Day. But the absentee ballot process, like almost every aspect of the American election system, differs from state to state. As Mr. Soori-Arachi experienced, the issues range from who can have one, how one gets the ballot, and the rules for return and processing.

In rules for processing, Florida, Georgia, Michigan, and Iowa share a flawed obligation to count a ballot: the signature mismatch law. Under this scheme, a poll worker receives an absentee ballot from an otherwise qualified voter. The worker then compares the signature on the absentee ballot to a signature the state has on file. Sometimes the signature is preserved from the original voter registration or from a driver's license. Other times, the worker uses another signature to prove a match. These are not poll workers trained in the art of signature verification or even in basic forensic studies. Although I have never used the absentee ballot process, I doubt I'd pass—like you, more than likely, my signature doesn't match from Kroger to CVS. Yet, states use this mismatch as a reason to disqualify otherwise eligible voters from having their duly submitted ballots counted.

In Florida, in 2018, former Democratic congressman Patrick Murphy submitted an absentee ballot using the same signature he'd used in the state's primary in September. Yet, this time around, the county board of elections disqualified his ballot for failure to match the signature on file. Worse, he learned about the rejection too late to fix it, what is known as "curing" a ballot or fixing the issue that put the ballot into question. He wasn't alone. Across Florida in 2018, forty-five county boards of elections threw out 3,668 ballots; and when estimates for the state's two largest counties of Duval and Miami-Dade were added, an estimated 5,000 votes got tossed out.

Conservative supporters of the signature mismatch process argue against changes to the rules, noting that in the razor-thin election for U.S. Senate with its margin of 10,033 votes for the Republican candidate, these 5,000 votes could not have swung the election. I take exception to that response on two fronts. First, any voter denied a say in democracy has been harmed, and a remedy is in order regardless of the effect on an electoral outcome. Second, voter suppression tactics operate in tandem, not in isolation. Florida's constraints on voter registration (like limits on third-party registration) and access to the ballot (such as closing early voting locations) must be added to the toll taken on a vote's outcome. However, by utilizing convoluted processes like signature matching, and then treating the harm as isolated, perpetrators of suppression can wash their collective hands of the terrible effect.

How big an issue are signature mismatches? Of the top ten reasons for rejecting absentee ballots—from otherwise eligible voters—the nonmatching signature is number *one*. According to the Election Administration and Voting Survey (EAVS), in 2018 signature mismatches accounted for 27.5 percent of rejections. In states with these laws, the problem starts with requiring untrained workers to assess the veracity of a signature. Forensic scientists have found that laypersons, like these poll workers, have a 26 percent error rate for judging the authenticity of a signature, even when they have access to six authentic reference signatures for comparison. Part of the challenge for laypersons is the inability to account for factors that can explain variations in signatures, such as age, recent illness, medication, or eyesight. Imagine a senior citizen who has recently suffered a stroke or a young voter who had a recent sports injury. External factors also matter, like the type of pen used, the lighting in the area, the surface used for signing, or the quality of the paper.[5] Any of these issues can alter a signature, but it only takes one mistake for a voter to lose their right to the democratic process.[6] Not only do the poll workers lack the skill to assess signatures; in these states, election officials often lack uniform standards or procedures for authentication. Instead, each county decides the process, denying eligible voters any consistency of democracy in states like Michigan and Georgia, both of which currently face lawsuits for their arbitrary processes.

Absentee ballots are intended to make it easier to vote, but, as is made clear with signature mismatches, a vote can still be denied by rejecting the ballot itself. In states with problems with voter suppression, the high rate of rejections of otherwise eligible voters is a strong indicator of voters being wrongfully denied their rights. The EAVS data highlighted the top culprits for rejected absentee ballots[7]:

- Arizona: 10,769 rejected
- Florida: 21,973 rejected
- Georgia: 13,677 rejected
- Ohio: 10,189 rejected

Compare those numbers to Nevada and New Mexico, where only 1,177 and 95 ballots were rejected, respectively. The reasons for rejecting an absentee ballot may vary, but the common ones exist across voter suppression states.

After rejections due to nonmatching signatures, missed return deadlines for ballots came in second as the rationale, at 23.1 percent. Failure to meet a return deadline, at first blush, appears to be the fault of the user. In various aspects of our lives, we are expected to get things in on time: taxes, college applications, loan requests. For the average American, the expectation of meeting a deadline seems a reasonable one. Yet, like so many other components of voter suppression, try as they might to meet the obligation, the system makes doing so nearly impossible.

In 2019, Voto Latino, an organization focused on increasing Latino participation in elections, joined forces with Priorities USA to sue the state of Arizona over its absentee ballot deadline.[8] Arizona has a troubled history of racial discrimination toward the Latino and Native American populations in the state. In fact, Arizona is one of the few states outside the old Confederacy states that faced oversight under the VRA. The state got added to the VRA in 1975 because of a pattern of racial discrimination in how they conducted elections. Prior to the preclearance obligations imposed in 1975, Arizona refused to provide election materials in any language other than English, which had a direct effect on its significant Latino population. Arizona had been a strong proponent of literacy tests to block Latino and Native American voters from accessing the ballot. The state also allowed for "voter challenges" where others could question whether a person should be allowed to cast a vote. This behavior, which functioned as legalized harassment, discouraged

Latino and Native American voters from trying to participate until the VRA banned most of the egregious practices.

In 2005, Arizona had four hundred polling locations; as of 2019, the number had dropped to sixty. Defenders of the 85 percent cut of in-person locations lauded the increase in mail-in voting, that is, absentee ballots, as the rationale. Yet, according to testimony given to a congressional panel examining voting rights, Native Americans face unusual obstacles to meeting the requisites for complying with the absentee ballot deadlines. Roads into reservations are poorly maintained, and the postal service is unreliable. And, in Arizona, a ballot mailed from a rural, Native American, or Latino community could even be routed to New Mexico or Utah before it reaches Phoenix. The complaints echoed the issues raised in the Voto Latino lawsuit, which points out that Arizona sets a receipt deadline of 7:00 p.m. on Election Day for absentee ballots to be accepted.

However, even the secretary of state of Arizona acknowledges that meeting this deadline often requires submitting a ballot five to seven days ahead of Election Day. But for those who live on reservations or in remote areas of Arizona, that may not be sufficient time. Several other states use a more reliable metric of postmark deadlines, which do not hold voters accountable for whether the mail runs slow. The disproportionate effect on communities of color in Arizona means that in rural counties, Hispanic and Latino voters are *five to six times* as likely to be disenfranchised as white voters. Even in urban counties, they face double the likelihood of not having their votes count. To put this in perspective once more, the 2018 U.S. Senate race was decided by 55,900 votes, and more than 10,000 absentee votes were rejected.

Georgia's high rejection rates reflect the challenges of Michigan and Arizona with both the lack of training and the deadline for receipt. Lianna Arah Kang, a super-volunteer on my campaign who showed up almost every day, willing to do whatever was asked, attempted to vote absentee from her college in Maine, and she submitted her application in early October. When her ballot finally arrived on November 4, she overnighted her ballot through the assistance of the college's nonprofit center that helped students cover the costs of absentee submissions. Despite meeting the deadlines, she could not verify that the county received or processed her vote, and she flew back to Georgia to address the elections boards that failed to protect her rights. Even armed with a tremendous education, knowledge of the system, and the resources to defend her right to vote, Lianna still found herself silenced and without recourse.

Voters who try to use the flexibility of absentee ballots do not always have the ability to cure the problem. Best practices and Georgia law require election officials to notify voters of any issue and to fix it—to "cure" the ballot. Voters make mistakes, especially when the process is unfamiliar or the standards change; therefore, the goal should be to let well-intentioned mistakes be fixed. The 2018 election saw a record number of absentee ballot submissions across the state. However, in Georgia, 159 different counties administer their curative processes quite differently due to no uniform standards or training. For example, Georgia law requires "prompt" notification of any deficiencies, but the law does not define prompt and neither does the secretary of state. Basically, the administrators are supposed to contact the voter and allow them to cure the mistakes, if possible. Yet, in Georgia and around the country, who gets to make it better differs from state to state. For example, in the rural, mostly white Georgia counties, absentee rejection rates were often zero. They didn't do a signature match, and if the voter's oath was missing information, the administrators would just give the voter a call. But in the state's most racially diverse county, Gwinnett, elections officials also had the highest rejection rate of any Georgia county, and the affected voters rarely knew until it was too late. How different counties interpreted the laws meant a different experience for voters within the same state.

A series of lawsuits led to changes in the format of the Georgia absentee ballot and a cure period of three days after the election; however, the state still does not mandate when the voter learns about the defect. For example, a voter may submit an absentee ballot weeks before the election but not learn about a signature issue until the morning of the third day after the election. If that voter works hours away from the county elections board or has limited transportation options, and the cure is to bring in a photo identification or to answer questions in person, the ability to fix the problem might as well not exist. Without set standards requiring who gets a chance to correct errors and when, the right to vote becomes a privilege of the connected or the desirable.[9]

AND THESE ABSENTEE votes do matter—a lot. In 2018, I received 60 percent of all the absentee ballots cast in Georgia (137,616 of the 223,576 absentee ballots cast), and the difference in the election was 54,723 votes. The number of rejected ballots totaled 16,377, insufficient to change the outcome on its own, but—when combined with other factors like polling place closures and voter purges—these missing voices matter.

An even closer race may have hinged on these processes, and

when the Seventh Congressional District became a competitive seat in 2018, the Democratic candidate received 57 percent of the absentee ballots and lost by a mere 419 votes in a district that included Gwinnett County. Again, we cannot prove empirically that she would have won with better, more uniform processes, but voters cannot rest easy until they know that the fight is fair.

HOW A SAFETY NET BECAME A TRAP:
PROVISIONAL BALLOTS

Following the tumult of the Bush v. Gore election of 2000, Congress passed the Help America Vote Act (HAVA) in 2002. Federal lawmakers wanted to limit the ways voting processes differed from state to state, and they picked high-profile problems to address, like replacing the infamous punch-card and lever-based voting systems, establishing the Election Assistance Commission, and setting minimum standards for voting across the country. One of those standards was mandating the provisional ballot, which required states to allow eligible voters who might be rejected to cast ballots anyway, especially in light of administrative errors. Prior to HAVA, a voter might be turned away from a precinct if his name didn't appear on the rolls or if her address had changed but not been updated in the state's records.

Intended as a fail-safe for voters, like most other election laws, the process for handling and counting provisional ballots differs by state. In the hands of vote suppression masters, the provisional ballot provides not safety but a guarantee against full democratic rights. In 2018, states with a history of voter suppression had high rejection rates of provisional ballots. Arizona rejected 14,902 provisional ballots. Florida canceled the votes of

8,345 provisional voters and Georgia refused 9,699 provisional ballots. North Carolina rejected 17,578 ballots, and Texas tossed out 40,834 votes. The rejection rate ranged from a low of 28.64 percent in Arizona to a high of 75.37 percent in Texas. For voters who are handed provisional ballots, the intent may seem benign, but when used improperly, these ballots are a legal way to deny the right to vote.

Tommie Hollis and her daughter Cassandra Hollis arrived at the C. T. Martin Natatorium in Atlanta, Georgia, on October 31, 2018, eager to vote. Mrs. Hollis had suffered from a severe respiratory illness for much of the early fall, and she had been unable to leave her home. When her daughter brought them to the early voting center, they progressed through the first stage of identification with ease. When they asked for their ballots, Cassandra received hers, but Mrs. Hollis was told she couldn't receive one because she had already voted absentee in person (Georgia's categorization for early voting) on October 16, 2018. Mrs. Hollis objected, pointing out that she had been confined to her home until recently, and there was no way she could have cast a ballot. Cassandra and her mom scrambled to find a poll manager who could resolve the issue. The issue moved from poll worker to manager to a supervisor for assistance. The only recourse offered was the use of a provisional ballot. Even though Mrs. Hollis knew she hadn't voted, the error-riddled Georgia system denied her the right to an actual ballot. Instead, she filled out the provisional form. Cassandra and her mother spent the next two weeks trying to determine if Mrs. Hollis's vote would count. Cassandra left messages for various elections agents, but no one returned her calls. In the end, Tommie Hollis may have been one of the thousands of rejected provisional ballots—one of a raft of voters left out of the election entirely.

Across Georgia, eligible voters reported tales of problematic provisional ballots throughout the general election's process in 2018. In Troup County, the site of the story of Otis Moss Sr. recounted by Oprah, we heard stories of black voters receiving provisional ballots rather than regular ballots. At an event for Supermajority, a group dedicated to enlisting women in the 2020 elections, Jobie Crawford, a Spelman student, recounted standing in hours-long lines only to be told when she made it to the front that she wasn't registered, despite having received a letter confirming her registration days before. When she asked for a provisional ballot, the clerk told her that she only had a few left, and she wanted to save them for "real voters." In another incident, in Gwinnett County, a new voter used the state's online system to register and received confirmation that she'd made it onto the voting rolls. But when the voter went to her assigned voting precinct, poll workers found no record of her. Under HAVA, she should have been permitted to cast a provisional ballot, but the poll workers did not allow her to and she left the precinct without voting.[10]

A poll worker in DeKalb reported the frustration of several elderly voters who had been instructed to cast provisional ballots but found that the only station in the precinct accepting them was understaffed. One had to leave to pick up her grandchildren, while another reported it was already his second trip to the location, having left the first time because the lines were too long and he had to get to work. One poll observer reported eligible voters being turned away because the poll manager thought it was too early to offer the recourse of a provisional ballot. According to another affidavit, Lisa Schnellinger served as a poll watcher at a local church where the line went out the door and the wait time was more than two hours. She watched several voters leave without casting a ballot and took it upon herself to inquire why they didn't vote a provisional ballot. To a person, they told her they had been sent to the wrong precinct and weren't aware they could do so. When Ms. Schnellinger approached the poll manager, she was told that ballots were not offered because the manager believed the voters still had time to go to the correct precinct—even if that was not so.

For thousands of voters who cast provisional ballots, because they could not fix the problem in the limited time allotted or with the information at their disposal, their votes did not count. Georgia law requires the voter to resolve the administrative issue within three days of the election. But as Tommie and Cassandra Hollis learned, fixing a bureaucratic snafu may take much longer than three days, despite diligent effort. For others, especially shift workers or those with limited transportation, getting back to the scene of the election can be impossible. Federal law requires time off for voting, but no laws give protection for righting problems in the election system. For families that could lose a day's wage trying to navigate bureaucracy, the cost of fixing what they didn't break can be too high.

In Georgia, the issues were so pervasive that federal judge Amy Totenberg stepped into the 2018 election and ordered the state to review the nearly 27,000 provisional ballots. In the end, 44.89 percent were rejected, and when combined with the other errors in the elections process, thousands likely could not exercise their right to vote despite being legally eligible and having tried.

Provisional ballots stand as a clear example of how federal election law administered on a state-by-state basis leads to dramatic variations in justice. In Georgia, for example, my organization, Fair Fight Action (FFA), has filed suit, alleging that lack of training, under-resourcing, and uneven standards mean a different democracy in each county in the state. My fear, though, is that it is much worse. In the end, certain voters are shunted aside with the promise of provisional ballots but without the assurance that their votes will ultimately count.

BROKEN INFRASTRUCTURE: MALFUNCTIONING MACHINES, HOURS-LONG LINES, AND OTHER BARRIERS

In late August 2019, a terrifying video began making the rounds on social media. Mississippi held its runoff elections for the primaries on August 27, and one voter captured his process on his cell phone. During the fourteen-second video, the voter selected the name of the GOP underdog, Judge Bill Waller. Yet, each time, the machine flipped his selection to the opponent, Lieutenant Governor Tate Reeves, against his will and his intent. Over and over, he tried to make his choice, but the voting machine made a different pick. He shared the video, and by the next day, widespread reports of vote flipping had been identified in Calhoun, Forrest, Lamar, Leflore, Lincoln, Pearl River, Scott, and Washington Counties, roughly 10 percent of the counties in the state and 11 percent of the state's population. When asked about the discrepancies, the spokesperson for the Mississippi secretary of state's office denied responsibility, saying, "Machines are county-owned and tested by local officials." But that Mississippi voter was not alone in his cartwheeling process. In 2018, a Georgia voter filed an affidavit in the FFA lawsuit, attesting that she too experienced vote switching. Three times, the machine flipped her choice from Abrams to Kemp, and three times she had to try to change it back.

The 2018 election had the highest midterm turnout in recent

years, demonstrating both the enthusiasm for the election and the failed infrastructure that governs our processes. With millions more voting in the usually low-key midterms, deteriorating machines made mistakes, an inadequate supply of equipment lengthened lines, and too few poll workers complicated voting for the least resilient citizens. Those who had to vote early or late, who did not understand technology, or who could not get answers to their questions experienced a flawed election—and for too many, it wasn't the first time.

The actual technology for voting differs from state to state, but most states use direct recording electronic (DRE) voting machines, optical scan paper ballot systems, or ballot marking devices (BMD). Thirty-eight states and D.C. follow some version of federally recommended guidelines; however, eight states do *not*, including Florida and New Hampshire, often considered presidential battleground states. Because federal law does not require compliance, and because there are no consequences for bucking the system, these states go their own way. And understand, the process of purchasing and maintaining voting systems varies from state to state. In Mississippi, the obligation is left to the local officials, while in Georgia the secretary of state chooses the equipment. These election machine companies rake in millions of dollars by promising to provide a seamless solution to how voters cast ballots.

One company in particular, ES&S (Election Systems and Software), has faced national criticism over their machines. One of their offerings, the TSX model, was cited as the offending equipment in Mississippi caught on video. But other machines face similar critiques. After the issues of election security raised in 2016, Americans rightfully expected action from the federal government to address how we protect access to the vote. Instead, the

U.S. Senate leadership, under Majority Leader Mitch McConnell, has blocked funding and the adoption of new standards to protect machines against hacking and tampering.

Malfunctioning equipment is only one piece of our broken infrastructure, unfortunately. According to analysis performed by a national group of researchers, one of the most obvious barriers to voting is the wait time in line.[11] As the researchers point out, "Relative to entirely-white neighborhoods, residents of entirely-black neighborhoods waited 29% longer to vote and were 74% more likely to spend more than 30 minutes at their polling place." (They utilized smartphone data from the 2016 presidential election to account for biases based on self-reporting or overreporting.) One key issue that could explain the disparity is how well-resourced polling locations are for black versus white voters. If a black location has fewer machines, fewer workers assigned, and higher congestion, then the effects of wait times are magnified. In 2014, President Obama's Presidential Commission on Election Administration found that no voter should have to wait longer than thirty minutes to cast a ballot. For the majority of Americans, this timing holds true. But for those who are infrequent voters or have inflexible jobs or have family commitments, the effect of a longer wait time can easily suppress their vote.

In 2018, Georgia posted the longest wait times in the nation for minority voters. One of the racial disparities study's authors commented that the state had "[a] big surge in turnout. You can go down the list before you get to the malevolent explanations." While true, this blithe response ignores the actual harm done to the voters who experienced wait times of four hours or more. Benign neglect as much as malevolent intent harms voters facing obstacles to participation. Multiple FFA affidavits attest to minority neighborhoods and low-income communities confronting an inadequate number of machines, broken or inoperable equipment, and an insufficient number of poll workers. In two polling locations, the deficiency was so bleak that a court extended the deadline to vote from 7:00 p.m. to 10:00 p.m. Still, many voters had no options, like those with jobs that didn't permit a four-hour break or who had to pick up kids or tend to sick family members. FFA confronted the state with the issue of long lines, and the state of Georgia retorted that these voters could cast absentee ballots and vote by mail. But in a sworn statement to the court, the state argued that voters do not have the right to vote by mail and having their ballots rejected does not mean they were denied the right to vote.[12] One of our attorneys, Dara Lindenbaum, attended a press briefing for us and summarized the state's position perfectly: "I'm pregnant with twins. I can't stand in line for five hours, and it is maddening that the state's response is that my option is to vote absentee. Then, if my absentee ballot is rejected, the state's position is that my right to vote isn't denied because I can go right back to that five-hour line and try again. Insanity." In a democracy, where the state refuses to fix either the problem or the solution, voters are well and truly suppressed.

CHAPTER 5

Taking Our Power Back

My parents raised the six of us in Mississippi, my mother an underpaid librarian and my father a dyslexic shipyard worker. With salaries that barely kept our family afloat, my parents earned the right to curse the systems of government that taxed their earnings but did little to remedy their lot in life. I don't recall my parents ever placing a political yard sign in our postage stamp of a front yard, nor do I recall ever seeing one in the yards of our working-class neighbors.

Yet, as a child, I remember following my parents into the school and down the hallway to the gymnasium, where the voting booths stood with their half-curtains fanned out across the vinyl floor. My parents would sign in at the table and then proceeded to the booths with my siblings and me in tow, like the chicks in *Make Way for Ducklings*, one of our favorite storybooks. They would disappear inside the curtains while we tried to crowd inside to watch. The process was usually quick—a few minutes of selection and then done. In Gulfport, Mississippi, the lines to vote were never terribly long. But my parents brought us with them to ensure we understood that speed or victory wasn't the issue; the act was the thing.

Despite never declaring their allegiances with a sign in the yard, politics, voting rights, and good government were a constant conversation in our house. We got dressed for school to the dulcet voices of David Hartman and Joan Lunden on *Good Morning America*. In the evenings, Peter Jennings would recap the day with *World News Tonight*. I was six when I got into my only fight in school, a skirmish over the 1980 election contest between President Jimmy Carter and Ronald Reagan. Carter lost, but I won.

When we would pile in the car and travel an hour north to see my grandparents, aunts, and uncles, I sat enrapt as my family members recounted the fight for civil rights in the 1950s and '60s. Mom and Dad seeing a movie as teenagers in the balcony of the city's only theater, relegated to the Colored section. Granddaddy, a veteran of World War II, forced to give up his seat on the bus or be called a boy by men younger than he was. As much as my family spoke about segregated schools, sit-ins at lunch counters, or hospitals that refused to treat them, the fight to vote stuck with me the most.

In 1993, when I was nineteen, a group of civil rights leaders chose me to stand on the steps of the Lincoln Memorial to speak at the thirtieth anniversary of the March on Washington. I led voter registration efforts on campus, and I worked with political campaigns to turn out young voters across Atlanta. A year before, I joined Students for African American Empowerment (SAAE), a college group borne of outrage at the Rodney King verdict. When protests swept the country, Atlanta had been one of the hot spots. SAAE made a list of issues that demanded redress from someone—anyone—in power. Youth poverty, gang violence, and inadequate resources topped our list of grievances.

But, as we saw it, a more symbolic sin hovered over the state capitol and City Hall, both housed along the same street downtown. In defiance of desegregation and *Brown v. Board of Education*, Georgia leaders had added the Confederate battle emblem to the state seal on the flag of Georgia in 1956. This was now our state's calling card to the world. For years debate raged about why African Americans and people of good conscience had to confront the racist emblem simply to do business as citizens. As the summer of 1992 dragged on with little change, SAAE decided to stage a symbolic act of our own: we set fire to the state flag on the steps of the Capitol. (Being my parents' child, I, of course, followed the law and secured a permit.)

On August 28, 1993, I stood on the stage at the March on Washington and tried to reconcile both halves of my activist self. Had I been chosen because of my work to register and engage young people across Georgia in voting or because I burned a state flag? In the end, I settled for what would become my lifelong approach to politics, knit together from what my parents had instilled in me: citizenship requires constant action, which includes voting, protesting, and participating; and without the combination, we are all in jeopardy. I burned the flag for the same reason I led Bill Clinton's campaign on Spelman's campus and attended city council meetings as a college freshman: no true success would be viable and sustainable without harnessing every aspect of the process.

Twenty-five years later, I launched my campaign for governor of Georgia. During my campaign, with his permission, I shared my brother's story of struggling with substance abuse and bipolar disorder as a way to connect. I wanted to demonstrate how voting for me could help families who have their own Walter—a loved one trapped by illness, addiction, or mistakes that seem to have no remedy within reach—from securing the basics of Medicaid expansion to guaranteeing health care to those with untreated mental illness to criminal justice reform that would allow ex-offenders to get jobs and housing.

More than once, voters clasped my hands and told me that while they didn't normally go to the polls, this would be their first time because someone needed to speak up. In this moment, they understood how the right to vote could shape their lives and those of their families. I know that not all of those men and women got a chance to take action in that election. In 2018, hundreds arrived at their polling place to discover that either it had moved or they had been removed from the rolls. Tens of thousands called our voter protection hotline to seek assistance or advice, and thousands more likely didn't even bother to try. These lawful voters, denied access, still have more than citizens like Walter. When my brother finally regains his freedom, in too many states, he will most likely be permanently barred from voting.

The 2018 elections shifted the power dynamic in ways that have yet to be fully calculated, but the effects have already begun to reverberate. Democrats retook the House of Representatives, electing the first Native American members of Congress, among a record number of women and people of color. In Texas, Harris County elected black women to a record seventeen judgeships. Michigan, New Mexico, and Wisconsin chose a coalition of white, Latino, and black executives to serve as governors and lieutenant governors, replacing hard-core conservatives who had rolled back protections and rights for millions. Yet for each tale of triumph, a corollary quickly follows.

Nearly 1.4 million ex-felons in Florida regained voting rights, only to have those rights snatched away by a gerrymandered state legislature. In Tennessee, Republicans passed a state law to criminalize voter registration groups like Black Votes Matter, after the organization turned in more than 90,000 registration forms in a single year.[1] New Hampshire imposed new residency requirements to disenfranchise college students studying in the state. In Michigan, state law makes it a crime to hire drivers to transport voters to polling locations unless they are physically unable to walk, even if the polling location is miles away.

The fundamental reason for voting is to secure rights and expand opportunity—the lifeblood of progress for most Americans. But in Georgia, four months after the controversial November 2018 gubernatorial election, women ringed the state capitol, dressed in crimson and white, to mimic outfits worn on *The Handmaid's Tale*, the acclaimed novel turned television show about forced pregnancy in a dystopic future. Beyond the reach of their silent protest, lawmakers—mostly white, mostly men—argued over HB 481, the proposed bill that would add Georgia to a growing list of states passing anti-choice legislation. I had spent the previous few days on the phone, nudging former colleagues who wavered on their opposition to the bill and urging action from business leaders afraid of the consequences. The authors had smartly tagged the law as a "fetal heartbeat" bill, alleging (falsely) that the echoes heard in a sonogram at six weeks amounted to proof of life.

Earlier in the month, the bill had eked out a narrow victory in the House of Representatives and increased its margin in the Senate. Back in the House, the vote count showed that a handful of legislators would tip the balance. When the Speaker called up the bill for final passage, the bill essentially banned abortions in Georgia. It passed 92–78, in a chamber where 91 votes guaranteed victory. While supporters and opponents waited for the governor's signature on the bill, voters learned more about the contours of the legislation. Under the new provisions, both the woman and her doctor could face criminal penalties for any abortions—even if a woman did not learn of her pregnancy until after the ban had been invoked or if a medical procedure led to a spontaneous abortion.

For women in Georgia, the issue of pregnancy is fraught with perils. There are no ob/gyns in 79 of Georgia's 159 counties, and the state has ranked highest in maternal mortality for years. The Medical Association of Georgia, nursing groups, and others raised alarms about how HB 481 would worsen our health care crisis, particularly in the rural areas where seven hospitals have shut down since 2010.

Despite scientific evidence and statewide outcries from worried women and outraged physicians, on May 7, 2019, Kemp signed the bill into law. He exercised his prerogative as the governor of the state and, in the process, went against the will of a majority of the people—49 percent who opposed the law and 44 percent who supported it.[2] The legislation barely passed and won only because of gerrymandering in 2011. The process of assigning legislative districts had drawn a map that allotted 68 percent of the state's seats to Republicans, although the Republican statewide candidates only received 55 percent of the vote in 2010. The imbalance in power meant that while nearly two-thirds of the state opposed HB 481, neither the governor nor the legislature had to listen. They had rigged the system to inoculate themselves against popular will.

Georgia is not alone as a state with this disequilibrium in elections, and in voter suppression state after voter suppression state, conservatives in power are trying to force through agendas that defy the will of the people. And they can because they've stolen their votes. But now that we understand how, we can take them back.

STAYING IN THE RIGGED GAME

At the core of our American democracy is the theory of representation. We believe the people should elect the leaders who give voice to their values and ambitions. The right to vote is the cornerstone of our democratic republic, yet we have seen partisanship overtake patriotism in our process—where one party maintaining power is used to justify stripping voters of constitutional rights. Across the country, Republicans have passed laws designed to block, deflect, and deny access to the ballot. Since 2010, according to the Brennan Center, twenty-five states have put heightened voting restrictions—almost entirely authored by Republican officials.

Voter suppression typically targets the marginalized, the disadvantaged, and the inconvenient—those whose decisions challenge the established order of things, like college students or ex-offenders. But the effect is broader and exponentially more pronounced. These communities tend to share a common belief that political leaders should pass laws to guarantee equity and justice, and they vote that way. However, the disenfranchisement of individuals and entire populations from democracy through the booby traps of registration, access to the ballot, and ballot counting works to divide groups, often leaving the privileged unscathed by the process but hurt by the outcomes. Representative democracy is a brute force exercise, where who counts *matters*. Rigging the game affects all the players on the team, even those who are not targeted.

Consider the four-decade-long trend of legislation designed to ban abortion, despite the national consensus that access is a public good. In states where voter suppression is common, so too is an aggregation of power in the hands of conservatives who have a shared strategy for stripping away abortion rights. Targeted restrictions on abortion providers laws, known as TRAP laws, have proliferated in recent years, accelerating in the past twenty. In 2000, thirteen states were considered hostile to abortion access. By 2014, the number had more than doubled to twenty-seven. Poor women, women of color, and women in rural areas are the most likely to be unable to reach a doctor when these restrictions are imposed by state legislatures. Wealthier women, particularly white women, can cross state lines or secure private services that mitigate the effect of restrictions. As the push to overturn *Roe v. Wade* has also gained traction, wealthy and middle-class women who could safely seek abortion services now wait in the same limbo as those poor women denied access by the TRAP laws.

When the most vulnerable communities become isolated from public discourse, especially from voting, their ills might appear to be contained as well. But like any dangerous contagion, the symptom of voter suppression serves as a warning for a more virulent and deadly disorder. When democracy is broken, the effects are national and even international. Recent elections prove again and again that our democracy is fragile. Here at home, we hear about Russian interference, hacked machines, and more and more people who doubt the system. Abroad, authoritarians and dictators win elections and reshape democracies into parodies of freedom. The same world leaders who once feared disappointing American leaders now use our compromised elections to justify their own behavior. When disinformation campaigns target black and brown voters to scare them away from the polls, the source might as easily be Russian as Republican.

Saving democracy is not an overblown call to action—we *are* in trouble. The changing demography of America speaks to more than whether Democrats or Republicans control political decisions. Young people will be financially responsible for the largest population of elderly Americans in our history, but without the resources necessary to provide for them. The increased frequency of extreme climate events costs billions of dollars that will not be spent on education or infrastructure. The past fifty years of public policy toward communities of color have consequences. For decades, black and brown children have had higher dropout rates, higher incarceration rates, and lower earning power. This very same population continues to grow in size and political might, but America has largely abandoned our tradition of civic education to help guide their decisions. And international crises will demand American attention, but without a cogent and consensus-driven electorate, we will likely by paralyzed by inaction or stupid decision making.

We are in trouble. But we do know what to do. America has always been a crucible for democratic innovation, and our hallmark is our willingness to learn and grow. Fixing our broken democracy stands as a foundational prerequisite to progress. Our work to achieve universal health care access, education parity, social and economic justice, and more—they each depend on the fundamental obligation that undergirds them all, eradicating voter suppression and ensuring that our elections are fair fights. Whether through supporting the Voting Rights Advancement Act in Congress, or advocating for ballot security on the local level, or holding every state-level candidate accountable for putting forth a plan to end this repugnant practice, together we can

establish an electoral system that is truly democratic, where policies of, by, and for the people truly flourish. And, in the process,
we can repair democracy itself.

HOW WE BEGIN

Before I lay out the path to ending voter suppression, I must dispel one persistent myth. When perpetrators are caught in the act
with the intent and effect of restricting voting, calling out their
undemocratic behavior has led to cries of innocence from Republicans and feigned outrage in conservative media. When absurdly
long lines kept black voters away from jobs for hours, President Obama convened a commission to study the problem. In
response, GOP secretaries of state and other Republican politicians and pundits argued that the lines were simply a result of
excitement rather than suppression. Because the Democratic candidate won, most Americans of both political stripes quickly moved
on to other concerns. However, when a number of us raised the
issue in 2018, the concerns resonated and ricocheted around
the country. In response, Republicans have tried to argue that
because high numbers of voters of color participated in the 2018
election, this is proof that no voter suppression occurred.

Employing this level of purposeful intellectual laziness and
gaslighting voters of color who were deprived of their constitutional rights is shocking but not surprising, given that it comes
from a crop of politicos whose primary strategy for victory is to
make voting more difficult. Their spurious logic is belied by a
simple thought experiment: on an obstacle course, more people
can sign up and decide to compete, but an increase in participation does not negate the fact that the coach puts out more hurdles
and the track has more pitfalls than before. Indeed, in elections

in the past twenty years, GOP-led states have used the laws to tack on administrative hassles, close off shortcuts, and generally ratchet up the difficulty year by year. And like any stumbles on a booby-trapped course, for too many, the injuries are real. While more voters of color successfully navigated impediments to registration and ballot access in 2018, we cannot ignore the tens of thousands of additional voters of color silenced by purges, rejected ballots, and closed polling locations. Both can be true, and both were true in 2018.

Turnout reached a higher level among voters of color in 2018 than in any previous midterm election in memory, including in Georgia. Voters of color turned out in droves because they were inspired by inclusive campaigns and progressive agendas. But those numbers do not reflect the gauntlet of problems faced by voters, too many of whom were rejected or denied before having their ballots counted. Equally worthy of investigation are the additional eligible voters who would have participated if the process hadn't shoved them away.

Higher participation means that more people are willing to try, not that they will succeed. Much like suppression itself, increases in participation are nothing new. Surges in minority voting and voter suppression are not separate and independent phenomena. They are tightly linked by a 150-year history, where trying to block the right to vote has almost always triggered its increase.

The black response to suffrage granted by Reconstruction elected black men at every level of government. Women gained the right to vote in 1920, reversing years of suppression, and their participation rates have continued to rise. The fact that black, Latino, and AAPI voters showed up in droves in 2018 is proof that voter turnout *and* voter suppression can operate in tandem, but in relation to each other. Research shows that when voters become aware of suppression activities, if they become angry rather than disheartened, they will take extra steps to defeat it, including by getting out to vote. I liken it to a toy or possession that a bully threatens to take. Human nature says we may not use it very often, but when the wrong person tries to steal it, we'll fight hard to keep it for ourselves.

Those of us who believe in the promise of democracy must become outraged about even a single act of suppression. In an honorable system, the loss of a single voter's right to participate is a wrong that cannot be tolerated—and as Americans, we should know that a failure in the system weakens us all. Still, too many Republicans accept voter suppression as the price for continued power, regardless of the damage it does to the machinery of our country. Although the 2018 election debacle focused mainly on the statewide races like mine, over in Habersham County, a Republican colleague of mine from the Georgia House of Representatives got to see suppression up close. Dan Gasaway, the incumbent, lost his 2018 primary election by 67 votes, but when he checked the voter rolls, dozens of eligible voters had been unlawfully removed. A do-over election was called, but the same problems happened again, leading to a third election. Suppression may target a select group, but when the process breaks down, we are all at risk.

Heading into the 2020 elections, targets of voter suppression also face the return of "ballot security" measures, one last element of denying the right to vote. In 1981, the Republican National Committee came to the aid of the GOP candidate for governor. Beyond the normal financial assistance, they bankrolled a National Ballot Security Task Force, complete with off-duty officers and official-looking arm bands. They deployed their teams to minority voting precincts, mainly populated by black voters.

The task force put up signs warning voters that they were being monitored, and they challenged voters standing in line, trying to intimidate them out of voting. The force carried two-way radios and firearms, patrolling the voting lines. The plan worked, and the Republican nominee became governor. In response, the Democratic National Committee sued the GOP, and a federal consent decree was ordered. The consent decree forbade the Republican National Committee from running one of these operations again.

For thirty-five years, the decree kept the umbrella organization for the GOP in check, although groups like the conservative True the Vote have been accused of stepping in to pick up the slack by intimidating nonwhite voters and trying to get them removed from voter rolls.[3] In 2017, a federal judge lifted the consent order against the Republican National Committee, finding that the GOP's three decades of "good" behavior warranted an end to the prohibition. The 2020 presidential election will be the first national test since the end of the decree, and voting activists and election experts worry that the GOP has not learned its lessons.[4] From once again hiring off-duty law enforcement, including off-duty Immigration and Customs Enforcement (ICE) officers, to posting false information threatening returning citizens with criminal violations, the potential for harm is grave. Conservative desperation to hold on to power will increase with each campaign, and as the law permits more and more egregious action, our responsibility is to do whatever we can to defeat suppression at its source.

FIXING THE SYSTEM FOR GOOD

Our nation has struggled with real, universal suffrage from its earliest days; yet across this nation, dogged citizens have found ways to make democracy real for as many as possible. Whether through the action of state legislators and thoughtful governors or through citizen-led ballot initiatives that take the politics from politicians, we have a range of examples about what should be done to make our democracy work. In Oregon and Washington, voters and leaders aligned on a range of best practices, including automatic registration, same-day registration, no restrictive voter identification, and ballots mailed directly to voters (Washington State even sends voters a handy guide to the election). There, the ease of voting has not been marred by rampant fraud or corruption. Instead, both states have seen high levels of voter participation and turnout in recent elections. The United States must no longer be a patchwork of good, bad, and worst states for voters, a degradation of democracy based on state lines and zip codes. Being an eligible citizen should be sufficient for full participation, and we have multiple examples of what and how this can be accomplished.

Change must begin at the federal level, where Congress establishes a bottom line for democracy rather than relegating the quality of access to the states. Political scientists and voting rights advocates know what works; and in the first act of the 116th Congress led by Speaker Nancy Pelosi, the signature legislation focused on expanding and securing the right to vote. While the bill, known as H.R. 1, goes beyond simply repairing our damaged voting system, core elements of how we improve and guarantee access are worth attention.

The place where most of our problems begin is voter registration. The United States is one of only a few industrialized, democratized systems that compels citizens to undergo such rigor to be eligible to participate in voting. In fact, in North Dakota, voter registration isn't a thing. Already, seventeen states plus D.C. offer some form of automatic registration and twenty-one states plus D.C. give voters same-day registration, including on Election Day. Federal law must go beyond the limited success of motor voter and require automatic registration, same-day registration, and preregistration for sixteen- and seventeen-year-olds. For automatic registration, the process should be designed for interaction with federal and state agencies with the broadest contact, such as expanding beyond DMVs to include courthouses, human services offices, state tax offices, and public housing locations. If states wish to follow the models in Oregon, Washington, and California, the jurisdiction can aggregate data from all sources to register eligible voters, and then citizens who get added must be able to opt out with ease.

Like automatic registration, same-day registration would eliminate the patchwork of state rules for when a voter signs up, particularly given the fluidity of twenty-first-century lives. Already, states with early voting allow voters to go to a central location to vote on issues for their neighborhood or district. This capacity should be available for all eligible voters, on the state and federal levels—including allowing countywide voting centers that let voters avoid crowded local precincts if they need to do so. These changes would help mitigate the disparity in quality of elections—where more affluent areas experience shorter wait times and fewer challenges.

Once a voter gets on the rolls, deciding not to vote cannot be a pretext for taking a voter's rights away in what is known as a voter purge. No state should be permitted to remove voters simply for choosing not to vote. States should absolutely continue to conduct list maintenance—that is, removing the dead, those who have moved out of state, or those who are otherwise ineligible. However, the issue of database inaccuracies and faulty determinations means that stripping someone of their rights should be harder than it is now. Losing the right to vote in a state should be the last resort, not an option for gaming the election.

The second prong of voter suppression is limiting access to the ballot. Federal law must prohibit restrictive voter ID laws, which serve no one except those seeking to curtail voter participation. Unnecessary restrictions do nothing to protect voters and instead create irreparable harm to the victims of these laws, namely people of color, low-income Americans, young people, and the elderly. The requirement of identification does not necessitate screening out otherwise eligible voters. Instead, states must be barred from requiring voter IDs that go beyond proof of identity to screening out likely voters: that means prohibiting impossible address requirements, demanding expensive or inaccessible records, or disallowing customary identification like college IDs or federally issued badges. Federal standards must be set for what states can require of voter identification, prohibiting suppressive requirements that exceed the most basic standards.

In addition to undoing the harm of strict voter ID, Congress should adopt restoration of the Voting Rights Act, as proffered in H.R. 4. This bill limits the closure of polling locations without preclearance by the Department of Justice, restoring a vital protection for targets of voter suppression. By requiring permission before voters are disenfranchised, communities of color, low-income communities, the elderly, the young, and the disabled will have a new tool to use to increase and guarantee their participation.

Access to the ballot should also set federal standards for ballot access—improving the diversity of candidates able to seek public office. In some states, the issue is political affiliation rules that set high bars for third-party candidates. In others, getting onto the ballot requires meeting petition thresholds that are nearly insurmountable for those who have no existing base of support. The idea that to be viable, a candidate must already have thousands of supporters, belies the intent of campaigns. The goal should be to encourage potential political leaders to reach out and build a support network—not require an existing network to reach the starting gate. Unfortunately, federal law bends to state law on ballot access rules, but doing so without setting standards means certain citizens will rarely be able to run. Whether the obstacle is financial or geographic or a combination, states should be compelled to meet baseline rules for opening access to standing for office.

The third issue is how we reform the act of ballot counting and ballot rejection. Our lives have become increasingly complex, and our options for how we vote need to keep up with the times. Making every vote count will necessitate changing how ballots are cast and who gets to do so. Dozens of states have adopted versions of early voting, voting by mail, and improvements to Election Day voting. But rather than leaving it to states to decide to support voter access, federal law should mandate minimum standards for early voting, absentee ballots, and equipment for polling locations. States can do better, have more days, have longer hours, and have more locations, but we need to have a foundational set of rules that don't change simply because voters change their state of residence.

Similarly, we need a set of standards for how polling locations are staffed with both equipment and people. Debate rages about the best equipment for voting, in part because of issues related to hacking by either hostile foreign governments or domestic attackers who want to game the system. Equipment for voting can run the gamut from the purely analog approach of hand-marked paper ballots to an array of digital options.

Until the federal government commits to both require and fund election security for all elections, or unless a state has demonstrated a high level of security consciousness, the best option is hand-marked paper ballots—with provisions made for those who require the accessibility of machine-assisted voting. Hand-marked paper ballots are difficult to hack, can be monitored and audited, and they can restore confidence in the process.

Voting equipment should be not only secure, but must also be available, along with adequate staff to support voter turnout. Progressives advocating for improvements in voter access do not discuss this often, but meeting a minimum number of machines or poll workers in each precinct is not sufficient. Our demand should be federal rules that require county election officials to increase resources at locations with historically long lines, regardless of the county average. Long lines can occur in locations with the same number of machines and voters for a number of reasons. One, the community served by the precinct may not be perfect voters. In low-income communities, large numbers of voters might move within the county, or within the precinct, and while not required to reregister to vote, they take additional time getting processed. Two, aging infrastructure in low-income communities might interfere with the operation of elections. Shortages or delays occur because the polling location may have insufficient electricity sources or other issues that cause machines to go down or make administering the election more difficult. Historic underinvestment in these instances is not solved by equality. Instead, federal law should maintain that to have equity among the precincts, each polling location must have its needs carefully considered—and that may mean more resources to those with less.

For absentee ballots, all states should be required to offer them without excuse to anyone who seeks to vote from home. The process for receiving the ballot should have federal guidelines to ensure that voters actually get what they ask for, and reasons for rejection, such as signature matches, should be federally prohibited. Moreover, returning the completed ballot should have uniform deadlines, as with filing taxes with the IRS: postmark deadlines that voters can control versus delivery deadlines they cannot. Waiting for absentee ballots may delay the call of a contest on election night, but that's not a good enough reason to restrict access to the vote. Americans may have grown used to instant results by 11:00 p.m., but we can learn to wait if a slight delay increases the legitimacy of the outcome. Though well-intentioned, provisional ballots have become a hindrance for certain communities, but again, standards for how provisional ballots are allocated and how they apply can mitigate many of the rejections. More important, by solving the challenges of voter registration, identification, and methods of voting, these improvements sharply reduce the number of ballots that fall outside the normal processes. A uniform federal ballot would even address the complexity of voting across the board.

It also matters if a voter can actually have time to participate. One option is to make Election Day a national holiday, which benefits most but not all voters. Of the thirty-six nations in the Organisation for Economic Co-operation and Development, a consortium of democratic countries from around the globe, the United States is one of only seven nations that hold national elections on a day when most of the country is at work; twenty-seven of those countries hold national elections on a weekend, and both Israel and South Korea designate Election Day as a national holiday. Only twenty-two American states offer paid leave for voting. Low-income voters could lose pay on that day if they are not otherwise compensated for holidays. Likewise, disabled voters may have difficulty securing support to get them to the polls. Another option is guaranteed paid time off on Election Day, with employees having the option to choose when they cast their vote, including during early voting periods. A minimum of five hours of paid time off for voting purposes would guarantee compensation for travel time and long lines at polling places.

Until we have a federal mandate, our corporate citizens can leverage their might in support of expanding access to voting and ensuring that all voters have a quality experience. Every business can take four simple steps to increase access to voting and to democracy.[5] First, companies of every size should provide voter registration info to employees and remind them to verify their current registration. The workplace is a guaranteed location where most Americans will visit at some point during the year. Registration is not a partisan activity, which should alleviate any concerns about undue influence or electioneering by the boss. Second, companies should take steps to ensure employees know when elections are occurring. Depending on the size and location of the company, this may become more complex, but groups like the League of Women Voters are available in nearly every state and can be good civic partners to keep workers informed. Third, every corporation that can should make Election Day a holiday with paid leave or guaranteed paid time off for workers who vote. Doing so sends a signal of civic engagement, and it relieves voters of the pressure of choosing between voting and earning a living. In America, this should be an unnecessary trade-off, and companies can lead the way. Fourth, businesses should encourage employees to be poll workers on Election Day. If more members of the workforce staffed polling locations, joining the ranks typically served by retirees, operations might increase in efficiency and transparency by adding staffing support. County officials have to spend considerable time recruiting poll workers, and this could help ease the burden. In Georgia, Arthur Blank and his companies, which include the Atlanta Falcons and Atlanta United, have adopted several of these policies.

While we are tackling the infrastructure of democracy, we also have to return to who is considered an eligible citizen with the right to meaningful political representation at the federal level. Taxation without representation led to the Revolutionary War, yet it has become acceptable to treat the citizens of Washington, D.C., and Puerto Rico as less than citizens. Both areas enjoy qualified citizenship rights, despite having populations that meet or exceed ten states with full citizenship. At a little over 700,000 residents, D.C. is more densely populated than Wyoming and Vermont. Puerto Rico has more than three million residents, placing its population above twenty other states. However, no resident in either of those areas has a voting member of the House of Representatives or a U.S. senator, and only D.C. has a vote in the Electoral College. As two areas with high concentrations of black and Latino citizens, the granting of statehood to both would recognize the historic injustices and offer a pathway for full inclusion.

The keys to creating permanent voting rights lies in major federal change. When the right to vote is left to the states, implementation is fragmented, racist, and plain suppressive. Still, short of major federal action, I firmly adhere to a code of *citizen* action. In 2017, the New Georgia Project spun off into a standalone organization still committed to voter registration and education, adding tens of thousands of people of color to Georgia's rolls each cycle and finding new, innovative ways to effectively engage low-propensity voters. After the 2018 election, I launched three organizations: Fair Fight Action to focus on voting rights and voter suppression in Georgia, Fair Fight PAC to assist in-state and nationwide, and Fair Count, to guarantee an accurate count of hard-to-reach populations in the 2020 census. All these organizations exist because I know that my lone agitation won't do much. Change demands broad-based engagement, and every moment of progress in our voting system has come about due to the work of many hands. At Fair Fight Action, we have a clear mantra: litigation, legislation, and advocacy. Nationwide, our political action committee works to help defend the right to vote wherever it is threatened. The recommendations I made above focus on federal legislative action, but citizens can force the question on a local level.

If you or someone you know has been a victim of voter suppression, do not keep it to yourself or assume that it's a one-off problem. Or worse, do not blame yourself. Know that voter suppression is designed to look like user error. Despite the complicated rules and the arcane provisions, voters who are denied their rights often believe they did something wrong. As the mantra goes, if you see something, say something. Contact organizations like the American Civil Liberties Union (ACLU), the Lawyers' Committee for Civil Rights Under Law, the NAACP Legal Defense and Educational Fund, Voto Latino, Asian Americans Advancing Justice, National Association of Latino Elected and Appointed Officials (NALEO), Fair Fight—and do so while it is happening. Not every problem can be solved by lawsuits, but laws rarely improve if they are never challenged. By collecting stories, demanding access, and pushing for more, we not only can help you or your friends, we can build a legal record to potentially force change at the local, state, or federal level.

Twenty-six states have a process for citizen initiatives or ballot initiatives,[6] and if you live in one of them, please follow the leads of Floridians, Michiganders, and Nevadans, who each passed sweeping voting rights legislation in the 2018 election. From restoring the voting rights of felons in Florida to creating independent redistricting in Michigan and same-day registration in Nevada, take advantage of the power of being an American and demand more from those who lead you. Groups like Bolder Advocacy support activists and organizations in launching and supporting citizen-led change.[7] If you live in a state without statewide initiatives, set your sights on local leaders. Reach out to your city and county officials about introducing legislation to give municipal workers Election Day as a holiday. Demand multilingual access if your town has a population that cannot fully participate due to language barriers. Push for more accountability in the redistricting process for your city council, county commission, and school boards, all of which face gerrymandering too. One reason good-hearted citizens stay out of this fight is how complicated it can be. As I've pointed out, we have fifty different democracies, and within each state, counties and cities operate in unique ways too. But it's important to remember that we're in this together. If you're in one of the twenty battleground states for Fair Fight 2020, we have set up voter protection teams that would welcome your help. Swing Left, Sister District, and Let America Vote are also excellent resources for engagement.

I believe the most important job of a citizen advocate is to first *educate* leaders about what you want and why you want it. So often, we assume that the issue that is top of mind to us is known to our leaders. It's not. Therefore, you can be the one to introduce the problem, tell them why it's a problem, and then share your ideas about how to solve it. Understand, however, that once they know the problem, the solution may differ from yours—and that is not always a bad thing. The second job is to *activate* others to help you press leaders to adopt rules to make it happen.

While it can sound daunting, all this really means is finding friends and allies who share your concerns and are willing to help to gather even more allies. One note of caution is the tendency to want people on your side to share both your passion and your solution. Sometimes, you get one or the other, but do not push away potential support. Figure out how to work together toward the common goal and go as far as you can together. And, when education and activation have taken your issue as far as it can, the final step is to *agitate* the powers that be. Bring pressure to bear until doing what you want is easier than resisting or opposing you. Use social media, traditional outreach, and good old-fashioned protests to raise awareness and push for action. Groups like Indivisible will provide training, resources, and support for electoral advocacy, and organizations like Planned Parenthood Action Fund, National Abortion Rights Action League (NARAL), the NAACP, Moms Demand Action, and others can help home in on particular policies with electoral implications.

I will admit, agitation is my favorite part of the process. The seat I held as a state representative had previously belonged to a civil rights legend, Hosea L. Williams. He once told a group of activists to think about a washing machine. What cleans the clothes is not the water or the soap, it's the mechanism that shakes the clothes and forces the water and soap to do their jobs: the agitator.

Federal laws only change when the leaders do, and state and

local laws have similar if smaller playing fields. But one of the barriers to change has long been that people didn't have the language to describe what is wrong, or have the information to prove that it happens. I know voting rights are complicated and messy, and voter suppression is infuriating and patently wrong. But we can only win our fights if we understand how they steal our power and when we resolve, each of us, to take it back.

CHAPTER 6

We Can See You and So Should They

Kimya met her future husband in 2006. By 2008, they were celebrating their first wedding anniversary and planning a family. In between that first kiss and the anniversary of their marriage, he started beating her. The violence, initially sharp flares, eventually became more routine. In 2011, Kimya picked up her daughter from day care, and her husband confronted her at the facility. Gun in hand, he shot Kimya four times and shot their young daughter once—in the head. Incredibly, Kimya survived, but years passed before the little girl learned to walk again, to speak, to feed herself. It would be years before Kimya would feel safe and whole. Those are years he stole with a weapon and with the tyranny of domestic abuse.

In the aftermath of her tragedy, Kimya started working with other survivors of domestic violence. She became an expert on how the system had broken down and failed her, her daughter, and millions like them. The statistics and challenges are staggering. In a single year, ten million women and men will experience domestic violence.[1] Advocates warn about how incomplete law enforcement training on partner violence leaves men and women like Kimya vulnerable to terrorization that gets dismissed too easily. Other legal flaws allow convicted abusers to regularly slip through background check loopholes, giving them permission to secure guns that heighten their threats and, to no one's astonishment, often kill their victims. Domestic abuse survivors warn legislators regularly about rental agreements that trap victims in place, too afraid to stay within reach of their abusers but unable to break their leases because they could be barred from renting anywhere else. And, as Kimya learned firsthand, America fails to invest in mental health treatment options, which affects both the abused and the abuser—spinning a vicious web with no escape and no recourse.

Kimya has become an advocate for gun safety, for better health care options, and for domestic violence protections for renters. She works to improve how the justice system treats victims of violence and how cycles of domestic abuse can be broken with access to mental health care. She now participates in electoral politics, holding candidates accountable for how they address the epidemic of domestic abuse that nearly took her child's life and her own. And she uses their responses to decide whom she will support and whom she will oppose. Her tragedy has become a filter for her political decision making—because Kimya practices identity politics.

Broadly speaking, identity politics describes when people, rather than using traditional categories like political parties, give priority to their racial, gender, sexual orientation, social, cultural, economic, or other identity affiliation when approaching political decision making. I don't know if Kimya would characterize herself this way, but I do know that one of the reasons she supported my 2018 campaign for governor was my stance on these issues, and I know because she recorded a video explaining her rationale. Voters like Kimya intentionally leverage their personal experiences and their engagement of systemic barriers to decide how they will vote and for whom they will use their democratic power.

As a young black woman in Georgia, Kimya picks her politicians carefully. She opposes those who refuse to support gun safety, like the legislators who refuse to expand background checks and restrictions for domestic abusers, even though guns are the most common weapon used in the murders of intimate partners.[2] (Statistically, the possession of a gun raises the risk of homicide in domestic violence cases by 500 percent.[3]) Kimya nursed her child back to health, but she understands that for nearly 500,000 Georgians, access to most health care is denied because the state has refused to expand Medicaid, the insurance program for the poor.

In the Deep South, as in much of America, race is the strongest predictor of political leanings, and Democrats are more likely than Republicans to share her values. Women are more likely to champion legislation surrounding issues that primarily affect women and children. Thus, if Kimya hedges her bets, the most likely politician to support her needs would be a black woman Democrat. Her politics—her voting decisions—are governed by who she is, what she has experienced, and how she needs government and society to function. In most ways, for her, identity politics just means common sense.

Electoral politics is often the *final* barrier to social change, especially in America. Social movements rise, force change, and achieve gains; however, until the movement's leaders can embed those wins into law and lawmakers, the successes are temporary.

Therefore, when a marginalized group can get one or more of their own inside the corridors of power, it is more likely that they will see permanent change.

The reality, though, is that electing someone to office cannot guarantee that they will stay loyal to the cause that got them there. More than one politician has become seduced by the power of the office and in turn refuses to jeopardize their position by taking action on the issues they once championed. When these leaders demonstrate that they have feet of clay, social movements quickly learn that quantity and quality are of equal importance. That is to say, politics can distract the most well-intentioned leaders from their purpose or, worse, weaken their commitment to the ultimate goal of social change. For a movement to use electoral power from inside the system, one person is not enough. So, to guarantee expanded access, social groups like women, people of color, the LGBTQ+, and poor communities quickly learn that they need a team of supporters—both agitating for action outside and pushing for legislation and policies inside the political process. One law, one representative, one strategy rarely succeeds in its quest for fundamental change.

Dozens of black men elected at every level of government during Reconstruction terrified the Southern white congressmen who knew expansions of black power would shake the cultural and economic foundations of the former Confederacy. Instead, the Southern white congressmen used the 1876 presidential election to end the transformation of the South and restore the discrimination that had served them so well. Those who rage against and work against expanding the electorate know what's at stake. The goal is to block access to the ballot and to policy making because letting the agitators inside might yield new laws to remedy inequality or injustice. The fear of these elected officials is a loss of power, grounded in an assortment of causes like racism, sexism, homophobia, religious intolerance, or an inchoate desire to keep the world as it was when they sat at the peak of influence. They forget that the bygone days of political tranquility never truly existed—the agitators simply hadn't amassed sufficient power to be heard. But they are getting closer to it every day.

We know the nation is rapidly diversifying, but the acceleration of demographic transformation is faster in certain areas, like the Sun Belt (the collection of Southern and Western states stringing from North Carolina across to Arizona). Still, changes are occurring nearly everywhere, affecting how electoral power is disbursed and what policies are expected in return. The power of democracy is concentrated in the right to vote, and voter suppression has been the most effective means of disrupting that ability. But who a person votes for matters as much as having the ability to cast a ballot. With candidates who reflect a range of experiences, outlooks, and, yes, identities, stepping up to be elected, voters have recently experienced an unprecedented array of choices. Now, from the most local to the highest federal offices, candidates are expected to reflect the mélange that is America. And voters believe they should be able to make a choice between more than two heterosexual white men. The increase in political activity outside of elections has raised awareness of who is in charge and what is being said or done to respond to community demands. The first step is election, but those new leaders are expected to show results.

During the 2018 congressional cycle, Alexandria Ocasio-Cortez and Ayanna Pressley became the highest-profile examples of this trend. Representative Ocasio-Cortez defeated a ten-term Democratic incumbent in New York City, partly as a result of the shifting demographics in the congressional district. In

Massachusetts, Representative Pressley also defeated a ten-term Democratic incumbent. Like Ocasio-Cortez, Pressley campaigned on a platform of being more responsive to the increasingly diverse legislative district. In Kansas, Representative Sharice Davids combined a cross section of identities to build a voting coalition for her bid to be the first Democrat to represent Kansas in a decade. She is the first openly gay person elected to the U.S. Congress from Kansas, one of the first two Native American women elected to Congress in history, and the first openly gay LGBT Native American ever elected.

This trio of new congressional leaders have each made their mark by advocating for legislative issues that propelled them to victory. For Representative Ocasio-Cortez, her promotion of the Green New Deal catapulted the resolution into national discourse. Representative Pressley, who ran on a platform of expanded access for the poor and minorities, has introduced legislation known as the Healthy MOMMIES Act to expand Medicaid coverage in an attempt to provide comprehensive prenatal, labor, and postpartum care with an extension of existing Medicaid pregnancy funding and tackle maternal mortality, which kills black women at a rate three times higher than white women.

Under its former secretary of state, Kansas developed a reputation for voter suppression that received little attention due to its solidly conservative leanings. In 2018, Kansas discarded provisional ballots at a rate 8.5 percent higher than the national average. Representative Davids authored the Count the Vote Act, which will give people the right to directly petition the Department of Justice to investigate voting complaints. Each of these elected leaders relied on a coalition of voters who saw their identities as clear indicators for the kind of political goals they would serve—a necessary factor for communities used to being isolated from power.

"Identity politics" has become a hostile phrase for some and a rallying cry for others, though the concept is as old as our nation, just like voter suppression. As a result, our politics, particularly around elections, often resolves into a dichotomy about how to win elections. The argument goes that we must talk exclusively either about groups that are explicitly excluded or only about those who feel as though they're going to be left out if the conversation changes. Presumably, we can't talk about both. Yet, our democracy has always been grounded in how we must investigate identity and work to include everyone, at least in theory. The best democratic acts are the ones that can bring people together, not by pretending we all have the same issues but by recognizing the obstacles that some of us face and the opportunities that all of us want.

To untangle the hysteria and fear surrounding identity politics, we have to understand where it came from, why so many fear it, and, most important, how to harness its power. To be clear, I believe we *must* embrace identity politics if we are to save our democracy and thrive. Both ardent opponents on the right and worried critics on the left tend to gloss over the history of who we are and how that experience shapes our engagement of public policy.

As a young black working-class couple raising kids in Mississippi, my parents had one clear path to ensuring us a quality education: carefully picking the street on which we would live. This choice defined the school we would attend, the level of violence and poverty we would endure, and the social exposure we would have. Economic policy dictated that they would be renters, as saving for a down payment was well beyond our reach. School zoning laws determined the kind of housing available in the neighborhoods available to them, as well as the trappings of the communities. To live in the zone with the best-rated schools, my parents would have faced exorbitant rental prices. The most affordable costs meant living in the poorest part of town. In a city school district with three elementary schools, that meant a Goldilocks choice. Lower-income neighborhoods traditionally have lower-ranked schools, less green space, fewer parks, and limited access to cultural programming.

My parents had limited options for increasing their standard of living. Labor laws in Mississippi did not guarantee equal pay for equal work for women; and as a right-to-work state, either one of my parents could be terminated without cause. Neither of their jobs—my mom as a librarian and my dad as a shipyard worker—offered health care benefits, which meant that as kids we rarely visited doctors except for medical necessity. Ultimately, my parents picked a three-bedroom home for our family of eight on a working-class street on the middle-class side of town so we could be zoned into a good (but not the best) school.

For my family and families like ours, the intersections of race, class, and gender affected us at every turn, from whether we could reach a grocery store without a car (no, we could not) or if we could participate in school activities like band, debate, or football (yes, but with sacrifice). While these micro-choices seem far removed from the more serious consequences of racism, classism, or sexism, the effects are cumulative and determinative. Food deserts, or the absence of healthy food options, tend to lead to higher food prices, worse health outcomes, and depressed property values. Depressed property values are directly linked to lower investments in public education, given that most school systems are primarily funded by property taxes.

When my parents went to vote, whether they expressed it tacitly or not, these issues underpinned their decision making. The school board members chose the millage rate (how much each renter, homeowner, or commercial property owner paid in property taxes) and they set the budgets for each school's spending. Mayors, city council members, and county commissioners set zoning rules, including the green-lighting of liquor stores rather than grocery stores in certain neighborhoods, and they determined if public transit would be available for those separated from jobs and opportunity. State legislators and the governor set the statewide educational budget and passed laws governing health care access, wages and labor, and public safety.

At every level of government, at every seat of power, a person stood to help or harm how I grew up, what I learned, how I lived, and what I became. And despite horrific or simply lazy political choices at every level, I turned out okay. Once, during a heated debate in the legislature, a colleague who disagreed with my position pulled me aside. In what seemed like genuine confusion, he asked why I supported increasing government investment in an education program. "You didn't have this stuff, and you're doing well. Aren't you proof that government should get out of the way? Let people do what your parents did." After a beat, I responded, "Yes, I did fine, but most people don't have Robert and Carolyn Abrams as their parents. My job is to look out for the rest of them."

I have been asked about the potential balkanization of politics where embracing identity means that we can no longer reach consensus on broader issues. Though the question is well intentioned, I find it somewhat naive. Those of us with identities that have long been ignored or, worse, weaponized against us, have successfully managed to work together to elect politicians to represent us. Long before women were seen as viable executives, or people of color could afford to run for Congress in great numbers, we used our identity politics lens to identify those who would get us as close to progress as possible—voting in tandem with others of different backgrounds and challenges. The difference today is that identity is no longer a sidebar; for millions, their concerns may be front and center as they vet those who would speak for them. When leaders refused to see my family, my parents voted for those who would, and the best metric was someone who looked like us and had experiences like us. Then, as now, identity matters. I embrace identity politics because for the marginalized, the disadvantaged, and the minority groups still grappling for purchase in our politics, identity is the strongest defense against invisibility.

CLASS WARFARE BEGINS

In the early history of the United States, the political players pretty much looked alike. The moniker we use almost says it all: the Founding *Fathers*. If we add the modifier "white," then the description would be accurate. To be fair, we have all heard the quiet role others played in the intellectual history of our fundamental documents, like Benjamin Banneker and Abigail Adams, but the principal architects were uniformly white men.

The U.S. Constitution reveals this original identity as the one to be protected at all costs. Social movements anchored by identity began nearly as soon as the country did, between the abolitionists opposing slavery, women demanding suffrage and equality, and the poor of every race being exploited for their labor. The fight over slavery led inexorably to the Civil War, Reconstruction and Jim Crow, and the civil rights movement. Women's suffrage became a multigenerational movement that culminated in the Equal Rights Amendment. Juxtaposed beside these fights over race and gender, Americans have long waged a political fight to use class as a centrifugal force, and, in several ways, class identity has had more success and a nearly parallel history.

Almost as soon as the country produced wealthy Americans, the overworked and underpaid railed against their lack of economic opportunity. A nascent political tradition called populism latched onto the disorganized fight for economic justice and, in short order, elevated the debate to the national stage. In the nineteenth century, the Know-Nothing Party denounced immigrants, Catholics, and minorities, insisting that their advancement came at the expense of white Protestants. For them, using the plight of the working white man cloaked an identity politics that shunned anyone who did not support white Christian supremacy, and they plied their ideology from 1849 until 1860. The Greenback Party, largely comprised of farmers, emerged in 1874 to demand an eight-hour workday and broader labor reforms. Like the Know-Nothings, they recognized the importance of political influence, and the party ran candidates for president until it dissolved in 1884. The remnants of the Greenbacks folded into the Populist Party, which also absorbed the Farmers' Alliance, emerging in 1890 as a prominent third party, winning seats in both the U.S. House of Representatives and the U.S. Senate. However, they shared the aims of the Greenbacks, such as support for collective bargaining and suspicion of the Know-Nothings, who reviled minorities. Despite seeking to build a wider tent—one that allowed white women to take prominent roles in shaping policy and organizing—the Populist Party largely rejected inclusion of blacks in their ranks, and, by 1908, their inability to cultivate urban support led to their demise.

William Jennings Bryan emerged at the tail end of one of the most intense clashes over class and economic security, and he became the most famous class warrior and populist of the nineteenth and twentieth centuries. A loyal Democrat, Bryan railed against moneyed interests and monopolies, promoting instead the needs of the "common man." He represented the state of Nebraska in Congress but rose to national prominence at the 1896 Democratic convention. The nation had divided over the issue of how U.S. currency would be calibrated. The Democratic incumbent, President Grover Cleveland, promoted the gold standard, which meant that the United States had a limited supply of currency. For populists, particularly those suspicious of foreign powers, the gold standard served the desires of bankers at the expense of regular folks, as proven by the Depression of 1893. With a single currency standard based on the more expensive gold metal, inflation increased and so did the cost of living for the average worker—prices went up, growth was less stable, and financial systems were less predictable. At the convention to determine the Democratic nominee for president in 1896, Bryan delivered his celebrated "Cross of Gold" speech, in which he argued for a more liberal monetary standard that included a more freely available precious metal, silver.

Bryan's brand of class consciousness as a political brand harnessed nearly fifty years of movement toward a class-based identity politics, functioning as an antidote to the wealthy who had benefited from working-class labor. In the speech, he laid out what still resounds through the class consciousness of modern-day politicians: "The man who is employed for wages is as much a business man as his employer; [t]he farmer who goes forth in the morning and toils all day, who begins in spring and toils all summer, and who by the application of brain and muscle to the natural resources of the country creates wealth, is as much a business man as the man who goes upon the Board of Trade and bets upon the price of grain."

Supporters of class-based identity will conflate their goals with those of the populists, but the ideas are parallel, not identical. Populist movements alternately either avoided or derided the issues of minority status. Their persistence throughout American politics has allowed *class* to serve as an acceptable form of identity politics. By folding in the economic struggles of farmers, miners, and laborers, the earliest constructs of identity politics nimbly evaded confrontation with the intersections of other identities, like race, gender, and sexual orientation. However, as those issues gained more prominence in the twentieth century, political activism demanded a broader discussion of who would be heard in the American polity.

The labor movements of the nineteenth and twentieth centuries merged into both civil rights movements and feminist movements, but often the class struggle pitted itself against the rise of these groups as separate enemies to be fought. The economic class struggle increased rights for white men but still denied women and people of color the right to own property. Later, as the prohibitions against ownership fell, the restrictions were replaced by limits on access to capital or even the right to purchase property in certain areas of town. Likewise, as public education expanded to include primary, secondary, and post-secondary options, marginalized groups were either segregated or denied access to educational achievement. Even in the wake of World War II, the G.I. Bill excluded blacks and other minority military men from benefiting from its educational investment. Across the board, economic class, as an identity, never fully included all the economically disadvantaged in its ranks. Instead, once class was established, new filters of race, immigration, gender, and sexual orientation weeded out those considered unworthy of its benefits.

MORE THAN THE SUM OF OUR PARTS

Race has been a constant source of identity politics; and in each century, politicians and average citizens have battled over which races counted and who belonged at the seat of decision making. The first wave of identity politics and race questioned the humanity of blacks and the treatment of Native Americans as the eighteenth century merged into the nineteenth. The Civil War, the Trail of Tears, the Chinese Exclusion Act, and the Mexican-American War had race at the center of the nation's determination of who held value. In the aftermath of the Civil War, the brief humanity of Reconstruction quickly gave way to the Redemption period, when Congress traded away the future of blacks for another century in order to resolve the election of 1876. In order to install President Rutherford B. Hayes, Republicans defending black citizenship withdrew their protections in the Compromise of 1877. Then the laws referred to as Jim Crow allowed for gruesome lynchings, mob riots that burned out black towns, and rigid segregation in education, in economics, and across all aspects of social life.

Native Americans suffered horrifically at the hands of federal leaders who vilified their identity as justification for the nation's most brutal acts. President Andrew Jackson commanded the removal and effective genocide of thousands of Creek, Choctaw, Cherokee, and Seminole via a 5,043-mile-long march over nine states: Alabama, Arkansas, Georgia, Illinois, Kentucky, Missouri, North Carolina, Oklahoma, and Tennessee. President Martin Van Buren completed the "Indian Removal" campaign, and in the northern states, the Sauk, the Fox, and other native tribes faced war or removal.

Out in California, Chinese immigration hit a peak in the mid-1800s, particularly after the gold rush of 1849. Chinese laborers took on work in mines, on railroads, and along the waterfronts. They represented less than 0.2 percent of the nation's population; yet, in response to demands for "racial purity" from white laborers and others, the 1882 Chinese Exclusion Act became the first federal law to prohibit an entire class of migrants. No Chinese person would be permitted to immigrate for ten years; and because of the Naturalization Act, no Chinese migrant living in America could be naturalized as a citizen.

For Latinos who inhabited the American West, the Mexican-American War ended with a grant of citizenship to all who decided to stay in the United States, under the Treaty of Guadalupe Hidalgo. However, soon thereafter, the reality of a significant Mexican American population began to result in laws stripping them of the perquisites of citizenship. In *Botiller v. Dominguez*, the Supreme Court refused to recognize Mexican Americans' titles to land in California. The decision came in the wake of the California Gold Rush, when the U.S. Supreme Court read federal law to strip Mexican American citizens of certain property rights in the 1800s. During the Great Depression, President Herbert Hoover oversaw the mass deportation of more than one million people of Mexican descent, an estimated 60 percent of whom were U.S. citizens. Like blacks in the South, the Latinos in the West also faced lynchings, segregation, and expulsion, including Operation Wetback authorized by President Dwight Eisenhower, which purports to have forcibly deported more than 1.3 million Hispanics living in the United States.

By the mid-twentieth century, though, racial minorities had begun to assert both their increased presence and their capacity for organizing to combat injustice. The civil rights movement of the 1950s and '60s led to a raft of new laws to address historical inequality. Likewise, the American Indian Movement, El Movimiento (the Chicano Movement), and court decisions to force language equity in schools and desegregation in housing benefited more and more people of color. Still, today, as we know, racial inequality festers in our politics, our economics, and the lived experiences of Americans of nonwhite descent.

Gender, like race, has been twisted into knots of both access and rejection. The movement for women's suffrage succeeded, and the second wave of women's rights seen in the Feminist Movement of the 1970s also yielded extraordinary change. Like people of color, women faced limitations on their very citizenship: the right to vote, to serve on juries, to work in the arena of their choosing, and the right to control reproductive choices. Through a series of movements, beginning with suffrage and continuing through first- and second-wave feminism, women built upon the compromises gained in earlier rounds. Yet, in each of these achievements, the intersection of race and gender left women of color behind, primarily black women. Sojourner Truth voiced legitimate outrage in her "Ain't I a Woman" tirade against a pale vision of suffrage, anticipating that the right to vote granted by the Nineteenth Amendment excluded black women.

Ida B. Wells faced rejection from white women when she brought attention to the lynchings of black men and women. For Latinas and Asian American women in the West, not to mention Native American women, their womanhood did not guarantee entrée into the debates of feminist objectives.

The development of an identity politics for the LGBTQ+ community has stretched over nearly 150 years in America, from the 1870s forward. As the acronym demonstrates, no single profile adequately describes the range of issues faced by lesbians, gays, bisexuals, transgender, queer, or other nonbinary individuals in the United States. Forced for most of American history into the shadows of daily life, the emergence of a social movement got its initial start during World War II, layering upon the underground freedom experienced in metropolitan areas like New York City in the 1920s. During World War II, the first iteration of "don't ask, don't tell" led to members of the LGBTQ+ community enlisting in the armed forces, and a relaxation of social constraints permitted more open behaviors. Backlash quickly followed, highlighted by Senator Joseph McCarthy's crusade against homosexuals employed by the federal government in the 1950s. The public demand for equality for the LGBTQ+ community coincided and intersected with the rise of the civil rights movement. The Stonewall movement, which began with a raid of a gay club in 1969, launched a more sustained effort to gain equality in mental health treatment, health care, housing, employment, marriage, and adoption. What remains a tension in the LGBTQ+ movement are the conflicts that race, class, and gender expose when wrapped into the national debate on sexual orientation.

Identity politics, a term originally used by black women in the 1970s, became a shorthand for combining the two most critical facets of achieving full inclusion in the United States—who you are and how you gain power. Black feminists in the Combahee River Collective used the term to describe how difference had made them the targets of oppression. But, more optimistically, they recognized that using the common experiences of that identity could allow a new political organizing strategy to end that oppression. Over time, more and more groups recognized the resonance of the term, and they used their own common experiences to build coalitions, define the inherent challenges of their struggles, and leverage their new collectivism to press for change. Arguments continue over what constitutes true "identity politics" as a philosophical construct, a public policy imperative, or a flawed means of picking candidates based solely on external characteristics rather than the candidate's own merit. Rather than engaging in a false choice, I opt to short-circuit the debate with a more simplistic view: identity is real and necessary and intertwined in our politics in such a way that there is no going back.

WHY WHO WE ARE MATTERS

To own the power that voting provides, we must be positioned to select and elect leaders who will support our ambitions and clear barriers to our inclusion in opportunity. More important, we must acknowledge and accept that we all practice our own form of identity politics. Every person comes into the public discourse with histories and challenges. The worst political spaces are the ones where voters are told that everyone has the exact same narrative and everyone faces the exact same obstacles. The myth of the self-made man coexists with the stereotype of the welfare queen and the homeless junkie and the Spanish-speaking laborer.

When political leaders homogenize our experiences or, worse, reduce them to insults or aberrations, they evade the hard work of understanding whom they represent.

Identity politics forces those who ask for our support to do their jobs: To understand that the self-made man got zoned into a good school district and received a high-quality education, one that wouldn't have existed if his zip code changed by a digit. To recognize that the woman on welfare with three kids is the product of divorce in a state where she risks losing food stamps if her low-wage job pays her too much. Or that the homeless junkie is an Iraq War veteran who was in the National Guard but lost his job due to multiple deployments and didn't qualify for full VA care. And that the laborer is a migrant farmworker who overstayed his visa to care for his American-born children.

Single-strand identities do not exist in a household, let alone in a nation. When America is at its best, we acknowledge the complexity of our societies and the complicating reality of how we experience this country—and its obstacles. Yet we never lose sight of the fact that we all want the same thing. We want education. We want economic security. We want health care. Identity politics pushes leaders to understand that because of race, class, gender, sexual orientation/gender identity, and national origin, people confront obstacles that stem from these identities. Successful leaders who wish to engage the broadest coalition of voters have to demonstrate that they understand that the barriers are not uniform and, moreover, that they have plans to tackle these impediments. The greatest politicians display both of these capacities, and they never forget that the destination—regardless of identity—is the same: safety, security, and opportunity.

The goals of social justice movements and the imprimatur of identity politics have a common objective: to create permanent, unassailable legal protections that guarantee no one can strip another of fundamental rights guaranteed by citizenship. Yet, as with the core issue of voting rights, without inviolate protections, no marginalized group is ever truly safe.

Demographic changes and broader public inclusion have hastened this latest wave of hostility in the past few years to people of color, immigrants, the LGBTQ+ community, and women. Antagonistic policies that penalize differences, like the Muslim ban, caged immigrant children, and forced pregnancy bills are clear examples of this vitriol. More subtle is the evisceration of protections like the social safety net through slashes to food stamps by the federal Department of Agriculture or the rescission of discrimination protections by the Department of Education and the Department of Housing and Urban Development. For Native Americans, the risks come from forays by the Trump administration into stripping federal lands of protections and weakened environmental controls that encourage encroachment on native lands. This even includes the refusal of Republicans in Congress to renew the Voting Rights Act, a repudiation of racial progress that was unthinkable fifteen years ago.

Our power to shape the future centers around the ability to cement rights but, more important, to understand the intersections of identity that deny access and opportunity. Difference is real, and to acknowledge such does no harm to the American identity as a whole. The vibrance of our identity politics reaffirms the complexity of our nation and the underpinning of our founding. People fleeing religious persecution did so because they required a safe space where difference would be tolerated. Our progress as a nation has been yoked to the complexity of who our people are. Knowing identity matters is the first step— but the harder part is knowing how to make identity count.

CHAPTER 7

How the Census Shapes America

Right now, a war over numbers threatens to reshape the next decade of American life, and almost no one is paying attention. Stephanie Hofeller certainly never expected to be a key player in the fight. Estranged from her father, Thomas Hofeller, Stephanie had not spoken to him or seen him in several years. As she tells it, she only learned of his death by searching for him on the Web while her car idled in the parking lot of a convenience store. Stephanie then trekked from Kentucky to North Carolina to her mother's home. During her visit, her mom allowed her to take several files belonging to her dad, perhaps hoping it would spark a reconnection. Stephanie dutifully combed through the hard drives and thumb drives, finding family pictures and other memorabilia. But the images of kids and happier days shared data space with work product from his day job as a redistricting consultant for Republicans.

The banal term "redistricting" has been added to the general American political diet in recent years, but how and why it happens remains murky. Indeed, most people have never heard of the conservative Thomas Hofeller or his daughter, Stephanie, the political independent. Fewer have visited the website she set up, known as The Hofeller Files, where she has published thousands of pages and spreadsheets of her father's work despite legal threats and accusations of theft. The documents she uncovered in her father's records, compiled over several years, tell the story of how the GOP has fixed itself on a singular goal: aggregating and maintaining Republican dominance in state and federal politics regardless of the will of the people.

The grasp for power should surprise no one who pays attention to the nightly news, but the methodical and vicious nature of Hofeller's advice might. He served as a national guru on redistricting, the process by which congressional lines, state legislative districts, and local political maps are drawn. For the Republicans, he was a savant on the art of gerrymandering: twisting and turning those geographic lines into unbeatable political districts for Republican candidates. In document after document, Hofeller taught a master class to lawmakers and lobbyists on how to use statistical data and legal tactics to block efforts to increase civic participation by people of color. He composed memos and reports on limiting the decennial count of nonwhite residents in the United States, as part of the nation's makeup.

In 2020, his work has increased in relevance, because since 2010, more Americans have learned the effect of gerrymandering on the composition of Congress and state legislatures. After three twentieth-century presidential elections where the winner *lost* the popular vote, a renewed discussion of the Electoral College rages on the internet and in small intellectual enclaves. But at the core of these debates, at the center of the maelstrom, is a single instrument of immense importance, one that shapes all the contours of power in America, and that's the U.S. census.

The U.S. census typically gets attention in the weeks leading up to its start, and in the days before it ends. A few blips capture America's attention afterward, like the announcement of how fast a state has grown or how many people live here now. Knowing who is in the United States has been a constant part of our national identity from the beginning. The Constitution calls for a count of all persons residing in America every ten years, with the first census conducted in 1790. Article I, Section 2, dictates an "enumeration" of people, regardless of citizenship, and it lays out who counts and why. From the outset, unsurprisingly, the count had caveats. The three-fifths compromise allowed Southern states to undercount enslaved blacks for the purposes of the census. "Indians not taxed" were also excluded as part of the national calculus, relegating most Native Americans to invisibility. Over time, the rules have expanded to count each person residing in the states, including citizens, noncitizen legal residents, noncitizen long-term visitors, and undocumented immigrants. Short-term visitors are not counted, and neither are Americans living abroad who are not directly employed by the U.S. government, like military personnel and foreign service officers and their dependents. Who counts matters a great deal, and the accuracy of the process has been a source of controversy from the start.

More than a simple head count, the U.S. census steers more than a trillion dollars for critical services like health care and education, guides the drawing of lines for political districts and school zones, and informs businesses and employers about opportunities for economic development. No one is exempt from the impact of these decisions, yet in each iteration, certain populations remain hard to reach. The most undercounted groups are people of color, low-income persons, LGBTQ+ persons, young children, ethnic minorities, undocumented immigrants, renters, and those in rural areas.

Referred to collectively as hard-to-count, these populations comprise more and more of the American majority. This undercount costs communities economic access and reduces their political power a decade at a time, and who we understand as our national population influences every facet of public life and is wound inside nearly every mechanism of election administration. Overall, the census is a trove of rich, useful data that can assess where a hospital should be built or where a business might locate a factory. Researchers, scientists, and social justice advocates alike turn to it for guidance. I have referenced its statistics as a legislator to bolster an argument and as an entrepreneur when making a pitch. No one is immune to the reach of the census, whether they try to be or not. In the decade that follows the upcoming census, more than $1.5 trillion will be allocated on an annual basis. Likewise, based on the numbers collected in 2020, political power will be distributed at nearly each level of government until 2030. But when it is corrupted by intent, or when efficiencies trump accuracy, the census becomes a weapon against the most vulnerable.

THE SIGNIFICANCE OF THE UNITED STATES CENSUS

It's no secret that political and economic power tend to be distributed unevenly in even the most democratized nations; however, the U.S. census ostensibly offers a cure to the problem. It's designed to count everyone and let the data tell the story. A bad census count steals from the communities that are not included. Federal dollars are distributed based on the number of people affected, and if a neighborhood is undercounted, the residents will not receive the funds allocated to solve their problems. And if they cannot elect representatives to speak up for them, they are victimized again.

Consider a low-income neighborhood with high birth rates and tragic rates of infant mortality. Decades ago, we decided to intervene by providing public health programs like Medicaid and the Special Supplemental Nutrition Program for Women, Infants, and Children, otherwise known as WIC. Each state receives an allocation based on a formula derived from census information. In places where at-risk mothers and babies are left out of the census, the missing information means a decrease in the amount of money the area receives. I have served communities undercounted in the census. During my career, I worked in local government for the City of Atlanta, at the state level as a representative, and in the federal government in the Environmental Protection Agency and the Office of Management and Budget. Because of those jobs, I possess a granular understanding of what an undercount can mean, like the difference between survival and opportunity.

In the aftermath of the 2018 election, I spent ten days between Election Day on November 6 and my nonconcession day on November 16 thinking about what would be next for me if I didn't win. Tackling voter suppression stood at the top of my list, an expansion of work I had been doing for more than twenty-five years. Somehow, though, launching Fair Fight's work struck me as critical yet insufficient. Another worry niggled at me, a reminder of my first days as minority leader. The 2010 census had led to a profound reshaping of political representation in

Georgia, and we were not alone. We know that 22 percent of Georgia's population is considered hard-to-count, and that challenge could cost the state more than $407 million per year in funding. For every person who does not participate in the census, Georgia loses $2,300. Across the country, there is a notable correlation that shows that when sharp increases in people of color occur in GOP-led states, those same states have seen voting become harder. I needed to focus on voting, yes; but I knew I had to address the foundational tools for how power is allocated. That was the bottom line. Thus, our Fair Fight operation was joined by a separate organization called Fair Count, dedicated to ensuring that hard-to-count populations were seen in the 2020 census—because the census was the core of it all.

The census sources the numbers and data points that construct our picture of America, which led us beyond the borders of Georgia with the Fair Count crusade, but the challenges posed to an accurate count in Georgia and across the country are significant and have been highlighted in an in-depth study by the Urban Institute.[1] The report cites issues including underfunding the Census Bureau, the unknown impact of moving the census online, and several other factors that could lead to the worst undercount of black and Latinx people in thirty years, as well as notable costs to the AAPI and Native populations as well.

And it's not just in Georgia, of course. The census's impact will be felt nationwide, and the risks are just as keen. We visited the Brooklyn Community Foundation of New York in late 2019, and the event organizers echoed my fear that a damning undercount loomed. Despite sitting in a blue city in a blue state, the composition of Brooklyn reflects the broader danger for marginalized populations. Over 80 percent of Brooklyn residents live in hard-to-count neighborhoods, and the area is home to nearly half of the five hundred census tracts in New York State that risk an undercount. History doesn't bode well for them. During the most recent census, Brooklyn had one of the lowest return rates in the country, with fully one-third of households not returning their forms. Energized by the organizers' interest in our work, we expanded our efforts to South Carolina, North Carolina, Massachusetts, Nevada, and Louisiana and cities across the country.

The expected undercount of the census will have the starkest effect on black, Latino, AAPI, and Native American communities, costing them money and legislative representation. A number of groups and organizations are focused on ensuring an accurate census for hard-to-count populations. The Census Equity Fund has convened philanthropists and leaders to target strategic investment to the most critical areas. Groups like the Leadership Conference on Civil and Human Rights and the Census Black Roundtable help focus attention on national trends on improving census outreach. Organizing 101 teaches that people respond best to those who reflect their experiences, and entities like the National Association of Latino Elected and Appointed Officials, Asian Americans Advancing Justice, and the NAACP have developed programs to engage recalcitrant or frightened residents. Fair Count, like these other groups, has coordinated with the Congressional Black Caucus, the Congressional Hispanic Caucus, and the Congressional Asian Pacific American Caucus—together referred to as the Tri-Caucus—and at least one Native American member of the House to boost participation in the 2020 census. At a briefing in December 2019, utilizing the Urban Institute–produced estimates detailing the anticipated undercounts, Fair Count calculated how it would financially affect the distribution of funds to the communities where people live, and we discussed the bad news in numbers: by population, over 1.7 million black people could be missed in the 2020 census, and their communities could lose $3.3 billion in federal funding annually for the next decade if black people are undercounted. Based on varying costs across areas, the losses range from $451,000 per year in Wyoming to $392 million per year in New York. For the Hispanic/Latinx demographic, 2.2 million people could be omitted, and their cities and states stand to lose $4.1 billion in federal funding annually. Comparative costs show the impact to be $1.1 million per year in West Virginia and up to $1.1 billion lost per year in California. The census could skip over 305,000 Asian/Native Hawaiian/Pacific Islander people, costing $590 million in annual federal funding. Alaskan Indian/Native American people risk an undercount of 130,000 residents, yielding $200 million in forfeited federal funding each year. These fund losses reduce the potential to address real needs in their areas, and the ripple effects flow out for ten years, compounding the dereliction caused by the last undercount and the one before that. Schools awaiting investment in the 1990s now house the children of those left behind. Neighborhoods desperate for affordable housing investment have become ghost towns haunted by those who cannot afford to leave.

THE CENSUS *COULD* SAVE US

The census is more than a statistical juggernaut; it is an organizing tool we can use to salvage democracy. As the fiscal impact of the census grinds at the lives of the undercounted, so too do the political realities that come from not having access to resources or the ability to elect leaders to secure them. A regional census director has repeatedly told the story of a community that had begged county leaders for a public park. With no public green space, kids played in the streets and in vacant lots. On a regular basis, neighbors reported near misses with oncoming cars and drug deals occurring on street corners where kids congregated. Outraged and desperate, community leaders organized themselves and put in a proposal for funding to convert one of the lots into a safe space for children to play, free from the dangers of the streets. But the county commission rejected the proposal despite pleas from their district's commissioner. The staff explained the denial: in the last census, a majority of families in that district had not participated in the census, and that meant an undercount of the children in the neighborhood. The commissioner argued that anyone driving in the area could see the streets teeming with kids in need of recreational space. But, the staffer responded, those kids were not included in the last census, and she could only go by the numbers.

The average American understands the basics of voting rights because elections are nearly annual occurrences with millions spent to remind them. Whole television series and films have been premised on elections and their outcomes. Even if a person does not participate or their candidate loses, they may shrug off the results because no one is guaranteed victory in an election. When it comes to the census, those who benefit from participation as well as those who stand to be harmed may not share the urgency of the matter. And that's because most people know the census as a once-a-decade intrusion by the government, one that can be discounted or ignored with little consequence. But as that community learned, showing up on a form can save the lives of their kids.

To collect the data about who exactly lives here, the U.S. Census Bureau begins by sending letters to households either with a written form or, more likely in 2020, with a code direct-ing them to an online form to complete. The initial form is sim-ply the first salvo in trying to increase participation. Residents who fail to respond will receive reminders; and if they still do not respond, census takers will be sent door to door to gather infor-mation. The Census Bureau has developed special processes to count groups that do not have regular addresses during the cen-sus count: deployed troops, the homeless, college students, incar-cerated people, those displaced by natural disasters, the elderly and others in nursing homes, and other groups that do not have typical housing arrangements.

What the census asks for is fairly straightforward. It begins with where the person lives and sleeps most of the time. Resi-dents are also queried on the name, age, sex, date of birth, and race of each occupant, as well as the relationship between each person and the head of household. In the earliest census takings, only the heads of households were listed by name, with other members being referred to by count rather than name. The cen-sus also asks about the status of the residents and their dwelling, that is, is the home owned, rented, or occupied and is there a mortgage for the homeowner. In recent census rounds, respon-dents have also been asked to identify if each person is of His-panic, Latino, or Spanish origin. This latter issue has become particularly threatening to the GOP as the Latino population expands both in size and location.[2]

In 2019, the Trump administration attempted to add a "citizen-ship question" to the census survey.[3] The backlash was immediate, spurring accusations that Trump wanted to have an undercount of people of color, namely Latinos. Defenders of the citizenship ques-tion argued that the accuracy of the census depended on know-ing the legal status of every American resident—documented or undocumented. They self-righteously asserted that the census has been asking the question for years.

Until 1950, a version of a citizenship question did indeed exist on the short form sent out to every household. At the same time, U.S. law placed hard limits on immigration to the United States from almost everywhere except Northern Europe, meaning immigrants were mostly white. That imbalance in immigration existed until the Immigration and Nationality Act of 1965. The quota system adopted in the 1920s to restrict other countries had limited newcomers from Africa, Latin America, Asia, and southern European nations like Italy and Greece. But the country had stopped using the citizenship question *before* immigration became a major source of modern debate. Instead, the census had shifted to asking that question on the long-form versions of the census, which only went out to a sampling of Americans. No census had used the citizenship question on the ubiquitous short form in fifty years.

Here's where Thomas Hofeller's research once again tries to game the system. His notes and reports clearly indicate that the citizenship question was intended to stoke fear into immigrant families, regardless of status. Rather than answer a question about citizenship that might lead to deportation or draw attention to a family with mixed documentation status (a combination of citizenship, residency, and undocumented status), Latino, African, and Asian immigrants would ignore the census process entirely. Which is exactly what those in power hoped for. Indeed, one of Hofeller's studies boasts that the inclusion of the citizenship question would be "advantageous to Republicans and Non-Hispanic Whites" and he urged Republicans to seek its addition.[4]

Trump took the bait and announced his intention of putting the controversial question on the 2020 census. Organizations and a number of states filed suit against the Trump administration. California secretary of state Alex Padilla helped lead his state's lawsuit, along with state attorney general Xavier Becerra. They argued that the citizenship question was intended to artificially suppress the count, and the consequences for California would be dire. Home to nearly forty million people, California runs an economy larger than all but five nations on earth, and it has one of the most diverse populations in America. Latinos comprise the largest ethnic group at 39.3 percent, followed by non-Hispanic whites at 36.8 percent, AAPI at 15.1 percent, blacks at 5.8 percent, and Native Americans and Alaskan Natives at 0.8 percent.[5] In an interview with NPR, Secretary Padilla laid out the potential effect: "The whole point of the census is to get an accurate count of the entire nation's population for a couple of important purposes. Yes, it does determine federal funding formulas for the next decade—transportation dollars, education dollars, housing dollars, and so forth. But more fundamentally, it is the census numbers that drive the reapportionment process and redistricting. So we're literally talking about California's voice in Congress and the level of representation being at stake."[6] With a state where nearly six out of every ten residents is in the category of hard-to-count by virtue of race, an undercount would be financially catastrophic. And without full political representation, clawing back those missing dollars is a tall order.

With a national population estimated in excess of 329 million, the census has evolved from the founders' original construction and processing. The advent of the internet has fundamentally altered most of modern life, and the census is no exception. Where once the process began and ended in a single year, the utility and consequence of the census's data led to an expansion of the governmental function, eventually leading to the creation of a permanent Census Bureau within the Commerce Department. For the 2020 census, the bureau intends to use online forms to collect data. Use of the internet can expand the efficiency of the census under the theory that replying online is faster than paper and is a simpler process than going to the post office; however, the approach carries high risk for problems due to limited testing and outreach operations, exacerbated by underfunding. In fact, the Government Accountability Office flagged the conduct of the 2020 census as a "high risk" government operation due to the complexity of the process. "For the 2020 Census, the U.S. Census Bureau plans to implement several innovations, including new IT systems. The challenges associated with successfully implementing these innovations, along with other challenges, puts the Bureau's ability to conduct a cost-effective census at risk."[7] The underfunding of the estimated $15.6 billion census project led to a protracted battle between the White House and Congress.[8] Congressional leaders successfully secured additional funds for the operation, but funding still lags the necessary amount to achieve an accurate and complete count as estimated by the Census Bureau.

For the first time in history, up to 80 percent of respondents will be expected to complete the census online. The new method is supposed to increase both cost savings and broader distribution. For hard-to-count populations, what looks like innovation creates the risk of being left out. With limited access to the internet, millions may be unable to complete the survey, despite wanting to participate. In mid-2019, I gave a speech in Athens, Georgia, on the future of rural health care, including telemedicine, where physicians serve their patients using computers and video technology. A young black student in the audience raised her hand. She questioned the likelihood of using the internet in rural places like her hometown to provide health care. "I had to complete my college application in the parking lot of McDonald's in the next town over," she explained to the audience. "Where I live, there is no internet." Her warning is accurate and an urgent concern for groups interested in supporting the census. According to the Federal Communications Commission report on broadband progress, "In rural areas, nearly one-fourth of the population—14.5 million people—lack access to [broadband] service. In tribal areas, nearly one-third of the population lacks access. Even in areas where broadband is available, approximately 100 million Americans still do not subscribe."[9] This issue has raised red flags for a number of organizations, including Fair Count. Our response has been the installation of 150 Wi-Fi hot spots in low-coverage areas across Georgia. We partnered with Bishop Reginald Jackson and the AME church leadership in Georgia, and we developed community relationships that allowed us to place devices in churches, barbershops, a Cambodian refugee shelter, and a medical facility for migrant workers.

The suspicions of the citizenship question, underfunding, and online deployment reinforce another controversy for potential census participants: the security of their data. In an age of Russian hacking into elections and ICE raids of entire cities, some vulnerable communities do not trust the census because they do not trust the government. One census advocate tells of visits to apartment buildings, where residents are cautious about answering the forms. One worry is that if they report more people in their household than their lease allows, will they be subject to eviction? Another concern among black and Latino communities is whether the census can be used by law enforcement, regardless of whether the respondent has any criminal history. In states where racial bias in incarceration is real, their fears carry weight.

To combat legitimate apprehensions, outreach organizations are going to great lengths to explain how the benefit of the census outweighs the perceived harms. Both the Census Bureau and social media platforms like Facebook and Instagram have committed to fighting disinformation campaigns that seek to stoke fears.[10] That means explaining the consequences for breaking the privacy of the census. Under Title 13 of the U.S. Code, anyone who uses confidential information from a person's response commits a federal crime. A respondent's private information will never be published, including the name, address (including GPS coordinates), social security numbers, or telephone numbers of household members. The law also states that personal information cannot be used against respondents by any government agency or court of law. Any identifying data is restricted for seventy-two years, and the consequences for violation include five years of imprisonment, a fine of up to $250,000, or both. As I like to explain to skeptics, if a person owns a phone or pays a utility bill, the government already knows how to find you. By completing the census, you can get the money for your community and power in your politics, but trust will continue to be an issue until our national leadership proves its best intentions.

COLLATERAL DAMAGE: GERRYMANDERING

State House District 151 in Southwest Georgia is predominantly black and predominantly Democratic. The longtime state representative for the area, Gerald Greene, has served for more than thirty years, twenty-eight of them as a Democrat. Then in 2010, when Republicans swept the elections, he switched parties. Representative Greene is a retired educator with a deep history in his district. Yet, he has also presided over the closure of two hospitals in this impoverished region, and the counties he represented lost hundreds of jobs. Representative Greene opposed expanding Medicaid, which would have infused funds and employment into the region.[11]

As Democratic leader, one of my jobs was to win his seat for my party, but recruiting a good opponent proved harder than I expected. In 2016, a retired African American deputy sheriff who'd grown up in the region stepped forward to run. We ran all the traps on his background, studying up on his history in law enforcement and any surprises that could hurt a campaign. James Williams came back as an ideal candidate, including his long history of voting in the district. During the qualifying period, Mr. Williams drove the three hours to Atlanta, paid his fees for getting on the ballot, and returned home to District 151. A few days later, I received an outraged call from him. Secretary of State Brian Kemp had disqualified him from the race by claiming he didn't live in the district. Our team pulled the district maps that had been in use for the region since 2011 redistricting, and we used our computer mapping programs to verify what we saw. For five years, James Williams had called District 151 home, but nearly overnight, the county board of elections decided that his house sat just outside the boundaries, placing him in District 154. But his house hadn't moved. The lines did—almost by magic. Faced with a well-organized, popular opponent, the GOP had decided that rather than win the election fair and square, they would redraw the district lines and disqualify him that way. This tactic, drawing legislative lines to benefit a party, typically only took place every ten years, but under the Republican secretary of state who would become governor, a five-year "mistake" got fixed overnight and Williams was out. Despite aggressive legal action, gerrymandering had won.

Gerrymandering has come to refer to the drawing of legislative districts in shapes and configurations that give a party or a person an unfair advantage in elections. The practice, which runs counter to U.S. constitutional goals of fair representation, got its name from the machinations of some Massachusetts legislators, when in 1812, Governor Elbridge Gerry signed a bill that drew district lines for the state. One hyper-partisan district in the Boston area took the shape of a salamander, and so the portmanteau of *gerrymander* was born, and with it came denunciations from the press of the time as well as the governor himself.

In the past two hundred years, both major political parties have leveraged the drawing of congressional maps to privilege incumbents and their parties. However, in 2011, the issue of gerrymandering captured national attention. The 2010 elections flipped control of Congress to Republicans. Voters also awarded the GOP control of state legislatures and more than thirty governorships. In states like Michigan, Ohio, and Wisconsin, the Republican sweep gave the GOP unprecedented power to redraw political lines based on the outcome of the 2010 census. In most states, redistricting happens the same year that the census releases its data, usually in February of the year following the count. In state after state, the Republican Party not only cemented its 2010 electoral victories; it ensured little would change in the next decade and beyond by drawing political lines to keep itself in power.

Political scientist and statistician Dr. Simon Jackman explains the problem that is actually at the core of gerrymandering: that it creates wasted votes. "Wasted votes are votes for a party in excess of what the party needed to win a given district or votes cast for a party in districts that the party doesn't win. Differences in wasted vote rates between political parties measure the extent of partisan gerrymandering."[12] Translation: gerrymandering intentionally runs up the number of people in a district who have *no say* in how they are governed.

In Michigan, the 2016 state House races demonstrated the effect of extreme gerrymanders. Voters split themselves almost evenly between Republican and Democratic candidates; however, the GOP emerged with 57 percent of the seats. Because of how the maps are drawn in Michigan, Democratic candidates received a majority of the vote overall, but their districts rather than the will of Michigan voters overall decided legislative representation. As a result, Democrats won only 44 percent of seats in the House and 31 percent of the seats in the Senate—a lopsided result. For the U.S. House of Representatives delegation, the mismatch was 35 percent. Nationwide, from 2012 through 2016, the Republican Party won an average of nineteen additional seats in the House of Representatives because of gerrymandered districts.

Swing states like Michigan, North Carolina, Pennsylvania, and Wisconsin have seen their statewide elections become more competitive, but legislative lines disproportionately favor the GOP. In almost every state in the country, a perverse version of this mismatch between the population and voting power occurs when the incarcerated are counted in a process known as prison gerrymandering. In all but six states, the incarcerated residents are counted not in their home neighborhoods but in the penal institution. This means their communities have no access to the fiscal windfalls that could come from including them in the area count and no resources return to their hometowns. From the inception of the census, this has been the practice. As the argument goes, prisoners should be counted in the prison beds where they sleep, not in the houses where they lived before imprisonment. The consequence of that decision, however, is that the often struggling, under-resourced, and desperate communities where many of these men and women start never benefit from the investments that could help deter crime and poverty.

Moreover, because only Maine and Vermont allow the incarcerated to vote, prisoners in every other state have no political voice. To put a finer point on it, America's mass incarceration has led to thousands of black and Latino bodies from Democratic-leaning areas being counted in rural white communities that are typically Republican, where most of the penal facilities are located. In a feature on prison gerrymandering, Hansi Lo Wang reported about a district in Wisconsin where an alderperson represented a district with 61 percent of the population incarcerated in a local prison. Despite housing more than half of his constituents, the alderman has never visited the prison. According to the story, when asked if he wanted to know how many people are in the prison he represents, the alderman replied: "There's no comment."[13]

Since 2010, a number of states have started to address the inherent inequity of the prison gerrymander system. Nevada and Washington have passed laws to require their prison populations be allocated to their address prior to incarceration. California, Delaware, Maryland, and New York had already done so. The Census Bureau solicited public input in 2016, and 99 percent of respondents advocated for an end to prison gerrymandering. Enter—once more—Mr. Thomas Hofeller, who strongly urged against a fairer system. He noted, "In addition, the removal of prison inmates housed from other states has been allowed in 3 states in the 2010 redistricting cycle (Delaware, Maryland and New York). This practice, often referred to as 'prisoner adjustment' also moves the counts for domestic inmates in state prisons to the location where they lived before being incarcerated (prisoners not from out-of-state). Democrat allies are now lobbying the Census Bureau to include this practice in the 2010 Decennial. Prisoner adjustment is generally believed to be favorable to the Democrats."[14]

Stephanie Hofeller's revelations of her father's work sent up flares for groups like the National Democratic Redistricting Committee, led by former U.S. attorney general Eric Holder, and others who understand how Hofeller and the GOP have exploited the consequences of their manipulation of the process. But the next prong in their attack is pushing forward Citizen Voting Age Population (CVAP) redistricting, which recommends that rather than count all the people in each state, legislatures should only count the ones eligible to vote. By federal law, congressional districts must be drawn based on the actual population of the state, and each district is designed based on an equitable number of people present. In 2016, the Supreme Court rejected an attempt to draw those lines based only on the number of citizen adults of voting age; but if the Supreme Court had agreed, federal representation would no longer include legal residents, the undocumented, or children. The court's decision, however, left the door open for states to draw legislative lines that intentionally exclude these non-adult or noncitizen populations.

In states like Texas and Florida, the effect on political representation would shift power dramatically. Districts with large Latino populations comprised of a mix of citizens, green card holders, undocumented migrants, and children would only include the citizens in their calculations. For example, a district with a thousand people where seven hundred are Latino and three hundred are white will likely elect a Latino representative. But under CVAP, if half of the Latino population are either residents or undocumented and another quarter are children, then the white voters would be the majority (263 Latino voters to 300 white voters). Multiply that example by thousands, and the effect is crystal clear. To emphasize his point, Hofeller wrote a study that explained the utility of the approach as increasing Republican gains in legislative seats by diminishing the participation of Latinos due to reshaping effective districts. But he did pose a question that should haunt CVAP proponents: "Would the gain of GOP voting strength be worth the alienation of Latino voters who will perceive a switch to CVAP as an attempt to diminish their voting strength?" He ignores his own query, stating, "That, however, is not the subject of this study."

Partisan gerrymandering was upheld by the Supreme Court in 2019, which will allow politicians to pick their voters rather than protecting the right of citizens to pick their leaders. And then there is racial gerrymandering—the drawing of districts to "pack" communities of color together or "crack" them into small groups too insignificant to affect elections, as redistricting experts describe the two practices. Right now, the only protection is in Section 2 of the Voting Rights Act, which Republicans are also challenging. But until the Supreme Court strips away this last protection, race cannot be used to diminish the voting power of minority communities. However, only an accurate census count can provide the necessary evidence to challenge a racially discriminatory map in court. Hofeller and his ilk gave Republicans the tools to rig the maps in 2010, and, as a result, the composition of the courts, the legislature, and every level of government has been affected. What they know, and we must guard against, is an undercount of people of color. Like the neighbors who wanted a park for their kids, invisibility robs communities of power. If people of color are undercounted, this will result in racial gerrymanders where the victims have no proof because they were not seen.

The consequences of gerrymandering extend far beyond a single election or the electoral successes of a party. In Georgia, a rigged map has led to a continued refusal to expand Medicaid and provide health care coverage to nearly five hundred thousand Georgians. In Michigan, the Flint water crisis, where lead poisoned the city's residents, came about after a GOP-controlled legislature gave the governor the right to remove duly elected local officials and replace them with his handpicked overseers. North Carolina lost billions of dollars when the hyper-partisan state legislature approved a bill banning transgender bathroom laws. Wisconsin slashed protections for labor unions, despite its long and storied history as a worker-friendly state. When voters are not represented in their districts, and when elected representatives feel comfortable ignoring the will of their citizens, the process is broken.

But solutions do exist. Nine states mandate an independent redistricting commission to draw the lines for congressional and/ or legislative districts. This practice creates a measure of distance between politicians and their ability to dictate the contours of their domains. H.R. 1 begins the process by mandating independent commissions nationally; however, independence does not mean best practices. The core standards for fair districts include looking at compactness (not creating sprawling, oddly shaped districts to pick up favored voters); contiguity (keeping cities or counties intact and not splitting neighborhoods or universities); equal population (all districts have the same number of people);

preservation of existing political communities; partisan fairness (if in the prior election a state votes 55–45 percent for Democrats or 65–35 percent for Republicans, the mapmakers include this in their determinations of districts to keep the ratios as close to accurate as possible); and racial fairness (no cracking districts to divide racial minorities into multiple legislative areas to dilute their ability to pool their votes, no packing minorities into fewer districts to force them into less power by reducing their presence in other competitive areas, and no scattering racial communities across multiple districts).

END THE ELECTORAL COLLEGE

I abhor the Electoral College, and I am not alone. Democratic candidates for the presidential nomination have called for its abolition.[15] Editorials from the *Washington Post* and articles in the *Atlantic* decry its origins[16] and its current purpose.[17] The process is an antiquated, racist, and classist gerrymandering of the nation's elections. Proposed as a compromise between the slaveholding South and the classist North, the Electoral College has long skewed elections away from active engagement of the nation. At the time of its conception in 1787, the North and South had roughly equal populations, but in the North, more of the nation's inhabitants had the right to vote. Southern legislators wanted to count the bodies of slaves for political power but refused to recognize their humanity or grant them suffrage. In the North, leaders fretted about whether immigrants and the uneducated should have a voice in selecting the nation's chief executive. Mimicking what had become the three-fifths compromise for the treatment of blacks held as slaves, the Electoral College offered the South a version of what had been delivered for congressional seats: the benefit of a population count without the need to grant freedom to the enslaved.

Today, the use of the Electoral College continues to dramatically undermine the outcomes of elections. In the past twenty years, two presidents have been elected despite losing the popular vote: George W. Bush and Donald J. Trump. For blacks in the South, the terrible twisting of voter intent continues, and in areas where blacks comprise 25 percent of the population, five of the six states have voted against the will of Democratic-leaning black voters in the recent elections. Those voters have no chance of aggregating their will with like-minded voters across the fifty states because votes only count for the state where they live. Thus, although 80 to 90 percent of black voters tend to vote Democratic, until they all move to the same state, their votes will be drowned out in Republican states and amplified in Democratic ones.

For 75 percent of the country, candidates for the nation's top job do not bother to show up and campaign, narrowing their pitch and their obligations to the states considered relevant for the next four-year cycle. According to the National Popular Vote campaign, which is trying to undo the Electoral College, statistics show how few of us actually get to participate in the process. Nearly 70 percent of all the general-election campaign events in the 2016 presidential race occurred in six states and 94 percent took place in twelve states. The Electoral College was never designed to protect small states against the tyranny of larger states—not at its inception and not today. Instead, it served to protect slaveholders from a loss of power then and to advantage a small coterie of states deemed competitive today.

During my time in the legislature, I cosponsored a bill to include the state of Georgia in the National Popular Vote Interstate

Compact. The compact attempts to do through state legislation what would otherwise require a federal constitutional amendment. Under the system, each state agrees that all its electoral votes will be allocated to the winner of the popular vote, but the compact only takes effect once a sufficient number of states—comprising a majority of the electoral votes—agrees. As Georgia is one of the states long ignored by presidential contests, my Republican cosponsor and I moved the bill successfully through the state house on a bipartisan vote, but the bill died in the state senate. Later that year, Donald Trump won the Electoral College vote while losing the popular vote by more than three million ballots cast.

Amending the U.S. Constitution is the cleanest way to eliminate the antiquated system that has recently allowed two presidents to take office against the expressed will of the people. Voters can lobby their representatives to introduce a constitutional amendment and pass it, but this is unlikely given the composition of Congress. The rules require a two-thirds vote in both the House and the Senate, which is a high hurdle. A two-thirds majority of states can vote for a constitutional convention, but if that were to happen, the entire constitution would be open to amendment. I propose that Congress should authorize the National Popular Vote Interstate Compact, settling any concerns about whether it would be constitutional. More important, a federal signal from Congress may speed passage by states that have hesitated to agree. By doing so, voters will finally have the ability to vote directly for president without hoping the rest of their state agrees.

Thomas Hofeller led a stealth attack on voting rights, federal funding for communities, and political representation throughout his career. But he did so at the behest of a Republican Party

apparatus that has seeded his vision into state and local governments, using the theory that maintaining hegemony for white
voters is their clearest path to power. The methods he prescribes
wreak havoc on our democracy, and it is our most vulnerable
communities that suffer most. He explicitly targets race and
ethnicity, but class and marginalization are also intertwined.
As a result, where Republicans follow his strategy or create new
versions of their own, people of color and the disadvantaged
consistently experience intimidation and disenfranchisement in
multiple ways. This leaves little trust in a democratic system that
was not built to serve or count them from the outset. To mend
these cracks, defenders of democracy must double down on participation. This will be an enormous, daunting undertaking, particularly when those who must participate are often those who
have been targeted, silenced, and, in some cases, erased.

If progressive groups and advocates wield it effectively, the
U.S. census can become the most resilient tool available for this
project, given its predictability, impact, and reach. The census
occurs every ten years, without fail. Rather than react to the
newest attack or spend the year before the count begging people
to participate, we should never stop the census engagement
work. Progressives who want deeper engagement can use census outreach to build long-term connections within marginalized
communities. Instead of treating the census as a once-a-decade
activity, we should use education and voting to directly connect
the census to the issues that matter.

That is not to say that philanthropists, activists, and organizations do not plan for the census. Hofeller's surgical precision
shows how sustained effort on the right has used the census to
divide communities, block access, and change the political landscape. For our power to be real, our side of the argument must

develop a strong, continual, philanthropic, and research infra-structure to arm our side with ways the census affects everyone's daily lives.

A census trainer told the story of a rural community in the midst of a food desert. The closest grocery store was miles away, and the area had no public transportation. For years, the community tried to attract a national chain, but no one took the bait. The rejection was always the same—not enough potential customers to warrant investment. Then a census survey showed the most accurate count in the community's history, which the town leaders could use to prove viability to the company. With a way to turn a profit, the national chain agreed to locate a new store there, and families could finally shop for fresh produce and healthy options.

Our networks should collect stories, share anecdotes, and keep our target populations informed when changes come because of the census and, more urgently, when power is lost because the census was used against them. Otherwise, in 2030, we will once again find ourselves playing catch-up, despite a ten-year head start.

Similarly, groups can harness the redistricting as a process that happens immediately after the census. But voters also need to be alerted that states and municipalities practice redistricting year-round, without the attention or advocacy that is needed to thwart bad outcomes. That means having a broader discussion of where redistricting operates: not simply congressional seats, but state legislatures, city and county government, and school boards. Lack of representation at each of these levels compounds the pathologies and difficulties groups then spend the next decade trying to tackle.

Efforts that address and wholly leverage the intersections

between the census, redistricting, and overall voter education
and mobilization do not exist at a comprehensive level—when it
is actually a natural fit to work with these three major pillars of
democracy in combination. To fix our democracy from the side
of those in desperate need of access, we must develop and expand
voter knowledge and participation throughout census and redistricting efforts, particularly in the hard-to-count communities.
Groups like the Black Leadership Roundtable, which convenes
dozens of organizations to tackle the census, can serve as a permanent convener of this project. The census occurs every ten
years, but we should focus on education and engagement during the nine years in between each count. Communities can be
mobilized annually around census data collection as it relates
to the fiscal year's budget in their towns; and during redistricting and afterward, we can connect the decennial Census to the
importance of local elections whenever they occur.

While national and statewide races are regularly emphasized,
elections for mayors, county commissioners, school board members, the state legislature, and so forth do not receive the resources
or the attention of high-profile votes. More important, voters are
rarely given the tools to hold their governments accountable in
the same capacity. From long-term efforts to underfund community needs through complex budget processes to unfair ballot
initiatives and utility rate hikes, communities deserve a deeper
understanding of their elected officials' power. Too often this
portion of the work starts too late, with organizers from other
areas parachuting in to secure votes, only to leave directly after,
provide no follow-up, and demand no follow-through. However, with sustained long-term engagement, using the census as
both an instrument and a catalyst for community empowerment,

democracy warriors can make sure organizing efforts never cease, they can reshape the political landscape, and ultimately they can secure power for vulnerable communities. Hofeller and his cohort may have weaponized the census, but we can use it to win the war.

CHAPTER 8

The Playbook

The Dalton Convention Center, in Whitfield County, sits on Dug Gap Battle Road, named for a series of military skirmishes during the Civil War that occurred in this northwest corner of Georgia. Whitfield, like Dade and Walker and Catoosa Counties, is majority white and hugely conservative—Donald Trump won 70 percent of the vote here in 2016.

My visit to the convention center in August 2018 came as the last stop on a daylong visit to the area, and that trip was not my first visit to Dalton. I'd driven the ninety miles several times before I ran for governor, usually alone, always at the invitation of the small clusters of Democrats who knew they were outnumbered. Back then, I'd sit in tiny venues with fifteen to thirty Yellow Dog Democrats (a Southern idiom for diehards who would vote for a yellow dog before voting for a Republican). Running for governor, I knew a trip to the Republican stronghold was a symbolic gesture to some. No way would a progressive Democrat swing the region leftward. But that wasn't my goal. To piece together victory across Georgia, I didn't need to win every county, but I had to solicit as many votes as possible from everywhere imaginable, especially here. That evening, I spoke to the hundreds assembled in the meeting space, and as I had throughout the campaign, I offered a bit of my biography before launching into the reasons I was running. In Northwest Georgia, credible candidates of either party typically steered away from mentions of guns, abortion, and immigration policy. But I had come north with a different mission.

Before I arrived at the town hall, I had spent time with a smaller group at Miller Brothers Rib Shack, a black-owned restaurant, as I had on prior trips. Each time, I smiled at the ease with which black, white, and Latino patrons mingled in the cozy eatery, bound together by their love of good food and a willingness to hear me out. Regulars made a point of telling me how much they adored the owner and his wife, and I agreed. Each visit, they greeted me warmly and plied my team with overflowing containers of food to carry back to Atlanta.

On this visit, voters peppered me with questions about the state's failure to expand Medicaid, among other concerns. There was a young black family raising the issue who had a child with a chronic illness; and while they had been able to take care of her, they worried for others without means. An older black woman reminded me of the hospital closures happening in the area, and she expressed skepticism that I could convince a majority white conservative legislature to change course. A white pastor asked me about whether I would continue the criminal justice reform efforts of the current governor, who was working to help an increasing number of white ex-offenders who had been swept up in the meth epidemic and found life as a returning citizen nearly impossible. A black pastor echoed his worries, reminding folks of what had happened when crack had been the scourge of the time. I told them about my parents' medical issues and debts, about my brother's own experience with incarceration and drug addiction. They'd seen my commercials and heard my speeches, and I assured them that I had a plan for their concerns. But I listened to the repetition because I understood the goal: not to get a solution from me—but to remind me of my promise not to forget what I'd said.

After managing to quickly eat a few forkfuls of macaroni and cheese, my team spirited me to the other side of town to visit Love Empanadas, a taqueria owned by a Latino entrepreneur. The linoleum flooring and white walls contrasted sharply with the wood paneling of Miller Brothers, but the camaraderie inside was familiar. Again, the customers reflected the unexpected diversity of Dalton, and the food had a well-deserved reputation for deliciousness. I nibbled on an empanada as a candidate for the Whitfield County School Board made her pitch. She would be the first Latina to serve on the board, and she had once been an undocumented immigrant. The issue of documentation became a recurring theme that afternoon because the carpet industry and the chicken processing plants of the region attracted migrant farmworkers and others to their employ.

The explosion of Latino residents across Georgia had occurred in the previous decades, ballooning to nearly 10 percent of the state's population. From 2000 to 2010, the Latino population had grown by nearly 96 percent, transforming a state that had long seen itself in stark terms of black and white. I soon took my turn near the makeshift speaker; and I fielded questions about raids by ICE, which had many residents on edge. In the age of Trump, ICE had become more aggressive about immediate removal of those without documents, sometimes leaving American-born children without parents or refuge. A Dreamer—a young person brought to the United States without documentation—asked me about her future after high school. She had applied to colleges in state, but Georgia's rules forbade her from being accepted to the flagship universities, despite her qualifications. Other state schools were required to charge her out-of-state tuition, at costs that could be nearly four times as high.

Health care came up as a constant worry here too. The physicality of manufacturing work, at a carpet mill or a processing plant, meant accidents happened. But without Medicaid expansion, workers making even minimum wage were too poor to qualify for Obamacare and too wealthy to get Georgia's Medicaid coverage. Inevitably, the conversation turned back to immigration. I shared my work at the state capitol where, early in my career, I helped block an English-only constitutional amendment. The seemingly benign change would have prohibited any official government correspondence from being printed in another language. On the verge of its passage, I took to the floor of the legislature to explain that schoolteachers could no longer send messages home to parents in Spanish. Public health officials would be forbidden to communicate with their patients in Korean. State boosters couldn't translate offers to potential businesses in their native tongue. We defeated the bill, but new versions of anti-immigrant sentiment cropped up all the time. I'd secured changes to the state's draconian laws about search and seizure for noncitizens, and I had pledged to appoint members to the state board of regents who would lift the ban on Dreamers in our colleges.

By my event at 6:00 p.m., I had answered dozens of questions, each probing the sincerity of my intentions. More, though, I understood that the voters wanted to get a sense of my capacity to withstand the rigors of the long campaign or an even longer term as governor. If elected governor, the state legislature would remain as solidly Republican as Whitfield County. They needed to believe I was up to the task of fighting for them against heavily stacked odds. After my stump speech with the assembled evening crowd, the Q and A followed similar themes about jobs, living wages, health care, education, and the environment—questions I had answered over and over across the state, tailoring my response to the region but never wavering in my answers, whether they were about early childhood education, equitable pay for teachers, or investment in local entrepreneurs cut off from a finance system that didn't take risks. Then an older white woman stood in the rear and waved for my attention. When I called on her, she didn't ask about how I would navigate the complexity of politics at the Capitol or if I had plans to diversify the regional economy. Instead, she asked about my position on Stone Mountain, the massive bas-relief of Confederate generals commissioned by the same men who restarted the KKK in Georgia. Specifically, she wanted me to justify my comments a year earlier about removing the carvings.

The room had reached capacity before I arrived, and reporters fanned out along the walls. The reaction to her question was mixed, but the focus on me sharpened. For many, I was a curiosity, not simply because I was a black woman seeking the highest office in the state but because I was a Democrat seeking their votes. In a general election against an opponent guaranteed to sweep the region, my visit struck many as a fool's errand. Traditional Democratic politics deemed that I (1) not go this far north in a tight general election and (2) dodge and weave in my response to her. I had already broken the first rule by coming to northwestern Georgia despite having little chance of winning more votes than those who had preceded me. The top of the ticket for Democrats in 2014 received roughly 3,800 votes. And at this point in a campaign, time was best spent running up the score in safer places. But I had planted a flag here. Answering a question about the Confederacy was even more foolhardy than investing campaign time. We had convened in the shadow of a Civil War battle, but I had every intention of responding to a question that might undo the goodwill I'd accrued.

Patiently, I explained my deep animosity toward the Confederate generals' carvings. The men glorified in the etchings had fought to keep blacks as slaves, and they had been willing to terrorize a nation to achieve their ends. I had grown up in a town where visiting the last home of the president of the Confederacy was a rite of passage for some, even though it meant tourists tromping around shacks where enslaved black men and women had lived in squalor and horror. Still, I explained, while I despised the monument to their evil, its removal wasn't top of my to-do list. I'd not campaigned on the issue, but I refused to mince words when the question had been put to me in the wake of the tragic death in Charlottesville, Virginia. My beliefs and my biography could not change because of controversy. Anyone who wanted me to do so should not want me to be the next governor of Georgia.

I began my campaign with the goal of centering communities of color, speaking plainly about the concerns of the marginalized and disadvantaged, and taking clear stands on divisive issues from gun safety to abortion rights to tax policy. However, the corollary to our approach was as radical as the first: that our campaign had to reach out to white voters—and not only those who shared progressive values but those disillusioned by the results of GOP orthodoxy or independents looking for clarity and consistency. Our multiple visits to Whitfield County worked to build a new electorate that defied past practices. I traveled to all 159 counties in the state, invested in every demographic group, and told the same story to each community. I didn't win Whitfield County, but I nearly doubled the vote total for Democrats. We achieved presidential-level turnout in a midterm election with support from the diverse communities of color in our state, as well as the highest level of white support for a Democrat in a generation.

In the process, we also altered the familiar dynamic of Democrats staying home during midterm elections. Presidential candidates buoy all races during their cycle. Billions of dollars are spent to remind Americans about the importance of the presidency. Millions show up at the polls, and while they are picking the president, most will also vote for the other races on the ballot. But 2018 broke the pattern. Record turnout occurred across the country to elect governors, state legislators, and those running for federal office. The national sea change occurred in part due to a surge of interest in state and local politics caused by greater demand from constituents.

State lawmakers have more of an impact on the daily lives of voters of color and the marginalized than Congress ever likely will. Just as they set the law overseeing the right to vote, they also determine criminal justice, health care access, housing policy, educational equity, and transportation. Governors set budgets, sign bills, and implement these ideas. Secretaries of state act as superintendents of election law, but in many states they also manage access for small businesses and a host of administrative duties invisible to citizens until the policies go awry. Attorneys general serve as the chief law enforcement arm of the state, determining statewide matters that can have local impact. The year 2018 brought new investment in voters that included education about the roles and responsibilities of these offices, and around the states, candidates and advocates used election tactics that encouraged voters to go down the ballot and vote in each race and to show up for elections even when the presidency was not on the line.

What we achieved in Georgia occurred despite voter suppression, but our success was neither new nor singular. In 2008, the Obama campaign revolutionized elections with heretofore unseen technological advances, unprecedented fundraising, and a charismatic, transformative candidate. In 2010, without his name on the ballot, Democratic investment and infrastructure faltered and voters stayed home. The secret to President Obama's victory remains the fundamental (and traditional) key to winning elections: organizing voters and turning them out to the polls. In our campaign, as in contests around the country, the changing landscape of who is running and who is voting does not change the basics of how to win. The formula for winning is clear: (1) reject the myths of who votes and why, (2) make early and sustained investment in outreach to an expanded voter pool, and (3) recruit and support candidates who demonstrate authentic and consistent beliefs. Together, this approach will improve performance, build on the dramatic support of 2018, and yield electoral successes for 2020 and beyond.

REJECT THE MYTH OF THE MAGICAL VOTER

Anyone who has watched *The West Wing*, *Veep*, or any fifteen minutes of MSNBC during election time has heard about the highly coveted swing voter. This creature of rare and unlimited power lurks on the edges of Democratic consultants' dreams, bearing the secret to landslides and permanent wins. The swing voter shows up in polls often in the category of undecided or "persuadable," a voter who will adhere to either party's ideology, a voter who regularly chooses a candidate based on the quality of the campaign's persuasive tactic, not the partisan label or the candidate's name. The swing voter defies convention because most voters, regardless of the party to which they pledge allegiance, have a set of policy preferences: how they feel about taxes, defense spending, or the role of government in health care may shift from time to time, but typically within a fixed set of positions. Swing voters rebel against these rules, going across the Rubicon to select candidates they once may have opposed. Pundits deify these more protean voters, and campaigns organize themselves to win them.

In our 2018 campaign, we were advised to focus on the swing voters like every campaign before us had. But in Georgia, as is true nationally, the universe of "swing voters" or "persuadable voters," voters who regularly vote but oscillate between parties or are just of unknown partisanship, is relatively small. Even voters who consider themselves to be independents will routinely cast their ballot for the same party again and again, and when their records are under close scrutiny, the reality is that they truly are not open to persuasion. Still, because we wanted to win, our campaign calculated the number of swing voters available to us in Georgia, and the total was approximately 150,000 voters out of the nearly 4 million who eventually voted. In an election typically won or lost by 200,000 votes, the narrow margin forced us to think strategically about how we could cover the spread in our contest.

Swing voters do exist, but in modern politics, garnering their support has often come at the expense of an equally elusive but important group: the *unlikely* voter. Depending on the political scientist you're listening to, these voters fall along a spectrum of behaviors, for example, unlisted, inactive, nonvoter, sporadic, low-propensity, or low-scoring. Basically, these are the voters who took time to register—or got automatically added to the rolls if they were so lucky. Some, like the unlisted or nonvoter, have the capacity to vote but have not registered or have been purged. Most of the registered voters have actually cast a ballot before, typically in a presidential race. They rarely show up for primaries, and midterm or off-year local elections are not regular fare for them either. Over time, as campaigns became more sophisticated, identifying these voters became easier and easier. Then, it became more and more acceptable to skip their houses, delist their mailing addresses, and scrub their numbers from robocall lists. During election time, these potential voters face a deafening silence from candidates and campaigns. No one knocks on their doors to ask about their needs or to share policies that could solve their crises. Their mailboxes never swell with campaign literature, and no one texts their phones during dinnertime to solicit their support. Their social media doesn't get targeted with digital content to grab their attention. This might sound like nirvana to super-voters who welcome the odd day without electioneering, but imagine if political leaders treated you like you didn't exist. Or matter.

I once served on a panel with political strategist Cristóbal Alex. He told the story of a low-income Latino neighborhood in the West that lived without paved streets or regular trash pickup. They paid taxes, like their more affluent neighbors in the county, but they could never get the attention of their county commissioner. A few of the residents organized and confronted him, demanding to know why he never visited and never responded to their requests. With a shrug, he told them that he didn't have to respond because they didn't vote. At election time, as long as the rest of the county liked him, he could keep his seat regardless of what he did in their area. Chastened and angered by his response, the community leaders canvassed door to door, sharing the news of an upcoming election and the disinterest of their incumbent commissioner. The families organized and voted en masse for the first time, ousting the incumbent for a lesser-known opponent. The following year, they got their street paved, and regular trash pickup is now a given.

Unlike swing voters, who could not be depended upon to vote for Candidate A over Candidate B, low-propensity voters are wrongly deemed wholly unreliable, and when engaged, they can transform the political landscape. But without stories like Cristóbal's or elections like mine, swing voters remain the gold standard and the mythology of who votes becomes gospel.

In a time of changing demography, the problem with this approach to voting is that the low-propensity voters shunned by politicians share fairly common characteristics. They are usually people of color, young people, or unmarried women, otherwise known as the Rising American Electorate or the New American Majority.[1] The terms are used interchangeably, but they refer to the same trend: unmarried women, people of color, and young people constitute a majority of voting-eligible citizens.[2] Since 1997, the share of non-Hispanic whites as registered voters has fallen from 83 percent to 69 percent. At the same time, the combination of black, Latino, and AAPI voters (plus Native Americans and people who identify as other) has grown to constitute 28 percent.[3] Add in the tendency for voters under thirty to identify as Democratic-leaning (59 percent),[4] and that unmarried women tend to vote more Democratic than Republican, across race, age, and education.[5] They are also the missing ingredient for Democratic electoral dominance.

Let's begin with the nonvoters. As Democratic campaigns gained the technology to weed out these nonperformers, they created a concomitant challenge of the *unlisted*. In political campaigns, including the time leading up to them and the period that follows, political parties, individual campaigns, pollsters, researchers, and others rely on the aggregation of voter data from voter registration lists and consumer data. In a 2015 Stanford University study,[6] researchers found that approximately 11 percent of the adults eligible to vote by virtue of citizenship are not listed in these databases. According to their findings, 20 percent of black adult citizens and 20 percent of Hispanic adult citizens are not listed in these regularly used files. In contrast, only 8 percent of whites are excluded.

The danger for Democrats is that these unlisted voters are three times as likely to share progressive policy preferences, as they tend to be younger, more Democratic, more liberal, and less affluent. Unfortunately, because they are not on voting lists or in consumer files, these potential voters rarely hear about elections at the rate of their registered counterparts. Mail firms that send out postcards and placards to remind voters of candidate positions never send their collateral to these homes. The field teams with their clipboards and digital tablets skip these doors because no data means no knocking. Harried calls on Election Day to show up at the polls do not reach their phone lines, and neither do pollster questions seeking their input. The Stanford research also showed that had unlisted voters participated at the comparable rates to their registered peers, these voters would have handed the 2000 and 2004 elections to the Democratic presidential nominees.

Not to mention the outcome in 2016. Democrats do themselves and the progressive cause a major disservice by trading efficacy for efficiency—by skipping over entire troves of potential voters, we unilaterally block ourselves from victories. Republicans are losing the demographic game, so instead they are rigging the system. But Democrats are forfeiting elections by refusing to reach out to all of the voters who could even the score or tip the balance.

The unlisted voters are just one category of electoral potential that Democrats have not fully activated. Another group are referred to as unlikely voters: those who *have* made it onto the lists but still demonstrate a lower propensity to actually cast a ballot by Election Day. These voters are sporadic in that they may only vote in presidential contests, or they vote in general elections but not primaries and never in off-year elections. Both parties have learned to aggregate data about these voters, including information about when they vote, how they vote, and what issues move them. Based on this information and loads of additional data points, voters are assigned a score that rates their level of partisanship and their level of participation. On both sides of partisan politics, consultants and data engineers have developed models that correlate to how likely a voter is to turn out at an election. Super-voters—those who never miss an election for their party—are in the 90s. Unlikely voters with little history get lower scores, sometimes hovering just above the score of a voter who is a super-voter for the other side.

Because campaigns are always strapped for cash, the logic of the turnout score is clear. By assessing the likelihood of a voter's response before pouring out resources, a candidate can deploy her dollars more effectively. As we discovered in Georgia, though, the efficiency of this approach did not bear out under closer scrutiny. Yes, a turnout score can be a guidepost, but the scores do not tell a campaign *why* a voter is scoring low. If voters simply haven't heard from campaigns or face voter suppression, they get treated identically to voters who routinely vote Republican. Consider, again, Georgia's 2018 electoral map. The state had roughly 150,000 swing voters, people who were in the dead center of a partisanship scoring model (and with a high likelihood to vote) because they could go either way. In contrast, the number of unlikely Democratic-leaning voters was 1.9 million—more than enough to cover the spread. Our unlikely voters were predominantly voters of color, including 69 percent African American. On the other hand, the swing voters of unknown voting ideology were predominantly white. Our campaign was encouraged by many to focus on the white swing voters and de-emphasize the unlikely voters, and we were chastised by pundits for wasting resources reaching out to both people of color and white voters.

This racial dynamic—opting to win white voters over voters of color—is not unique to Georgia, and it often explains the devotion to the swing voter to the exclusion of other viable paths. Latino voters are held up as the missing ingredient in elections in the Southwest, but colleagues who run these campaigns complain bitterly about fundraising hardships once they tell supporters that these are their targets.[7] For AAPI or Native American voter groups, the challenge is often getting Democratic candidates to take their votes seriously.[8] One myth of elections is that white voters are more reliable than voters of color and that investing in the elusive white swing voter is a dollar better spent than the more complex but ultimately heavier yield of unlikely voters of color. That is central to the narrative of the rural white voters as the lost saviors of the Democratic Party.

Worryingly, debunking this myth spawns a second argument,

nearly as absurd: that to win white voters, a campaign cannot invest in voters of color. Indeed, when politicos celebrate my 2018 effort, they focus almost exclusively on how we achieved an unprecedented high turnout from Georgia's diverse voters of color. While we did accomplish this feat, the media attention to those numbers led to a falsehood that I abandoned white voters, despite trips like Dalton and field and communications investments around the state. What then follows is a shaking of the head that we lost white voters *because* I talked about and to voters of color. Political leaders who embrace this binary reinforce the stereotypes of bygone eras. Yes, white voters are predominantly Republican or Republican-leaning by a 52 percent to 39 percent swing, but that 39 percent remains a vital part of any electoral contest.[9] Democrats would do well to remember, however, that 86 percent of black voters and 64 percent of Latino voters identify with us.[10]

The glib summations miss the point of our grand experiment. Expanding Georgia's electorate among voters of color did not require a zero-sum strategy where talking to marginalized communities equaled losing white support. We did better with both groups because we worked hard to reach them all. We tripled Latino turnout among Democrats. We did the same among the AAPI Democrats. Our campaign recorded increased youth participation rates at 139 percent. We also dispelled the lie that the black vote had reached its peak in Georgia in a midterm election. Instead, we increased black participation by 40 percent. In short, in 2014, 1.1 million Democrats voted for the candidate for governor, but in 2018, four years later, 1.2 million black Democrats voted for me. At the same time, our campaign engaged white voters and achieved success in doing so, winning the highest percentage of white voters in a generation, even when third-party 2016 support is added to the mix.

This last statistic is critical. Our unusual approach to aggressively contest for both voters of color and white voters also created a false narrative that I performed poorly among white voters. But in fact, our campaign achieved historically high support from white voters; overall 25 percent of white voters supported the Abrams campaign for governor. Among them, college-educated white women supported my candidacy by over 31 percent, an improvement from the roughly 24 percent support rates at the top of the ticket in 2014. We surged in white support because I remained consistent in my message while campaigning aggressively in all areas of the state and targeting white voters through such mediums as mail, digital content, and rural country radio, along with television ads.

When we look back at the 2008 election as a singularity, an unrepeatable phenomenon, we miss the brilliance of the Obama election. His approach was no shooting star to be marveled at and recalled with nostalgia. The goal of reaching everyone, and meeting them where they live, is the essence of good campaigning. The most efficient election is not the one where campaigns save money by carving out choice parts of the electorate, and then pour money and resources in with the hopes of changing a narrow contingency of minds.

Winning an election is the most efficient way to campaign. Not scoring voters without regard to why they are lower on the charts or eliminating whole categories based on past performance. In 2020 and beyond, victory requires that we change who we see as our allies. We can reach out to rural voters, but only if we understand that rural includes voters of almost every race. Our identity politics can work to fix the plight of the working class, but the working class must expand beyond the prototype of a white guy in manufacturing. Today's effective, efficient campaigns see his Latino wife, who works as a nurse, and their next-door neighbors, a black couple surviving on a teacher's salary and a beat cop's pay. When we reject the myth of one way to win—one voter to chase—we open our pathways to victory into wide thoroughfares where more can join and everyone succeeds.

PUTTING OUR MONEY AND INFORMATION WHERE OUR VOTES ARE

Tram Nguyen serves as codirector of New Virginia Majority (NVM). When I first met Tram in 2014, she'd been at NVM for six years, working on an electoral strategy that would build on President Obama's 2008 and 2012 sweeps in the commonwealth. Like the New Georgia Project, NVM responded to a changing electorate that had to be harnessed to be effective. Democrat Tim Kaine had served as governor during his 2006 term, but in 2010, Republican Robert McDonnell won the hotly contested election. In a few years, he had earned his reputation for conservative policies, aided by a GOP-dominated legislature. He signed into law a bill requiring every woman seeking an abortion to undergo an invasive form of ultrasound. But in 2014, Terry McAuliffe won the race for governor, reinstalling a Democrat in the top job. Working alongside NVM, he targeted progressive actions without waiting for legislative authority. On April 22, 2016, he signed an executive order restoring voting rights to every felon in Virginia. A Virginia Supreme Court decision blocked the automatic grant of clemency, so he used his autopen (an automatic device to allow him to sign documents at a higher rate) to individually grant a restoration of rights to nearly 175,000 Virginians. But his work on ending felony disenfranchisement required more than holding the governor's office; a permanent solution meant holding the governor's power and taking over the legislature.

Enter NVM. Working with groups within the state and across the country, Tram shepherded funds into Virginia to target and flip state house and senate seats. The takeover plan was dramatic, ambitious, and historically implausible. Yet, in 2017, using early and deep investments in candidates and organizing campaigns, NVM helped usher in a tidal wave of change. The House of Delegates had been governed by a 66–34 GOP majority. The November 7, 2017, elections flipped 15 seats to Democrats, shifting the balance of power to 51–49 GOP to Democrats. While Democrats did not win the majority, these elections changed more than the head count. Danica Roem was elected as the first openly transgender candidate in a state legislature, and she did so by defeating a conservative incumbent. Elizabeth Guzmán and Hala Ayala notched victories as the first Latina members of the House. Along with Guzmán and Ayala, Delegate Kathy Tran won her seat as the first Asian American woman in the Virginia House, flipping a Republican seat. And Dawn Adams became the first openly lesbian state lawmaker in Virginia, again by taking a GOP-held seat. These victories presaged a dynamic 2019 state legislative election cycle, when Democrats swept both the House and Senate elections, placing control of the legislature and the executive branch in Democratic hands for the first time in more than twenty-five years.

What happened in Virginia has occurred multiple times across the country since 2016. The efforts of thousands, including organizations like Black Voters Matter (BVM), seized a U.S. Senate seat in 2017, delivering a sharp rebuke to conservatives who presumed Alabama to be impenetrable by Democrats. BVM ignored the prognosticators and instead fielded the Alabama Grassroots Mobilization Project. They seeded eighteen Alabama counties with organizing efforts, including mini-grants to more than thirty local, community-based organizations. Using a diffusion strategy, the organizations were then charged with outreach in their specific communities of interest, armed with funds for paid canvasses, resources for transportation, and the kind of outreach materials that raise awareness and visibility. And it worked, to elect Doug Jones over Roy Moore—a victory that would not have been possible without the deep investment in underserved and underrepresented areas.

This ethos of going deep into communities to transform their political participation has also driven BLOC, an organizing and mobilization group in Milwaukee, Wisconsin, that engages black voters to understand their electoral power and prepare for the 2020 elections. One of their novel tools is the silent canvass, where candidates and elected officials are taken on a tour of Milwaukee but cannot speak. They are encouraged to experience the city with their full senses, but also to encounter the everyday lives of voters without the filter of their position or power. On the other end of the country, New Florida Majority invests in the broad diversity of Floridians, particularly the ever-expanding and internally diverse Latino populations. By understanding the real cultural differences among Venezuelan, Dominican, Puerto Rican, Cuban, and other Latin American communities, NFM has made early investments in meeting each community—and each voter—at the point of its interests.

The shared theory behind each of these organizations and more besides is the realization that elections cannot be won in the last quarter of a campaign. Nor can policy change be realized without consistent engagement, a robust infrastructure, and early investment. It must begin long before elections start, in communities that lag behind in performance and resources. New Virginia Majority will almost certainly deliver its electoral votes for the 2020 contest to a Democrat, and Black Voters Matter's Alabama insurgency likely will not shift the race to the Democratic nominee, even with Senator Jones retaining his seat. But in Wisconsin or Florida, Pennsylvania or Minnesota, these efforts can be the difference made in elections that vacillate by roughly 1 to 2 percent in a presidential year. In the Southeast and Southwest, organizations are receiving early and consistent financial investment from aggregation groups like Way to Win, a consortium of organizations and individual investors who contribute to those willing to give primacy to on-the-ground engagement of unlikely voters. National donors too have begun to recognize the high impact of routinized, steady-state giving to groups building their way to power. Rather than simply bolstering the proven paths to winning certain elections, progressive organizations expand the playing field, leveling the odds in places progressives once ignored.

In 2018, as my campaign closed within 1.4 points of victory, Kyrsten Sinema led Arizona Democrats to a U.S. Senate victory. Her coalition of white, Latino, Native American, and black voters upended decades of Republican dominance. Arizona is now firmly on various pundit lists of swing states; but, like swing voters, our obligation is to look beyond the last election toward the potential of the unlikely voter pool. Investment, time, and attention operate alongside demographic changes and voter access to shift states from red to purple to blue. Arizona, like Georgia, has been making this bid for years. In 2018, Senator Sinema benefited from heavy national investment that generated increased turnout by voters of color and Democratic-leaning white voters, given that she lost white votes but prevailed by 54,000 votes. Arizona's victory validates a 2020 investment, but in Georgia we continue to wave our hands. Despite massive resources and a long list of states receiving those resources, national Democrats made a strategic decision not to invest in Georgia in 2016. In 2018, we did not have a federal race like Arizona, but the gubernatorial metrics are comparable. Despite no investment relative to other competitive states, the Clinton campaign held Trump to a 5-point victory, closer than the Ohio margin of 8 points and Iowa's 9-point loss, where national Democrats invested $70 million and $32 million, respectively.

North Carolina, which received national support in 2008, 2012, and 2016, has slowly demonstrated progress too. Although the Democratic nominee for president won only in 2008, the investment in the state continued even after the drubbing of the 2010 midterms and a hyper-gerrymandered map. With the support of resources and infrastructure, North Carolina elected a Democratic governor in 2016 while Secretary Clinton lost by 3.7 points. As one of Georgia's leaders in 2016, I challenged national operatives repeatedly about why North Carolina, but not Georgia, received the investment and support of a battleground state. Like me, other Georgia leaders heard a familiar mantra: Georgia isn't winnable yet. We pushed back on the argument with two proof points: (1) polling showed Clinton to be competitive in both Georgia and North Carolina and (2) Georgia had a much larger pool of infrequent voters of color but had no sustained support. Eventually, operatives acknowledged that they were catering to the myth of white voters versus voters of color. More than one admitted to the belief that white voters were more winnable in North Carolina and thus the state merited investment that

Georgia's predominantly black and brown voters did not. In the end, Hillary lost North Carolina by 3.7 points and Georgia by 5.1 points. The close call becomes a painful lesson when the dollars dedicated to the races are considered. National Democrats spent $91.8 million in North Carolina compared to around $8.8 million in Georgia: a difference of $83 million to secure a margin just 38,000 votes closer.

The 2020 elections are key to reversing the erosion of our body politic, restoring our national cohesion, and rebuilding trust within our communities, but long-term transformation in politics demands a strategy that looks beyond a presidential cycle to a sustained architecture of engagement. Democrats have done this before, most notably in the 1930s by following the Great Depression with the New Deal. We've also done it on a smaller scale, like the 1960s response to civil rights. But for the twenty-first century, we cannot create progressive policy-making unless we understand and reverse engineer how conservatives secured electoral dominance in the mid- to late twentieth century.

Over the course of decades, conservatives learned to connect voters' ambitions to the level of government that could make it so. Want to block sex education? Take over school boards. Oppose taxpayer dollars funding public transit? Win legislative offices. Strip workers' rights? Elect union-busting governors in industrial states. Putting our money where our votes are means going beyond presidential and federal contests to also battle for state legislatures, secretaries of state, attorneys general, and governors. Key ammunition in the fight will be ensuring our armies of voters know the issues, know who has the control, and know how to agitate for quality leadership.

While my 2018 campaign for governor engaged, organized, and inspired traditional voters and brought new voices to the table, the work began long before my name went on a ballot. Central to my theory of service is civic education as a precursor to engagement. Years before, as a state legislator, I surveyed my district and recognized that it contained some of the wealthiest, most educated neighborhoods in the state, as well as some of the poorest. The Druid Hills community is nestled just outside Emory University and within a stone's throw of the Centers for Disease Control and Prevention. Professors, doctors, and scientists are clustered in verdant neighborhoods with manicured boulevards and picturesque homes. But if you travel along the stretch of state road that cuts through the center of the district, structural poverty shouts its permanence from dilapidated schools, crumbling sidewalks, and vacant storefronts in South DeKalb.

For eleven years, I represented a cross section of Georgians who either voted for me, voted against me, or had no idea I existed. Like my colleagues, one method of outreach to all of them was a monthly newsletter. My version did not include tidbits about the neighborhoods in the district or spotlights on citizens doing good. Instead, I compiled all the key bills we'd voted on in the legislature at the time. I would categorize the bills, typically into groups like education, budget/finance, judiciary/law enforcement, and so forth, and then briefly explain the substance of the bill. But what followed in bold print set me apart from others who did the same; I listed my vote, why I voted that way, and what the other side likely believed. The purpose was twofold: I wanted voters to know what was happening, but I also wanted them to understand why I took the positions I did. I held the Democratic line more often than not. Sometimes, I voted with the Republican majority, and other times I joined those of more libertarian tendencies to defeat a bill.

For those who wanted to see me in person, I leaned on my

parents' experience as pastors on a circuit charge—where they ministered to multiple churches every month. Instead of going neighborhood by neighborhood, I moved my monthly district meeting around the area. The attendees looked like the district, about half white, half black. In a district of 53,000, a good turn-out meant 50+ folks showing up on Saturday morning. When controversial issues were on the table, the meetings swelled to between 75 and 100. To hear my political updates, the affluent had to traipse across town to an aging church basement. Activists from the most economically challenged parts joined me in wide, clean gymnasiums at newly refurbished schools. Together, they heard the same reports, and they listened to each other's concerns. However, all comers understood after their first few visits, I always dedicated some portion of the meeting to discussions about taxes, budget, and finance.

Before I ran for my first office, I practiced tax law at a white-shoe law firm in Atlanta. I'd studied tax law at Yale Law School and written my master's thesis about an obscure tax issue. Understanding tax policy, to my mind, was a key to unlocking voter engagement. It may be the least sexy part of government, but I understood that taxes had the highest impact on voters' lives. Eventually, I sat on the Ways and Means Committee, which set tax policy, from corporate tax to property tax to income tax. I was also a member of the House Appropriations Committee, which allocated those revenues. On any given day, the Appropriations Committee meeting room could be filled with attendees eager to hear whether their project would be funded or cut. Ways and Means meetings attracted mostly lobbyists protecting their interests. I wanted my constituents to understand the mechanics of government: where we got our money largely dictated how the state spent it. I included details in the newsletter, and we discussed the minutiae at the town halls. I broke down the budget into a single dollar, then identified how fifty-five cents went to education while only four cents went to natural resources. Over time, folks who lived in my district became savvier about the tax policies. By my fourth year in office, I regularly got questions from the audience about obscure topics like freeport exemptions (how goods are taxed at warehouses) and the difference between taxes and fees (they're basically the same thing). In areas facing gentrification, they learned to ask about how property taxes could help them live in the neighborhoods they had long inhabited and anchored. Unfortunately, though, they also learned that conservative state legislators controlled the means to fix the problems but often had no interest in doing so.

One of my proudest accomplishments remains the launch of Fair Fight 2020, a twenty-state strategy to finance the infrastructure of voter protection during the 2019 and 2020 election cycles. In our target states, we fund voter protection directors, deputies, and hotline managers to answer voter concerns, as well as organizers dedicated to voter protection to recruit and support volunteers across each state. We selected our twenty states based on presidential battleground status, but a look at our selections reveals a focus on flipping state legislative chambers as well as winning the U.S. Senate, picking up House races, and supporting down-ballot jobs like governor, secretary of state, and attorney general. Imagine, for example, an Obama presidency where Democrats maintained control of the House and the Senate, which would have saved thousands of state legislative seats—thus protecting the Supreme Court at the federal level and forestalling the current assaults on reproductive rights generated by recalcitrant states. Immigration reform, climate action, and the progressive agenda would have still generated rancor and division, but the fights would have focused on scale rather than existential questions about who we are. Elections matter, but voters matter more if they are the targets of engagement and education, not quick contacts or disregard. Long-term, sustainable electoral change requires that we have a comprehensive strategy that tackles the mythology of how we win and the problem of underinvestment with equal ferocity. Otherwise, notable wins like 2008 quickly become Pyrrhic victories without a plan for replication and expansion.

RUN AS YOU ARE

During the campaign, I joined Trevor Noah as a guest on *The Daily Show*. He pointed out the narrative building up around me, asking, "You know, people will ask you, they'll say, well, how do you plan to get out the white vote? They don't ask it the other way. So, like, what do you stick to when people ask you that type of question?" My short answer to his complex question was that I talked to everyone about my plans, and when I tailored a response, I did so to signal that I understood the particular challenges someone faced. I didn't have black answers or white answers or Catholic answers. I refused to hide my own story because issues of debt, incarceration, and mental illness in a family affect everyone. I ran the kind of campaign I thought would convince my nonvoting cousins to go to the polls.

By and large, our strategy worked, with the unintended consequence of perhaps working *too* well. One of the most persistent questions I have faced since 2018's seismic shift is about replicability. As Georgia geared up for two U.S. Senate contests, I was courted to run, in part on the assumption that our electoral achievements were solely the result of one historic candidate. I'm a good candidate, but my point is: everyone running for office can try this at home. In addition to our rejection of myth and our investment in voters, what voters responded to can be practiced by any candidate standing for office. All they need is an authentic communication of values that is strong, clear, and unafraid, backed up by an aggressive and strategic campaign.

Our campaign spent a significant amount on research of issues, voters, and me. Focus groups vetted me. Twitter investigated me. Facebook scoured my connection to almost everyone I'd ever met. As we traveled the state, as we synthesized our findings, we found that my personal story and identity alone could not woo voters, especially black women. Identity politics that focuses solely on externalities rarely succeeds, although they are a critical point of entry for many. People tell themselves stories based on what they see, making race, gender, age, and physical ability part of the candidate's narrative. Voters like to know that a candidate has similar experiences, and those immutable characteristics say a great deal about how that person has navigated society. But, more than who I was, voters of all ages and all races wanted to know what I would *do*. I had detailed plans to improve life for Georgians and to strengthen the state at the ready.

To really connect with voters, I adapted my storytelling to relate to specific audiences, and to acknowledge the particular barriers they faced. But, as in Dalton, I talked about the same issues in small rural towns as I did in the Atlanta metropolitan area, not changing my approach based on where I was or to whom I was speaking. And it worked. We had huge growth in turnout from all Democratic-leaning voters. Even in a high turnout and watershed Democratic year, Georgia stood out.

The true takeaway from what we did is not that campaigns must have a singular person at the top of the ticket in order to win hearts and minds. An effective campaign—or broader election strategy—can win by talking directly to people and by being authentic and honest about policy positions. Voters will never agree with everything you say, but they get excited to know that a politician is willing to tell them the truth. They want to trust that a candidate won't suppress their values to try to appeal to a specific group. A voter wants to know that the one in whom they invest their time and trust is an authentic candidate who stands on the values that they hold.

In practice, this process of authentic communication must scale beyond coffee klatches and dinner discussions. In Georgia, our target was 1.9 million unlikely voters plus the smaller pool of swing voters. We launched our campaign with an extensive voter contact effort through a volunteer field program in the primary. We ran the primary campaign like a general election operation and tested our messaging. The testing did not ask if I should soften my platform or pivot to less controversial issues. We tested how effectively we could share our goals and differentiated how we deployed our message. From digital videos curated by our young interns to why vote videos led by volunteers, we delivered our cogent platform to the widest swath of potential Democratic voters. We put together handouts that explained what a governor did. Volunteers held house parties to discuss our platforms, and others wrote postcards highlighting how policies would affect their community. Like most campaigns, we had television and radio ads, but we also had a dedicated field staff and hundreds of volunteers knocking on doors and having deep conversations with voters about their priorities. Our victory on primary night was staggering: we won 76 percent of the vote and 153 of 159 counties, with the highest non-presidential primary turnout in Georgia history.

In the general election, we again dove deep into research on every segment of the electorate: from multiple focus groups of African American unlikely voters across the state, to online qualitative testing, to traditional polling, to polling of infrequent Democratic and Republican voters. At the same time, we launched a paid canvass in July 2018 covering all major cities as well as the rural micropolitan hubs that dot the Southern Georgia Black Belt. We paid our canvassers a living wage, and we trained them on scripts that spoke about jobs, health care, justice, education, the environment, and housing. The campaign scaled up our already large and diverse in-house filmmaking and digital team, again using core, consistent messaging with the widest array of communication tools.

By using previously untapped or underutilized channels of communication, we defied the curse of under-resourced campaigns or ones strategically reliant on television. Our approach, and the approach to messaging, was: let us be nimble in our outreach. It didn't hurt that we raised more money than any gubernatorial campaign in Georgia history. For example, we ran an unprecedented, large-scale vote-by-mail program that resulted in a 50,000-vote lead in mail ballots, running up the score going into the three-week early voting period. We went big and early on digital investments to target all segments of our 1.9 million pool with diverse and compelling content. Then we layered on digital radio, conventional radio, multiple flights of mail, and paid and volunteer door knocks and texts. From the small rural markets to massive efforts in Atlanta and to Alabama, Florida, South Carolina, and Tennessee media spill markets, we brought to bear every available method of communication. Every single region of the state was reached through mail, digital, field, and media.

Our unusual approach to messaging and communication did draw skepticism—and an unexpected visit from Washington, D.C., operatives to question our unorthodox approach in the primary and general elections, as well as "friendly fire" from local Democrats on the evening news during the primary election and grousing from consultants who had previously advised Georgia Democrats but were not involved in our efforts. Democratic traditionalists did not trust our methods or our math. They feared we would lose a winnable race by bucking the regular rules. Other pushback included anxious advice when we rejected targeting recommendations from experts to trim low-turnout-scoring Democrats from our universes; repeated befuddled questioning about why we weren't saving every dime for TV advertising; general strategy questions from opinion leaders in Atlanta and Washington, D.C., asking, "How do you know talking to voters will work?" and the list goes on.

In the end, Abrams for Governor and the Coordinated Campaign spent a combined $42 million, outraising our opponents in both the primary and the general elections. We spent about $14 million in the general election on TV (Atlanta's media market is one of the top ten most expensive in the United States), and we also spent millions on digital, millions on mail to Democrats for vote-by-mail, early voting, and Election Day, and over $7 million on organizing. The results were historic—the governor's race was too close to call on election night, we broke the 200,000 margin curse, and we won substantial victories down ballot with sixteen new members elected to the state legislature and Lucy McBath elected a new member of Congress by a few thousand votes. Indeed, 2018 was a high turnout year across the country; but in Georgia, we changed the expectations of candidates and campaigns.

Victory must begin to mean more than winning a single election. Our obligation, in Georgia and across the nation, is to seize the high road by changing how we campaign and to whom. Demography is not destiny; it's opportunity. We have to expand our vision of who belongs in the big tent of progress, invest in their inclusion, and talk to them about what's at stake. This formula is no guarantee of triumph—but I can promise that without it, we don't stand a chance of conquering the future.

CHAPTER 9

Populism and the Death
of Democracy

I met Will Dobson in Liberty, Missouri, in 1994 at the annual
welcoming week for the newest class of Harry S. Truman Scholars. Will and I had been picked from our respective colleges and
states; the following summer, we were invited to D.C. as part of
their policy institute. We interned for different departments in
the federal government as a precursor to graduate school. One
day, Will invited me out to lunch, and our conversation turned
to the primacy of foreign policy over domestic policy. I pushed
the domestic policy side, the argument that we had to solve our
problems first before venturing abroad. I had taken international
studies courses as part of my degree at Spelman College, but I
was headed off to grad school to steep myself in domestic public
affairs. But what he challenged me with was, "Look, if you want
to be a leader, you have to understand more than your space."
And he said, "You do that in every other part of your academic
life and your intellectual life; why are you closing yourself off on

the foreign policy side?" I couldn't effectively rebut him, which was really annoying—so I started learning.

In college and in grad school, I kept up my focus on civic engagement in the United States, and, due to Will's influence, I started studying social policy in Brazil, of all places. Through him, I learned about the Salzburg Global Seminar, and I applied to become an international fellow on civic engagement, investigating how increasing youth participation affected political regimes. All the fellows lived together in a schloss in Austria. My two closest companions were my roommate, Claudia, from Colombia, and Tejan from Sierra Leone.[1] Claudia studied in Bogotá, and she led protests against government corruption. Sitting in our room one night, she told me about death threats she'd received for her organizing work and that she might be arrested when she came back from Austria. Frightened for her, I marveled as she dismissed the danger she faced. She believed in the democracy promised by her nation's constitution, and it was her duty to show her fellow students their capacity for leadership.

A former child soldier, Tejan had escaped from his captors and found his way to his decimated village. After years of civil war, he had come to Austria to learn how to translate his trauma into democratic reforms. Like Claudia, he faced police surveillance and death threats, but he knew his work affected the future of his younger siblings and fellow emancipated fighters. In their company, I worried about whether my work in Georgia really meant anything. I centered my efforts around eradicating youth poverty through civic engagement, not the persistent violent crises they lived with daily. Midway through our time together, we huddled over a table in the common room after dinner. With a twinge of embarrassment, Tejan confessed to me that he had not expected to see a black American at the event, and Claudia quickly agreed. They could recite the ignominies of Jim Crow and black sufferings under '80s economic and social policy. Much of their efforts was informed by the civil rights movement, and they delighted in peppering me with questions. I did the same, and to this day, I draw on their lessons of how universal and difficult it is to get those most harmed by public policy to take ownership.

From there, I participated in an East Asian studies program to examine how their economies and political structures shaped the future of globalization. Hooked, I worked with the British-American Project, the Council of Italy, the American Council of Young Political Leaders program, and the Council on Foreign Relations, among others. In 2004, I traveled to Bulgaria as part of the German Marshall Fund's program. I sat in a small office in Sofia, meeting with representatives of the Roma people. I listened keenly as they described the arc of their community's history, marginalized and isolated from power. Nearly a decade later, I had a similar discussion with an Aboriginal leader who pressed me for details about the cause of civil rights in America. Whether I was meeting with executives in Seoul, Korea, or entrepreneurs in Tel Aviv, I developed relationships that leaned upon my life as an American as a point of entry to discussion. While foreign policy seemed to stray beyond my focus as a state legislative leader and a voting rights advocate, I intentionally worked to build a robust understanding of international complexities. Moreover, Will was right that any leadership in America must understand the international approach to global questions as well as the intersectionality of our policies. Plainly said, we have to understand the effect we are having on the world, and vice versa.

The 2016 election and the tumult that has followed heightens my conviction that we are obliged to reclaim our democracy now. I no longer believe there is a bright line between domestic and foreign policy. What has played out in the last few years has shown us just how thin that line is, if the line exists at all. The New American Majority stands to inherit the consequences of authoritarian populism here, and we can shape our response to its legacy abroad. Authoritarian populism should not be confused with the type of progressivism that uses the language of economic dignity and labor to galvanize political change.[2] Its American progenitor, William Jennings Bryan, helped shape the modern Democratic Party with his calls for more inclusive politics that centered the needs of the economically vulnerable. However, populism, like most theories, can have different strains. In modern politics, progressive populists have argued a more inclusive message than the fearmongering of the Know-Nothings. Think Huey Long, Jesse Jackson, Sherrod Brown, or Bernie Sanders. While some characteristics cut across populism, the dangerous kind seeks to dismantle and destroy rather than advance and uplift. My deep concern lies with the current expression of destructive populism in America and abroad—the type that seeks authoritarianism as its end.

The rise of populism is a direct threat to our political, social, and cultural fates, whether it occurs in the White House or in Poland. Populism challenges and pushes into relief the tensions that exist in a democracy; taken to extremes, it tends to presage a slide into flawed democracy and then into authoritarianism. Despite our sanguine belief in the permanence of the U.S. system of governance, according to the annual Democracy Index, we have fallen to number 25 on the list of functional democracies, below Canada, Mauritius, and Uruguay, to name a few. The international scale rates us as a flawed democracy in the twenty-first century, a terrible slide from our preeminence as a world leader. And less than twenty years ago, Turkey had a thriving democracy that now struggles to hold on to the claim.

My deepest fear is that it will take too long to restore our position in the world because our moral credibility has been diminished. It is difficult to articulate ideals of who we should be and who we expect the world to be when we are not living those ideals at home. When the president authorizes family separation of immigrants or tramples minority rights based on religious beliefs, when his handpicked judiciary shrugs off the corruption of self-dealing or hiding witnesses, American leaders cannot then go abroad and espouse a different set of ideals. The hypocrisy of barring transgender people from our military undermines our arguments against countries like Azerbaijan that seek to criminalize the LGBTQ+ community. It is a matter of degree, not of difference. We have failed to recognize the suppression of minority rights. We continue to have a Muslim ban on entry, and we have also undervalued and mistreated voters right here at home. Like Modi's India, we have allowed the blossoming of laws that have systematically suppressed minority rights and minority votes in the United States.

By succumbing to the lure of populism made real by a combination of the Electoral College and voter suppression, we now have the most reckless foreign policy that we've had in modern history. I may have disagreed with George W. Bush and George H. W. Bush and Clinton and Obama on things, but I never disagreed fundamentally with the position the United States held in the international order. I do now. The persistence of Trump's style of populism has an effect on how safe we are as Americans, both physically and economically. For example, during most of 2018 and 2019, the U.S. president launched the largest trade war in a generation. Though played out through goods and services rather than bullets, a trade war has a real effect on everyday lives. The U.S. consumer bears the majority of the costs passed along to businesses and hidden in the prices we pay. Economically struggling Americans feel the results in daily life, especially those who face stagnant wages that have not grown despite having the lowest unemployment we've ever had. The average American cannot recover from a trade war with the same resilience that a corporation can. The only solution will be to actually engage in trade policy that is not based on populist brinksmanship, which is what we've seen play out for the last few years. As Trump positions China front and center, our country is also embroiled in trade battles with historic allies such as Germany, Britain, France, and Canada.

As with trade, our immigration position has weakened our stature abroad, at a time when international civil wars and climate refugees begin a new wave of transmigration. Authoritarian populism grounded in alienation of outsiders eviscerates our ability to call for international cooperation when the crisis peaks. America will have to restore the humanity of our refugee policy. Demographic changes like slowing birth rates, automation, and shifts in industry anchors mean we also have to anticipate a changed labor market. With harsh, divisive rhetoric that casts immigrants as the enemy, we undermine our national security by weakening our economic security. Our only solution will be, again, to finally have a robust and real policy for immigration that recognizes America's deep reliance on foreign labor and our history as a nation of immigrants. That is our responsibility. But we must have a Congress and a president who are willing to actually confront these issues and cease worrying about the next election and actually worry about the next twenty years of American life.

Once he leaves office—regardless of when—the actions carried out under Trump's banner of "America First" will affect any international interventions we attempt. Thus, we have to recognize that the iteration of populist-driven policy is not going to simply be tied off with a new leader. We are going to have to rebuild and restore our credibility, and that means that we're going to have to confront the very real harm that's been done to our foreign policy by our current administration. America's role as a model of democratic norms, moral leadership, and global problem-solving are required now more than ever. The presidency under Donald Trump will not necessarily revert to type with his ouster. His command of the authoritarian populist playbook is strong, but he has not yet fully completed the process. His successors might. Which is why we must reaffirm why America must aggressively defend its role in the world.

TAKING POWER FROM THE PEOPLE

The ringing of the phone startled me from sleep. And though the call came around 8:00 a.m., I had not yet roused myself from bed because I'd had a long week. The legislative session was in full swing, and I spent my weekends visiting traumatized Democrats around the state.

It was the start of 2017, the beginning of the Trump administration, and the anti-immigrant fervor of the newly inaugurated president had swept into Georgia. A GOP state representative had proposed HB 66, a piece of legislation that would tax wire transfers to other countries. Or, more precisely, it would tax remittances that the undocumented sent home to their families. The punitive taxing scheme could generate an estimated $100 million each year.[3]

I'd already warned the immigrant-rights groups and small businesses affected by the proposal, some who processed the wire transfers and others who used them. But on Sunday, January 29, 2017, the phone call raised a new alarm. A civil rights activist needed me to mobilize attorneys to gather at the Hartsfield-Jackson International Airport. Trump's Muslim ban had taken effect against immigrants, refugees, and people from six Muslim nations; and at the world's busiest airport, families were being harangued and turned back from the homes they knew. I quickly coordinated with leaders at the ACLU, Asian Americans Advancing Justice, and others who needed lawyers to help field the panicked appeals for assistance. The counter-response to Trump's edict was immediate: all day and into the night, protesters gathered at the airport and around the nation in a spontaneous rejection of this new American cruelty.

On Monday, January 30, back at the Georgia state capitol, I drafted a letter for our senior U.S. senator, Johnny Isakson. Though we came from different political camps, he and I had worked together on a number of issues over the years. I emailed the letter to my executive assistant to place on letterhead for my signature. In particular, I wanted her to see my request, as she served as the only Palestinian Muslim employed by the Georgia House of Representatives. "America is a nation grounded in its globalist capacity, rooted in a fierce memory of our founding by those who sought to flee oppression," I wrote. "My ancestors arrived through enslavement, but I hold the American history of open doors to be a profound counterpoint to our bleaker impulses. To isolate believers of the Muslim faith and to validate disparagement of their contributions to our nation is to invite the scourge of religious persecution against others around the world, led by our example." It was simply a letter, but I felt compelled to show my assistant and our senator what I saw. I don't recall if I received a response, not that one would have changed the course of the Trump administration. Eventually, the ban—weakened but still pointed at the Islamic faith—gained approval from the U.S. Supreme Court.

Fast-forward to Sunday, January 12, 2020, three years later. That morning, my phone pinged with a text message at 9:59 a.m. The sender, an immigrant rights leader, wrote, "Sorry to bother u on Sunday morning but we have an Iranian student detained at the airport. She goes to [a Georgia university] on a student visa. She's going to be deported today." Again, I quickly acknowledged the message and began calling Democrats in Georgia's congressional delegation, and they agreed to help. Before they could intervene, though, the young woman was deported back to Iran, away from her studies and her friends. In Boston, in New York, across the country, similar deportations sent students, doctors, and others away from the lives they'd built here. All on the orders of an American president in the twenty-first century.

In the lead-up to the 2020 presidential election, no one can turn on the television or open a newspaper without confronting a sharp panic about the ideological divide in the Democratic Party and how it might play into the outcome of the contest. Think pieces abound about the cleaving of the Big Tent party, where all are welcome, into rabid factions that will tear each other apart in the run-up to the election. According to the breathless analyses, the Left and the Farther Left share a deep disdain for the Center Left while despising one another. Medicare for All or Medicare for All Who Want It confront Obamacare for Now as though the latter signals the presence of moral infirmity. A commitment to climate change proves insufficient if the timeline for action strays by a year or so, or worse, if the hierarchy of the cause isn't ticked high enough on the list. Even I am not immune to it all, despite the fact that I am not running for anything. On Twitter and Facebook and screeds in some left-leaning publications, I am denounced as a corporatist and a faux progressive. The angst spills out into daily conversations I have with voters, which are underpinned with a sense of depression that worries it is already too late.

Winning in 2020 and beyond depends on candidates who recognize that they are not running against Donald Trump or the darker impulses he represents; they are running *for* America. And there is a difference. If a campaign is waged solely against the current occupant of the White House, then his behavior becomes the fulcrum against which decisions are made— pettiness to match pettiness; incivility for incivility.

On the other hand, a candidate intent on winning over Americans leads with the kinds of conversations we need to have about contentious domestic policy issues and complex foreign policy. That candidate rejects the well-worn tradition of fearmongering and demonization as a way of swaying voters to their cause. The Democrat who takes back the White House must refuse to cater to the underbelly of vicious populist anger in our nation. Instead, the victor will bring more people to the table because, for so many of us, fear has always been a part of how we navigate America, especially as minority communities. Fear is a given, but fear is not a reason to vote. Hope is a reason to vote: a visible, visceral compassion for those who worry for the future and fret about the now. The triumphant candidate weaves together these reasons without casting fellow citizens as villains. But in politics, as in life, there is nothing new under the sun, particularly blaming the marginalized and disadvantaged for the wrongs of life. Always, authoritarianism and the death of democracy wait in the shadow of populism.

The strains of populism that have bolstered class identity in American politics too often become entangled with racism, misogyny, and a hatred for others that leads to sustained hostility and violence—but this is nothing new. The original populists, the Know-Nothing Party of the early 1800s, turned their cries for equity for poor whites into vitriolic attacks on minorities. Trawl social media today and the same animosity wrapped in righteousness has resurfaced. Whether fully embraced by a majority political party or not, in the United States, both parties have welcomed the sleight of hand used to engage populism's promises of relief to the underdog—often by victimizing another group instead. What has kept the threat of unchecked populism in the United States at bay is democracy itself. Democracy protects the expression of minority needs while supporting majority gains. Trump may win the presidency, but the women's marches can fill the streets of dozens of cities. The urgency of fighting the corrosive version of populism the Trump administration has heightened (but not created) in America cannot be reduced to simply defeating him in an election. Under his government, our moral standing has weakened, our rule of law has fractured, and our checks and balances have failed. But we must accept this truth. He is not a singularity, and what he represents will continue even after his defeat, so our ambition must be larger than fighting him.

THE RISE OF AUTHORITARIAN POPULISM AS DEMOCRACY'S ENEMY

Democracies, in every region of the world, are straining. The liberal democratic order that arose from World War II and reached its pinnacle in the years after the end of the Cold War faces new threats. Authoritarian regimes seek to unwind the new world order Americans have come to take for granted. Consider the democratically elected leadership of Taiwan, which stands firm in its freedoms under the narrow gaze of China's authoritarian empire. The people of Taiwan understand that the independence they have fought to maintain holds no guarantees. Or, take Ukraine, a former Soviet-bloc nation that broke from Russia and yet has to fight constantly to fend off Russian assaults. With their respective military and economic might, China and Russia stand as formidable external risks to these two democracies on their doorsteps.

But the greater threat is the one that has emerged from within liberal democracies across the globe: the threat of populism run amok. Beyond the United States' first brushes with the phenomenon, in Russia, the Narodnichestvo of the 1860s and '70s founded a similar populist movement that sought to replace the urban elites with the true power found in the farmers of the rural countryside. The 1950s and '60s birthed variations in Latin America, Africa, and Asia. Survey current economic unrest on nearly every continent that has experimented with democracy, and exemplars of populism abound, which should terrify Americans who believe in the system of government designed to provide a degree of equity to society.

Democracies rarely fall today because of military coups or foreign invasion. Instead, their death is gradual, coming slowly and over time with an erosion of rights and an accumulation of attacks on the institutions that form their backbone. From Hungary to India, from the Philippines to Venezuela, the corrosive power of populism wielded by authoritarians—an illiberal political current that tramples on democratic institutions while claiming to speak in the name of the people—has made deep inroads across the globe. And what is so pernicious about populism is that it arrives in disguise. While it comes to fruition through democratic electoral politics, it simultaneously has an utter disregard for liberal institutions or norms. The authoritarian populist succeeds at the ballot box but, once in power, chips away at the very architecture of democracy.

The populist attack usually follows a standard playbook. The first step is the entrance of a charismatic leader. He—and it is almost always a "he"—offers himself as someone new and different, unbound by the rules and norms that have guided others. Whether he is gliding down a golden escalator or standing on an overturned milk crate, his language and style attract and hold attention. The delivery may be coarse, but that deviation from the polished, professional leader only adds to the appeal of making him appear like everyday people, one unafraid to speak "truths." By defying conventions like vetting officials or holding press conferences, he seeks to have a direct and unmediated relationship with the "people." The charismatic populist chooses a variety of tropes to launch his romancing of the crowds. Jair Bolsonaro won Brazil's presidential election by promising to exploit the Amazon rain forest and mimicking the behaviors of military dictators. The specifics of the leader's message do not matter, because it isn't about specific policies—his message is the politicization of social resentment and exploitation of people's fears. He will craft a message based on people's grievances, as President Rodrigo Duterte did in the Philippines by promising to kill thousands of drug traffickers and criminals without trials. And he will lambaste and promise miraculous results in any of the areas in which government has failed to be responsive to people's concerns (real or imagined).

Once he has the attention of his targets, the populist must polarize politics. He may wrap himself in the mantle of a particular cause, but he does not care about ideological divisions or a polarization based on political beliefs. To the populist, his

aim isn't an argument between competing political visions—
the authoritarian populist was never truly motivated by ideas in
the first place. Instead, to captivate and hold his audience, he
casts his fight in moral terms: good versus evil, light versus dark.
Embedded in his rhetoric are plaudits that give his supporters a
rationale for their anger. Those who stand with him are patriots; and his opponents are enemies, traitors, or terrorists. Cast
in this light, his political opponents are no longer viewed by his
own supporters as champions of an alternative political vision
with which they disagree. Instead, the opposition is stripped of
any claims to national loyalty. Indian prime minister Narendra
Modi has cemented power through not only stoking the fervor
of Hindu identity; he has publicly stripped the Muslim minority
of their place in India's secular state. Upon democratic reelection
in 2019, Modi nullified Article 370, the agreement that had protected Muslims in the Kashmir region since 1949, shortly following the division of Pakistan and India in 1947. Months later, his
parliament offered citizenship to refugees in India, except those
of Muslim faith. Through tirades, bombast, or acts of the legislature, opponents to the populist's aims are transformed into
menaces, enemies of the people. When the opposition speaks up,
denounces the populist's pronouncements, or attempts to resist
the populist's moves, their warnings only feed his narrative that
he is the one true leader against the corrupt elites.

To maintain his hold, he must ratchet up the polarization of
politics to a sustained fever pitch. He must take more strident
and uncompromising positions, over and over again. The aim is
simple: to prove his mettle and whip up his supporters, he has
to challenge his opponent on the field of battle. By doing so, he
makes it appear as though society is irreconcilably at odds with

itself, that there are sharp and deep rifts between his camp of true patriots and those who mean to harm it.

Take Nigel Farage, the former leader of the United Kingdom Independence Party who advocated for Britain to leave the European Union by declaring that those who sought a break achieved "victory for the real people."[4] In that declaration, he decried the 48 percent of British citizens who rejected Brexit as the enemy, not real Britons.[5] The populist doesn't just want conflict; he requires it. The visible wrestling match depends on clashes that draw the attention and maintain the emotional connection stoked by his charisma. His chief enemy is anything approaching reason, consensus, or moderation. So, he convinces his followers to reject any logic that questions his own. He feints toward compromise to get attention, then blows up any potential for joint action. And he draws lines in the sand, only to vault over them, thereby resetting what seemed normal.

But polarization is merely one tactic, and the populist understands that he has to create permanent rifts that threaten to reassert the normal order. Thus, once the charismatic leader has effectively polarized politics and taken power, he must set to work to attack all democratic institutions and rob them of credibility. His most valuable targets are the basic building blocks of democracy: the media, the judiciary, any independent authorities that might constrain his power. Preemptively discrediting the media is a first-order imperative because he knows full well that good journalism will shine a light on his abuses. Hugo Chávez and then his successor, Nicolás Maduro, leveraged Venezuela's 2004 Law on Social Responsibility in Radio, Television, and Electronic Media to censor media and limit coverage of demonstrations and critics of the government. By bringing suits against both traditional media and social media, populist leaders have muted coverage of state actions, even as recently as the oil and food crisis of 2019 as thousands filled the streets. And effective populists also create new direct connections with their supporters, from weekly radio programs to reinforce the polarizing messages to aggressive Twitter feeds to stoke outrage and reshape reality.

For the authoritarian-in-training, the next target will likely be courts. In democracies, a judiciary willing to uphold the rule of law is the most potent direct constraint on his power. In response, he will politicize their work, question their agenda, and fill their ranks with cronies or sympathizers. Having silenced critiques and manipulated the law, the final act is dismantling the machinery of democracy through undermining the institutions and laws that act as guardrails against the personalistic accumulation of power. In Hungary, Prime Minister Viktor Orbán, democratically elected first in 1998 and again in 2010, quickly moved to weaken the judiciary and install his allies in newly created institutions.

Having destroyed so many institutions, the populist must now build a new, resilient regime through patronage politics. Since he never had any true beliefs or policies, he is not circumscribed by an actual agenda. Instead, he will fill the ranks of government and any perches of political influence with cronies, patrons, or backers. This extends beyond the pinnacles of power. What policies he does design or support will reward his core supporters, however he perceives them. Turkey, for long a parliamentary democracy, established an executive presidency in 2017, rather than the more ceremonial role of president. This constitutional change allowed its former prime minister to imbue the newly charged role of president with expansive authorities. As the first Turkish president of this type, Recep Tayyip Erdoğan has the authority to dissolve the federal legislative body, appoint his cabinet, issue decrees, and essentially operate without monitors, as he also appoints the courts and the bureaucracies. For the authoritarian populist, the faster traditional monitors of democratic norms can be discarded or eroded, the better.

GETTING OUR CREDIBILITY BACK

The first steps to restoring our nation's standing are electing a new president, protecting the processes that can deliver a representative and active Congress, and removing the barriers that hinder an engaged citizenry. We must also anticipate the next populist leader's emergence, which means we must strengthen our democratic institutions, we must fortify our voting rights with permanent fixes in law and the constitution, and we have to live our values and hold leaders accountable when they fail to behave.

America today is approximately 51 percent female, 13.4 percent black, and 18.1 percent Hispanic.[6] Under the Trump administration, however, the nation's leadership does not reflect its composition. As of 2020, of the twenty-four cabinet or cabinet-level positions, only three are held by women and three are held by people of color, and of this group, one is a woman of color. Observers blasted his all-white, all-male lineup of military leaders as he announced attacks on Iran.[7] The foreign service corps has a similarly dismal composition: 6 percent Hispanic, 5.6 percent black, 6.8 percent Asian, 0.3 percent Native American.[8] His judicial appointments are record-breaking. By January 2020, Trump has appointed 185 judges to the federal bench, and his confirmations include two Supreme Court justices, dozens of circuit court judges, and more than 100 district court judges. In the populism playbook, reshaping the judiciary is a key metric, and Trump's alliance with the GOP-controlled Senate has confirmed a slate of judges that are 76 percent male and more than 85 percent white. These appointments are not at all reflective of the composition of our country. And when people are checking us for our values, they can see that our representation in the domestic and international order does not reflect who we are, which negates our ability to criticize their own discrimination.

Diversity informs and expands a nation's capacity to groom effective leaders, and history has proven that it is a helpful thing to have better and more effective leaders. Our greatest weakness in our democracy stems from our treatment of minorities, which serves as a cornerstone of democracy's utility. To reclaim our standing, we must be able to show the world that we actually value minorities, as then we have a moral leg to stand on when we tell them the participation of minorities in their body politic is important. Survey when autocracies and authoritarian regimes come into power, and their first act is to eliminate minority rights. Populists succeed by treating the other as the enemy, which makes it much easier to do the work of strongman leadership. And that's part of what we're seeing in the nation-states that are retreating from their democracies—what happened in the Philippines, what happened in Turkey, what's happening across Eastern Europe. The suppression of minority rights is the first hallmark of the end of liberal democracy and a grave danger to those communities. Therefore, there is a public benefit and an international good to minority representation in America's democratic institutions. We cannot demand that others value minority rights elsewhere when we fail to demand it of ourselves.

Voting rights are essential and fundamental to democracy, and we are facing an existential crisis in the United States. Our democracy is shredded by naked pursuits of power that allow states to suppress the right to vote, and we face a crippling challenge to our leadership here and abroad. What we have seen play out in the last twenty years has been an aggressive attempt at voter suppression that is directly targeted to communities that have long been outside the body politic, and it began when they started to enter and affect elections in real and tangible ways. Yet, the international consequence is that we are no longer credible as election supervisors and election monitors when in our own country some of our largest states are engaging in voter suppression as a native good. Political power evolves when new people come into the process. An increase in minority participation halts the advance of populism, and minority voices often lead to progress because typically they are upset that they were left out of previous transformations. In the twentieth century, blacks were excluded from the New Deal programs, the G.I. Bill as former soldiers, and housing programs due to federal prohibitions on loans and where they could buy houses. Latinos and Asian Americans faced educational discrimination at the public school level, and they also faced housing discrimination. Voter participation blunted their complaints, and as more have become civically active, greater attention has been paid to their needs. The same is true for other disadvantaged communities. Populists understand that the corollary to energizing the base of their power is the suppression of the other. Americans like to think that we're invulnerable, but we are not. Our systems are not. Our democracy may be resilient, but it is also fragile. And that fragility is what is at stake now.

When I think about the next generation of elections, my deepest fear is that we are going to face not just voter suppression but that the more insidious part of voter suppression will take effect and people will believe that they no longer count. When people self-select out of participation, that is actually a much more effective consequence because increasing difficulty is one thing, but making participation seem irrelevant has a much more pervasive and permanent effect. In a putative democracy where the majority of the minority decides their voices no longer matter, we are in a dire circumstance. This threatens democracy for the United States and thus is a threat internationally. By restoring the Voting Rights Act and undertaking the raft of proposed voter engagement legislation presented to Congress and to the various states, we can reassert our leadership and demonstrate how to recover from the hazards of suppression.

Our institutions and our voting rights feed into the most visible example of our decency. How we treat our people is a beacon for how we intend to lead. The metrics of health, education, economic security, climate action, and national security hold long-term consequences in the international context, which means that if the ideals and the values we espouse abroad are not enshrined at home, then our ability to call for that liberal democratic order is eroded. American credibility has been threatened before. During the Cold War, the USSR very effectively used the propaganda of America's presence in Latin America, in Asia, and in Africa. They told those nascent democracies emerging from colonialism, "This is a country that tells you to trust them, but they are purveyors of inequality and racism. Why believe them?" Our credibility was deeply damaged in the 1980s, having a president who supported apartheid as an acceptable political and economic system. So, it's not that our credibility hasn't been damaged before. The stark difference is how Trump and his political supporters have undertaken a sustained attempt to abrogate our systems in the ways we have seen since 2017.

Nations watch what we do, and they emulate our behavior,

even now. America's authority to question Russian president Vladimir Putin's treatment of dissidents weakened when President Trump refused to hold Saudi Arabia accountable for the murder of an American resident and journalist. International calls to accept refugees from Yemen, Syria, and elsewhere go unanswered when the Trump administration offers individual states the right to refuse resettlement. To the extent that they are emulating the behavior of America and the erosion of democracy, we have to recognize that democracy is not a permanent good.

One of the ways to reclaim our moral center is for America to show that we want something better. An absolute good happens when we change our national leadership, when we reject the current order. That restores, at least, an intentionality on our part. The next president is going to have to revisit the Paris Agreement and our national commitment to action on climate change. The next administration must reexamine what we've done with Iran and the international accord, as well as repudiate dictators and populist bullies around the globe. The immediacy of our response to what has been done in the name of American citizens will speak to the world of our intended direction moving forward.

We restore credibility when we demonstrate that the United States has a new crop of leaders, reflective of the values we espouse, who are willing to do the work of building those relationships again, and that there is a sustained opportunity to fix what was broken. Equally critical, we must examine our laws to assess how any demagogue could infiltrate and shift our nation this quickly and assuredly. We must ensure that we can never lose ourselves or our place in the world again.

CHAPTER 10

The Next Best Version of America

'm angry. More than a year after the 2018 election, I can scarcely stand to watch footage from the campaign without my mouth tightening and my eyes narrowing. I'll see the faces of Georgians illuminated on the screen, some cast in the bright sunshine of an outdoor rally, others in the artificial glare of gymnasium lights, and I remember the press of an elderly kiss to my cheek in Sandersville or a spontaneous hug from a gangly teenager finally old enough to vote. I have dug through footage of voters sharing their stories in order to capture them here; and more than once, I had to press pause to give myself a moment—because I believed Jordan when he told me about his passion for early childhood education as a protective shield for our youngest citizens, when Isabella and Kenneth claimed our common values in Spanish, when Kristy and Amy gave me my name sign in ASL. I believed we had a fair shot at winning.

But in Georgia (as in other states like Florida and Texas), the winners staked their campaigns on using disgust for immigrants, and—in my beloved Georgia—my opponent promised to sign legislation to demonize the LGBTQ+ community. In all three cases, oppression won with voter suppression pushing away black and brown voters, young people, the elderly, the poor, and new citizens. At the end of the day, the victims of these campaigns saw how little their needs influenced elections. And that too enrages me.

In the intervening months, I have done interviews and podcasts and penned op-eds, but I don't believe I have yet fully captured what I learned in 2018—especially in those ten days after the election. The morning after the election, our core team met in the dining room of the suite at our hotel. My parents and siblings had gone back to their rooms at around two a.m. I fell into a restless sleep closer to four, and I was up again a few hours later. A cold I had been ignoring for days pounded through my head. But I had to focus on our game plan for the next phase.

In most contests, Election Day is the end unless the state has runoffs. Georgia is a runoff state, but that morning, the Associated Press still refused to call the race. Rather than check the secretary of state's website, I waited for my campaign manager, Lauren, to update me. Before we'd gone our separate ways, I'd authorized a series of television ads to encourage voters to cure their provisional ballots and call our hotline if they experienced voter suppression. When Lauren arrived, a little past eight, she was livid. Thousands of calls had poured in already, and by the end of the process, the hotline would log more than 80,000 calls. Soon, Dara Lindenbaum, nearly four months pregnant with twins, joined us, followed by Allegra Lawrence-Hardy. The duo comprised our legal brain trust, and they'd been advising Lauren and me since our 2014 fights with Brian Kemp.

Over the next few hours, we plotted our strategy and made

assignments. None of us cried at the table as we plowed through our options, but the meeting had an air of unreality. Eighteen months of campaigning. Three years of planning. And still no answers. Eventually, our conclave broke up because Allegra and Dara had to see about extending their hotel reservations. The candidate suite transformed into our post-election War Room. I handed out extra keys and waited patiently for everyone to leave. Then I crawled back into the rumpled hotel bed, ordered up *Sorry to Bother You*, and waited for tears to come.

They didn't flow when my parents came by to check on me. When my brother Richard brought me breakfast. Or when my older sister told me she'd postponed her flight home to Kentucky for another day. I hugged Andrea harder than necessary, but I refused to cry. Part of me knew that tears would mean I accepted defeat, that all our work was over. The stoic part of me never liked crying, and I was proud that I held it in. It wasn't until my brother Walter called from a prison phone, more worried about me than himself. After I hung up the phone, the sobs didn't seem to stop. But I quickly had to tamp them down when I saw the time and realized I had another call to do with donors to raise money for overtime.

Over the next ten days, I tried to speed myself through the seven stages of grief. I'd read about them coming in turn, but they seemed to attack me all at once. Shock, denial, bargaining, and testing got funneled into a series of lawsuits I authorized or learned about, and though we won most of them, there was no relief. With each victory, the numbers between me and my opponent got closer, but with no clear answer.

Anger was ever-present, along with rage and its variations. Until this election, I had never considered myself an angry person. Almost every job I have ever held required navigating warring factions, picking among competing visions, or simply surviving the low, steady hum of bigotry. My temperament is low-drama and even-keeled, and, to be honest, sustained anger always struck me as a weakness. A person loses focus or, worse, becomes defined by that emotion alone. But I was mad and I couldn't shake it.

I sat with depression, rereading favorite romance novels, assured of a tortured relationship with a happy ending. I watched reruns of sci-fi shows as I camped out on my sofa at home. My youngest sister had been designated by our family as my minder, so she found an excuse to visit almost every day for the next week. Like clockwork, my campaign manager reported the election news daily, and while the gap closed, I had a feeling the distance would be insurmountable. By day six, I decided to skip over acceptance and go straight to a new stage that I like to call plotting.

On a legal pad that I kept on the coffee table for Lauren's daily reports, I sketched out three new ways I could continue to do the work that has fueled me since I was a teenager: fighting for the rights of those who are too often left behind or ignored altogether. The results were Fair Fight Action and Fair Fight PAC to tackle voter suppression and engagement, Fair Count to address the census and beyond, and the Southern Economic Advancement Project to still generate the progressive policy ideas I likely wouldn't be able to promote as governor.

I talked to my friend Will about the closing window of the election, and he asked if I planned to concede. I tried to respond, but I couldn't form the words. The idea of accepting what happened to 80,000 disenfranchised voters—that I knew of—was unbearable. On the night of November 15, when Lauren and I realized we'd gotten as close as we could, I used that same legal pad to sketch out my speech of non-concession. Yet, as I rejected the tradition of conceding, as I developed these groups and raised millions of dollars to fund their efforts, as I stood before America delivering the State of the Union response, the constancy of anger dogged me. Its permanence unsettled me, still catching me unawares at odd moments.

In the end, I forced myself to confront the awkward, sullen feelings that burned and chilled inside me at the same time. Losing the contest for governor wasn't my first defeat, and I had prepared myself for the possibility. Chelsey Hall, my onetime special assistant, now adviser, had the job of staffing me as I reemerged into the public eye. As I made my way through airports, grocery stores, and hotel lobbies, I realized what kept me so irate. Over and over again, people who'd never met me rushed up to thank me for running. Chelsey would hold handbags and watch luggage as they hugged me. The first few times, I was nonplussed by the attention. I'd prepared myself for humiliation, for people avoiding eye contact or offering me advice on what I *should* have done. But that never materialized.

Instead, I found flight attendants who passed notes to me that they'd written on napkins, grateful that I spoke up for them. Maintenance workers pushing their carts through office buildings clasped my hands or hugged me spontaneously, whispering that they voted for me and their votes got stolen. Well-wishers from outside Georgia asked for selfies to show their kids because the campaign had ignited a passion in their households. I sat in a waiting area between trips and spoke by Skype to the overworked, underpaid women of the National Domestic Workers Alliance, and I marveled as they celebrated the 250,000 volunteers they had amassed in 2018—cheering their newfound power instead of bemoaning the election's results. I visited with labor leaders who had poured into our campaign, from early endorsements to thousands of volunteer hours to financial support that placed hundreds of field workers on doors. To a person, they thanked me for our campaign without a hint of resentment for its bitter end. On a connecting flight through a midwestern state, a middle-aged white man in camo saw me come off yet another plane. He stood just past the gate, stolid as a tree trunk. Chelsey had been a few rows behind me, so I waited alone, watching him as he watched me. After a few seconds, he marched up to me. "You Stacey Abrams?" Knowing I couldn't lie, I said, "Yes, I am." His rugged face broke into a grin. "Can I give you a hug? You kick ass." I embraced him, just as I had the group of young black and brown students at the college where I spoke, kids who told me they knew the vote was rigged but they weren't going to stop. My rage exists because they deserve more, but our nation is in trouble and I know why.

America, like much of the democratized world, stands at a crucial moment in history. Concepts of justice and fairness have become more fragile, and now the core elements of our democratic system of government are under siege. While the United States has always fumbled in its pursuit of social equality, what we accepted as basic principles have been eroded, and truths about who we are as free people have shifted—and not for the better. Whether it's the stories of police brutality against blacks, migrant children dying for lack of care in American detention centers, attacks on food stamps for the poor, or the emergence of authoritarian regimes where proud democracies once stood, a disconnect is spreading between who we say we are and how our systems behave. The cause is clear: a massive and inevitable change in the demographic makeup both in the United States and abroad.

America's rapidly changing population has hit a diversity

inflection point, one where a new political majority has fully emerged. Rumblings about this multiracial, multiethnic, youth-driven majority's clout have grown over the past twenty years. Yet prognostications of a sea change toward a progressive movement have been met with skepticism about whether such a coalition could actually be realized. We first saw glimpses of this progressive promise in the 2006 midterm rout that swept in the first woman Speaker of the House and became manifest in the 2008 election of President Barack Obama. But with the failed elections of 2010, 2014, and 2016, most of us started to believe that a coalition of the marginalized and our allies could never assume real power. Proving the point, political candidates and the Democratic Party have struggled to reliably engage this new demographic group—nibbling at the edges of success but refusing to put the weight of an election on their turnout.

Part of the challenge is external: a pervasive, systemic process of stripping the right to vote from some and building obstacles to access for others. The power of voting is real, as are the policies that mute the humanity of our fellow citizens like Trump's screeds against people of color and a political financing system that preferences the white, old, and wealthy. But the threat is also coming from inside the coalition itself: citizens grappling with racism, sexism, homophobia, and poverty are the least likely to trust in or utilize their votes. Worse, they are told that it's wrong to seek out candidates who look like them, share their experiences, or speak aloud about solutions for them. Underlying it all is shortsighted planning that responds to the problem at hand rather than constructing long-term solutions.

In the end, we expect voter suppression, voter disengagement, cheating, and factionalism; and the candidates who should engage our burgeoning cohort to win victories are afraid to reach out. We see these wins when they come as political singularities, admirable but not replicable. This dismissal of a treasure trove of voters persists despite transformative victories around the country and across multiple years, where women, people of color, LGBTQ+ candidates, and young people became the visible hope of the New American Majority. Close losses in unexpectedly competitive territories also demonstrate that demographic changes have come to fruition as a political road map. Yet, as we fight against those invested in the status quo and our friends too afraid of the potential of this mélange of opinions and needs, we must come to grips with our victory. What comes next is the how: how does a progressive movement become a permanent political force when neither its enemies nor its allies truly believe it's real?

We have to reclaim the notion of what democracy means. A major part of this project is that we have to stop thinking about elections as being about candidates. One of the things I say that infuriates the Right, but I mean it sincerely, is that in Georgia, we *won*. I didn't see victory simply as my getting across the finish line and getting a title. Winning is about ensuring that people who do not think they matter in our system believe that they can lift their voices up. For too long, politicians have treated elections as a single night of results. But as long as we make winning the only thing, when we make crossing that finish line and getting the crown the only metric, we are going to continue to lose our democracy. When winning is all that matters, how you win has less and less relevance. My mission is to remind us that it is not about getting a job. It is about helping the voices of our people be heard. And that's what democracy is. The power and the purpose of our system is to enable the people with the ability to have their values represented and to select their leaders. Any time we erode that capacity, we are eroding the very republic we seek to protect.

Yet, in a democracy, the fundamental objective is driven by math: get more votes from those who share your views, your values, and your priorities. While casting a vote rarely guarantees an expected outcome, each vote serves to tally the intent of the governed. Of course, beyond voting for elected representatives, we cast our ballots for a host of other items. In some states, ballot initiatives allow citizens to write their own laws of the land, and the elected and appointed governmental officials are supposed to be bound by the will of the people. A number of jurisdictions require citizens to vote before bonds are issued or taxes raised, to set limits on how much can be collected, or to dictate how the dollars are spent. We hold elections at nearly every level of government, from school boards and city councils, to judges and state legislators, to Congress and the presidency; and if you live in Duxbury, Vermont, you can vote for dogcatcher. Regardless of the level of government, the impact of the role, or the breadth of impact, voting is power.

Identity politics reflects how we filter our choices. In the current age, what has become controversial is how distinct identities are and how effectively both candidates and voters have leveraged identity to make strides for their values. Recent elections now routinely include the mention of a first: first Muslim mayor, first Native American congresswoman, first transgender state representative. This effective use of identity—either to pick a candidate or to rally a voter—has upended the traditions of American politics, and with that transformation has come a resentment from those who do not see themselves in the description. Academics have parsed the legitimacy of identity politics, and pundits have written think pieces decrying its salience. More frequently, critics use a revulsion of identity politics—ones based on marginalization or disadvantage—to scare voters into believing their particular choices cost them victories in elections. However logical the argument may sound, though, the reality is that as those outside the norms of politics rise, so too do various rationales for their level of success or defeat. Candidates do not win or lose because they express concern or solidarity for otherness. They win or lose because they ignore it or because some voters are afraid of it. But in the midst of demographic upheaval, the rise of voter suppression and the denouncement of identity politics by the marginalized share common cause. Voter suppression serves to block access for those who are not considered full citizens because of race and status. And rejecting identity politics tells the same groups that their difference not only doesn't matter, it is harmful to their progress.

But the integration of voter access and identity is the fundamental purpose of democracy. As a nation, we organized ourselves to delegate authority over both the most profound and the most mundane policy matters to the people. In reaction to the tyranny of a monarchy, we established an inclusive, independent process that, in theory, assigned equality to all citizens by virtue of the vote—not by race, class, gender, sexual orientation, national origin, or physical ability. The only hurdle was supposed to be gaining citizenship. Yet, as history and current-day behavior show, we continue to struggle to believe that full citizenship belongs to all who are entitled to hold it. Instead, for more than two hundred years, we've seen the act of voting thwarted based on identity. And we've witnessed the very identities thrust upon communities by the majority used as a justification for suppression and oppression. The result has been a silencing of voices and, worse, a silencing of ideas and a disconnection from what people need to actively participate in our nation's future.

In a democracy, if we do not hear from everyone, the

complexity of our communities goes unaddressed and our national ambition is incomplete. When citizens feel unrepresented or, worse, exorcised from the process, disengagement follows. Often, those potential voters who sit out elections are decried as apathetic, and too many of them would agree with the description. I recently saw a YouTube video by a hip-hop artist named YelloPain. The opening sequence broke my heart as he tours his neighborhood and bitterly describes how useless voting seems. He invokes the promise of the Obama presidency, then laments all the ways life failed to improve. His damning indictment of the act of voting seems at once logical and tragic. But with his next verse, he rips into the fiction of voter apathy, and in his rapid-fire poetry, you come to understand that his reaction is more aptly treated as despair and disillusionment. Like him, eligible, silent voters tend to come from communities that have traditionally been ignored by politicians and by policies. He details the travesties of a system that fails to connect the dots between voting and change.

When I answer questions about why the most oppressed citizens do not vote, I describe the eighteen-year-old growing up in intergenerational poverty. She can be forgiven for not believing a campaign slogan that promises a quick fix to the housing and hunger crisis she has lived through her entire life. The same is true for a middle-aged man who lost his manufacturing job and, with it, the health insurance that provided coverage for his family. Or the black family burying a child killed in a police-involved shooting. As our country shifts in its economic production as well as racial and ethnic composition, disengagement will likely follow its traditional pattern and become disaffection. Whether the result is Occupy or the Tea Party or Black Lives Matter, our current age has seen what happens when people don't feel represented.

What YelloPain does next is a stroke of artistic and activist genius. He deftly illustrates how understanding and engaging in the political system is an issue of survival. Like a modern version of *Schoolhouse Rock!*, he explains the three branches of government, connecting their failures to our own. From health care policy and climate action to the social safety net and high finance, our votes determine how the public and the private sectors operate and where they intersect. More important, like YelloPain, we must internalize that the ferocity of our engagement in every branch of government, at every level, decides whether those in charge pay any attention at all.

The difference in how we approach questions of access and opportunity depends heavily on how one sees the role of government. If a pollster queried the average person, most would say they don't think that anyone should be homeless if they work a full-time job. They would say that Americans shouldn't die from curable diseases because they lack health insurance. Our nation ostensibly frowns upon theft, and we encourage education. Yet, these common beliefs require public action to guarantee implementation and permanence. For voters, political party labels serve as shorthand for candidates, in lieu of full-fledged investigation. And parties serve as guideposts for policy making. Whether the choice presented is to elect an official or to defeat legislation, the act of casting a vote remains the key. It is a key that unlocks access to opportunity, to change, to the interconnected webs of commerce, politics, and social justice we know we want, and they want us to keep that door closed. But there is absolutely no change if we let the door stay locked. Only if people vote will their voices be heard and their lives change.

Our time is now. We have the numbers, the mission, and the opportunity to start constructing the next best version of

America. Each of us has the obligation to defend our democracy. This week, every one of us can ask five strangers if they have registered to vote or if they've recently checked their registration. If they haven't, direct them to Vote.org. If they check and are missing, or if they have ever faced voter suppression, contact FairFight2020.org. This month, we should identify and contact our city councilmember, our county commissioner, *and* our state representative. Yes, all three, because each manages a distinct set of laws that govern our lives. If all you do is send a quick note to introduce yourself, or leave a voicemail about an issue you care about, then that's good enough. Elected officials work for us, and they do their best when they know we are paying attention. If you want to up the ante, ask them how they plan to support fair redistricting for your community. Finally, this year, volunteer to reach out to unlikely voters through a campaign or an organization. Whether you help out a presidential campaign or a school board race, ask specifically to be assigned to the lowest-scoring voters, the ones who haven't shown up in years. They are the ones who need to know they matter. And don't worry if you hate knocking on doors or prefer phone calls or you'd rather send postcards. Pick your lane and then invest in someone who thinks they are invisible. If you're reading this after the presidential election, no worries. There's always a campaign happening somewhere in America.

With our collective commitment, the best version of America is within our grasp: one where we guarantee a fair chance to shape the discourse, knowing that victory is not a given; where we understand that sometimes, the fight is the thing. But unless we are committed to the battle for the soul of America, we will forever be held back by our weakest moments.

I believe in more. Because I believe in us.

Afterword

As this book goes to print, the world is grappling with the COVID-19 pandemic, a novel coronavirus that has spread to nearly every continent, and whose victims cut across race, class, gender, and creed. Responses to the threat have varied, and resources to battle its attack have been in high demand. Testing protocols, economic supports, and health care regimes have been stretched to their limits. Worse, information flows that could have prepared countries to respond more quickly and effectively have been stymied by distrust and gamesmanship. The United States, a nation always called upon to lead such efforts in decades past, has fumbled its own defense to COVID-19. Although President Trump was warned by his own experts for months, he responded to the crisis with half-truths coupled with a blasé attitude about what was to come. Health officials went unheeded or were silenced, while political action focused almost exclusively on the virus's toll on the stock market. As the pandemic spread across the country, governors found themselves battling not only the disease but an erratic, incurious, and ill-informed president who regularly contradicted or undermined what the best science could recommend.

Our arrival at this critical moment is not a surprise. For forty years, a conservative juggernaut of ideology and special interests has eroded trust in government, defunded the capacity of our institutions, and undermined people's belief in science as an independent, reliable tool for fact-finding. What began during the Reagan Revolution found true believers in the Bush years and flourished when the GOP took power in 2010. The fall began with the constant jeering of bureaucrats as unnecessary drains on citizen resources rather than essential personnel to operate the machinery of our sprawling national exercise in governance. The workers responsible to the American people became easy punchlines. Elected leaders mocked their usefulness, and constituents believed them. Government employees became targets of mistrust, rather than members of a vital delivery system of public goods.

But convincing Americans not to trust government served as step one. Grover Norquist famously explained the ultimate conservative mission, "to get [government] down to the size where we can drown it in the bathtub." For decades, congressional Republicans have executed this second step by stripping crucial bureaucracies of funding, sometimes aided by cowed Democrats. Waves of privatization, deregulation, and sequestration had their desired effects: fewer hands on deck. But those hands are needed to deliver critical services, such as public health, and we now have thinning ranks of service providers in times of disaster.

The third step has been replacing scientific fact with profit-driven opinion. From the climate change deniers to the congressional prohibition of unpopular scientific studies, modern conservative ideology has rejected research as a necessary ingredient for decision making. Where Richard Nixon strengthened the role of the United States in environmental action, Republicans who have followed have systematically destroyed our faith in facts.

The weakening of our public administration infrastructure has reached its pinnacle in the Trump presidency. Trump and his cabinet have consistently derided the very institutions they lead. Americans have become inured to the churn of cabinet officials and staff departures. Trump's steady stream of lies has half of the country turning a deaf ear and the other half ingesting false information. Trump's actions have built on the GOP's intentional destruction of institutions, and have left America weakened in a time of international crisis.

This erosion of public confidence has clear consequences. Our leaders need our trust in order to compel swift action in a crisis. Otherwise, rather than operating in the collective interest, citizens defer to their own personal concerns. For COVID-19, we have had a uniquely ineffective leader who told a nation not to act, despite an international call to arms. Our president frittered away precious weeks, which meant our national reaction lagged far behind more competent responses in South Korea or Taiwan. When the CDC called for social distancing, thousands of young people, reared in an age of government distrust, flocked to the beaches of Florida to enjoy spring break. They are not alone in ignoring warnings. Across America, the disdain for evidence is the result of trained cynicism that has affected young and old alike. Without the ability to share a common narrative, government has little chance of producing a successful solution.

Unfortunately, America has not only a disbelieving public; its ability to respond has been hollowed out. Budget cuts on the federal, state, and local levels have gutted our public health systems. And privatization—where private companies take over public services—has left a public sector unable to perform essential services. Instead, we find ourselves turning to the private sector to step into public roles. Current debate swirls about invoking World War II–era legislation to force the private sector to act even more aggressively; however, the histories are not parallel. What America faces today is a self-made crisis, where too many elected leaders abdicated responsibility for public duties. The fault lines of this overreliance on the private sector are already showing. The demands for private sector testing solutions for COVID-19 in Walmart and Target parking lots will inherently privilege those with access to cars. Those who rely on public transit or who are homebound may be left behind. The availability of medical care typically flows first to the more affluent facilities, those private hospitals that can afford top-notch care. The most endangered patients are those reliant on government-funded clinics or under-resourced rural hospitals, or the undocumented who are wholly outside any organized healthcare system.

Still, America has an opportunity to remedy this debacle. The 2020 elections will hire our next federal leaders, and across the country, state and local officials will be up for a vote. First and foremost, these elections must occur. A democracy cannot abide a trade-off between security and participation. The future of our country depends on elections that protect voters, poll workers, and the right to vote. As we adapt to new norms to protect ourselves from COVID-19, we must also adapt how we conduct our elections. Voter registration should be made available online, and paper registration must be made easier for the millions who do not have access to the internet. In every state, vote by mail is already in place, though some states restrict who can access it; in 2020, it should be universally available. The gold standards for vote by mail include postage-paid or prepaid ballots, counting all ballots postmarked by Election Day, reforming signature match laws to protect voters, and allowing community organizations to securely collect and deliver completed, sealed ballots. States should also prepare to conduct in-person elections that conform to CDC guidelines. Certain communities (particularly Native Americans and rural voters) have slow or unreliable mail, and black and Latino citizens often prefer voting in person.

Likewise, the 2020 census must also proceed, with keen attention to and investment in full participation. The Census Bureau should extend the timing for responses, deploy more digital and phone-based outreach, and expand its educational campaign to amplify the importance of the census. There is a direct connection between an accurate count and access to the financial and political power conveyed through the census, and political leaders of goodwill should demand adequate funding to ensure the work is done right. Despite the COVID-19 pandemic, the Constitution does not allow for a do-over. We have one shot for this decade's future.

The 2020 elections should become a referendum on how to restore trust in government by rebuilding competent public systems. We should press candidates on their commitment to the urgent issue of true disaster preparedness. That requires a plan to strengthen public health systems in every state and vulnerable community. To do so requires a consistent, appropriate funding stream that is not subject to ideological whims or propaganda. Our international obligations should be central to this renaissance. In 2018, Trump effectively dismantled the Obama-era global health security system that had been recommended by Ron Klain, Vice President Joe Biden's chief of staff. The objective—to understand how viruses move beyond borders and to prepare a communications and response strategy for transnational health crises—had its genesis in the nation's multilateral engagement on the Ebola virus. Swift, worldwide action had not only accelerated treatments to countries facing infection, it slowed transmission to other nations, including the United States. Trump's shortsighted decision, while devastating in this current crisis, should galvanize a restoration of the global health security system and prompt a deeper rethinking of what constitutes genuine national security threats.

COVID-19 demands immediate response to defeat an intercontinental enemy to our health, our economies, and our futures. But the CDC designation of "COVID-19" refers to corona (CO) virus (VI) disease (D) of 2019 (-19), an indication that this is simply one of many novel coronaviruses that have and will affect human populations.

America once stood as the world's defender, as an exemplar of the competency of democratically led governments. Now is the time to reclaim our world standing by restoring our democracy to its full operating force and reentering the global arena as a true leader of nations. We cannot afford to wait.

Author's Note

As we head into the political circus of 2020, I spend more and more time offering words of calm and patience. Combined with the current coronavirus pandemic, concerns quickly spiral into near-panic. A fumbling response from the Trump administration amplifies the deepest worries about the state of our national capacity to grapple with future disasters—natural or man-made. People ask: if our government cannot formulate a basic plan to address a public health crisis, why would it successfully execute the 2020 census or a transformational presidential election? The underlying confidence in our systems is fracturing.

Elections are always messy operations, but the breakdown in time-honored norms has collided with a very public debate about what progressive really means. I hear the worry from seasoned operatives who should know better, and I get peppered with questions by those shaken by the 2016 election. To a person, they all seek a way to understand what has happened and what is to come. *Our Time Is Now* is my longer, more complicated answer to how we can frame and revise voting rights and the architecture of American democracy for the current age. My hope is that they can read this book, written by a sojourner like myself who has seen glimpses of our possible future. Like a Magic 8 Ball or a weather forecaster might say, the outlook is hazy, but with the potential for good.

We will not get there unscathed. The friction in our nation is not simply between right and left. What we face is a more fundamental shift of changing norms and wholly upended ambitions that can no longer coexist. Our current political moment reflects existential challenges coming to a head. And it is the progeny of twentieth-and twenty-first-century assaults on the role of government, the legitimacy of elections, and the intent of those elected to lead. But no matter who we elect as president, one person alone cannot fix what ails us or forestall what is to come. We will have to grapple with liberal ideals in real time, and we will have to marry our promise of freedom with the reality of what that means in a society strained by the speed of change.

What will hold us together, though, is the stability of our institutions—if we can restore them. Writers like Ari Berman, Jon Ward, and Spencer Overton have waved red flags of warning about voter suppression. Historians Carol Anderson, Kevin Kruse and Heather Cox Richardson remind us that we've been here before. Hansi Lo Wang has doggedly educated America about what's at stake in the 2020 census, and Nikole Hannah-Jones has educated America about the consequences of 1619 and the arrival of slavery on American shores. Political journalists like Jason Johnson, Rachel Maddow, Joy Reid, Jorge Ramos, Chris Hayes, Yamiche Alcindor, Jennifer Rubin, Jamil Smith, and Rebecca Traister show us a broader sweep of this political moment. Podcasts from the crew at *Pod Save America*—Jon

Favreau, Dan Pfeiffer, and Jon Lovett—the duo of Roxane Gay and Tressie McMillan Cottom, or teams like *Five Thirty Eight* or the *Slate Political Gabfest* trio of Emily Bazelon, John Dickerson, and David Plotz highlight weekly where we are most at risk. Whether we need to fix our elections, our leaders, or our census, we can no longer claim not to know where the problems lie and how we can solve them.

Our Time Is Now is equal parts synthesis and prognostication. I don't know who will be the Democratic nominee for president in 2020; and though I think Democrats will win, I honestly can't know. Foreign interference, disinformation campaigns, the fractured communications network and a soul-deep fatigue will work against our highest goals. But what is also true, though, is that the recipe for victory is neither secret nor out of reach. What I have attempted in these pages is to create a sense of urgency, buffered by ways to ensure we make the most of what is coming at us. We cannot stop the future, but if we are wise, we will prepare for the variations in outcomes. And if we are smart and nimble, we will shape the future as we can—because our time is now.

Notes

INTRODUCTION

1. "Georgia Medicaid is currently only available to non-disabled, non-pregnant adults if they are caring for a minor child and have a household income that doesn't exceed 35 percent of the poverty level (for a household of two in 2019, that amounts to under $6,000 in total annual income; only six states have lower income limits for Medicaid eligibility for low-income parents)." Louise Norris, "Georgia and the ACA's Medicaid Expansion," healthinsurance.org, November 4, 2019, https://www.healthinsurance.org/georgia-medicaid/.

2. As of April 2019, the Georgia Maternal Mortality Review Committee reported that of pregnancy-related deaths, 18 percent occurred while pregnant and 55 percent occurred within the first 42 days postpartum. Additionally, data shows that black, non-Hispanic women were 3.3 times more likely to die from pregnancy-related complications than white, non-Hispanic women. "Maternal Mortality in Georgia," Georgia House Budget & Research Office, April 2019.

CHAPTER 1

1. Chris Joyner and Jennifer Peebles, "AJC Analysis: Absentee Voting Pitfalls Tripped Thousands of Ga. Voters," *Atlanta Journal-Constitution*, December 20, 2018, https://www.ajc.com/news/state--regional-govt--politics/ajc-analysis-absentee-voting-pitfalls-tripped-thousands-voters/5Qu6ynxydaKrT4le1edtPL.

2. Bruce Hartford, "Alabama Voter Literacy Test," Veterans of the Civil Rights Movement, https://www.crmvet.org/info/littest.htm.

CHAPTER 2

1. Laura Williamson, Pamela Cataldo, and Brenda Wright, "Toward a More Representative Electorate: The Progress and Potential of Voter Registration Through Public Assistance Agencies," Demos, December 2018, https://www.demos.org/research/toward-more-representative-electorate.

2. Heather K. Gerken, "Make It Easy: The Case for Automatic Registration," *Democracy*, no. 28 (Spring 2013), https://democracyjournal.org/magazine/28/make-it-easy-the-case-for-automatic-registration.

3. Medicaid also provides health care to the blind, the infirm, and a certain population of the elderly.

4. Ron Shinkman, "Effect of Rural Hospital Closures Lingers in Communities," FierceHealthcare, April 12, 2014, https://www.fiercehealthcare.com/finance/effect-rural-hospital-closures-lingers-communities.

5. Their findings control for type of election year (municipal, presidential, midterm) as well as turnout activities, and serve as a baseline to understand what we can expect from a voter registration drive focusing on underrepresented groups.

6. Josh Israel, "Georgia Secretary of State Laments That Democrats Are Registering Minority Voters," *ThinkProgress*, September 11, 2014, https://thinkprogress.org/georgia-secretary-of-state-laments-that-democrats-are-registering-minority-voters-8b9d677c6b32/.

7. Skyler Swisher, "Hillary Clinton Chides Gov. Ron DeSantis for Tweet Calling Voting a 'Privilege,'" *South Florida Sun Sentinel*, January 17, 2020, https://www.sun-sentinel.com/news/politics/fl-ne-desantis-voting-privilege-20200117-udndv6mb2vhdlmwpbhslgeei7y-story.html.

8. Christopher Uggen, Ryan Larson, and Sarah Shannon, *6 Million Lost Voters: State-Level Estimates of Felony Disenfranchisement, 2016*, The Sentencing Project, October 2016, 15, table 3, https://www.sentencingproject.org/wp-content/uploads/2016/10/6-Million-Lost-Voters.pdf#page=17.

9. Angela Caputo, "A Southern Strategy, Redux," *APM Reports*, November 1, 2018, https://www.apmreports.org/story/2018/11/01/former-confederate-states-purge-felons-from-voting-lists.

10. Russ Bynum, "Georgia Stops Voting by Felons Using Broadest Reading of Law," Associated Press, May 28, 2019, https://apnews.com/44f3c3bd33dd4877b7a27a1592aed0d4.

11. Daniel Rivero, "Everything You Need to Know About Florida's Amendment 4 Lawsuit," WGCU Public Media, October 7, 2019, https://news.wgcu.org/post/everything-you-need-know-about-floridas-amendment-4-lawsuit.

12. "Florida Amendment 4," CNN Politics, December 21, 2018, https://www.cnn.com/election/2018/results/florida/ballot-measures/1.

13. Jeffrey D. Morenoff and David J. Harding, "Incarceration, Prisoner Reentry, and Communities," *Annual Review of Sociology* 40 (July 2014): 411–29, https://www.ncbi.nlm.nih.gov/pmc/articles/PMC4231529.

14. "Ensure Every American Can Vote: Vote Suppression: Voter Purges," Brennan Center for Justice, https://www.brennancenter.org/issues/ensure-every-american-can-vote/vote-suppression/voter-purges.

15. *NASS Report: Maintenance of State Voter Registration Lists: A Review of Relevant Policies and Procedures*, National Association of Secretaries of State, 2009, updated December 2017, https://www.nass.org/sites/default/files/reports/nass-report-voter-reg-maintenance-final-dec17.pdf.

16. Rachel Frazin, "Judge Restores Kentucky 'Inactive' Voters to Voter Rolls," *The Hill*, October 15, 2019, https://thehill.com/homenews/state-watch/465868-judge-restores-kentucky-inactive-voters-to-voter-rolls.

CHAPTER 3

1. Jon Ward, "How a Criminal Investigation in Georgia Set an Ominous Tone for African-American Voters," *Yahoo! News*, August 6, 2019, https://news.yahoo.com/how-a-criminal-investigation-in-georgia-set-a-dark-tone-for-african-american-voters-090000532.html.

2. Ibid.

3. Tom Kertscher, "Mark Pocan: 'More People Are Struck by Lightning Than Commit In-Person Voter Fraud' by Impersonation (True)," PolitiFact Wisconsin, April 7, 2016, https://www.politifact.com/wisconsin/statements/2016/apr/07/mark-pocan/which-happens-more-people-struck-lightning-or-peop.

4. Justin Levitt, "A Comprehensive Investigation of Voter Impersonation Finds 31 Credible Incidents out of One Billion Ballots Cast," *Washington Post*, August 6, 2014, https://www.washingtonpost.com/news/wonk/wp/2014/08/06/a-comprehensive-investigation-of-voter-impersonation-finds-31-credible-incidents-out-of-one-billion-ballots-cast.

5. Douglas Keith, Myrna Pérez, and Christopher Famighetti, *Noncitizen Voting: The Missing Millions*, Brennan Center for Justice, May 5, 2017, https://www.brennancenter.org/our-work/research-reports/noncitizen-voting-missing-millions; Justin Levitt, *The Truth About Voter Fraud*, Brennan Center for Justice, November 9, 2007, https://www.brennancenter.org/our-work/research-reports/truth-about-voter-fraud.

6. Wendy Underhill, "Voter Identification Requirements: Voter ID Laws," National Conference of State Legislatures (NCSL), February 24, 2020, http://www.ncsl.org/research/elections-and-campaigns/voter-id.aspx.

7. "History of Voter ID," NCSL, May 31, 2017, https://www.ncsl.org/research/elections-and-campaigns/voter-id-history.aspx.

8. As of 2019, eleven states have strict photo identification laws (Georgia, Indiana, Iowa, Kansas, Mississippi, Tennessee, Virginia, Wisconsin, Arizona, North Dakota, and Ohio). Both Pennsylvania and North Carolina have also passed strict ID laws; however, both laws have been struck down by the courts. See Underhill, "Voter Identification Requirements," table 1, http://www.ncsl.org/research/elections-and-campaigns/voter-id.aspx#Table%201. Note that Iowa has also adopted a voter ID law that has been challenged in court as a restrictive ID law. The National Conference of State Legislatures (NCSL) does not include Iowa on its list of strict ID states; however, the author does, given the timing and similarity to other strict ID laws. See Anna Spoerre, "Judge Upholds ID Requirement at Polls but

Strikes Down Other Parts of 2017 Iowa Voting Reform Law," *Des Moines Register*, October 1, 2019, https://www.desmoinesregister.com/story/news /crime-and-courts/2019/10/01/judge-rules-portions-2017-voter-reform -law-unconstitution/3829470002.

9. Theron "Scarlet Raven" Thompson, "ND Senate: Heitkamp Wins! Native Vote Mattered, Again!," *Daily Kos*, November 7, 2012, https://www .dailykos.com/stories/2012/11/7/1158318/-Heitkamp-Wins-Native-Vote -Counted.

10. Michael G. DeCrescenzo and Kenneth R. Mayer, "Voter Identification and Nonvoting in Wisconsin—Evidence from the 2016 Election," *Election Law Journal: Rules, Politics, and Policy* 18, no. 4 (December 2019): 342–59, https://www.liebertpub.com/doi/full/10.1089/elj.2018.0536.

11. Cameron Smith, "Voter ID Tied to Lower Wisconsin Turnout; Students, People of Color, Elderly Most Affected," *Milwaukee Journal Sentinel*, September 30, 2018, https://www.jsonline.com/story/opinion/contributors /2018/09/30/voter-id-tied-lower-wisconsin-turnout/1480862002.

12. One Wisconsin Institute, Inc. v. Thomsen, 198 F. Supp. 3d 896 (2016).

13. Since 2014, Alabama and Arkansas have both imposed new photo ID requirements; however, because of alternatives that remain available to voters, NCSL does not categorize these states as having strict photo voter ID.

14. *Elections: Issues Related to State Voter Identification Laws*, United States Government Accountability Office, September 2014, https://www.gao.gov /assets/670/665966.pdf.

15. Mark Niesse and Nick Thieme, "Precinct Closures Harm Voter Turnout in Georgia, AJC Analysis Finds," *Atlanta Journal-Constitution*, December 13, 2019, https://www.ajc.com/news/state--regional-govt--politics/precinct-closures -harm-voter-turnout-georgia-ajc-analysis-finds/11sVcLyQCHuQRC8qtZ6lYP.

16. Matt Vasilogambros, "How Voters with Disabilities Are Blocked from the Ballot Box," *Pew Stateline*, February 1, 2018, https://www.pewtrusts .org/en/research-and-analysis/blogs/stateline/2018/02/01/how-voters-with -disabilities-are-blocked-from-the-ballot-box.

17. "Religious Entities Under the Americans with Disabilities Act," ADA National Network, 2018, https://adata.org/factsheet/religious-entities -under-americans-disabilities-act.

18. "Voting Outside the Polling Place: Absentee, All-Mail and Other Voting at Home Options," NCSL, February 20, 2020, http://www.ncsl.org/research /elections-and-campaigns/absentee-and-early-voting.aspx.

19. Alexander Gonzalez, "Report: Missing Absentee Ballots in South Florida Affect Young People, Democrats," WLRN, November 25, 2018, https:// www.wlrn.org/post/report-missing-absentee-ballots-south-florida-affect -young-people-democrats#stream/0.

20. Tony Doris, "Did Missing South Florida Absentee Ballots Turn the Tide?," *Palm Beach Post*, November 10, 2018, https://www.palmbeachpost.com /news/20181110/did-missing-south-florida-absentee-ballots-turn-tide.

21. Actual affiants in Fair Fight Action, Inc. et al. v. Raffensperger, https:// fairfight.com/wp-content/uploads/2019/07/2019.02.19-Amended-Complaint -File-Stamped.pdf.

22. Tia Mitchell and Mark Niesse, "Mystery of 4,700 Missing DeKalb Ballot Requests Gets State Review," *Atlanta Journal-Constitution*, March 22, 2019, https://www.ajc.com/news/local-govt--politics/mystery-700-missing-dekalb-ballot-requests-gets-state-review/v2bSkLQrcayxPy803QGZoL.

23. "Cutting Early Voting Is Voter Suppression," ACLU, https://www.aclu.org/issues/voting-rights/cutting-early-voting-voter-suppression.

24. Michael Wines, "The Student Vote Is Surging. So Are Efforts to Suppress It," *New York Times*, October 24, 2019, https://www.nytimes.com/2019/10/24/us/voting-college-suppression.html.

25. Rashawn Ray and Mark Whitlock, "Setting the Record Straight on Black Voter Turnout," Brookings Institution, September 12, 2019, https://www.brookings.edu/blog/up-front/2019/09/12/setting-the-record-straight-on-black-voter-turnout/.

26. Jordan Misra, "Voter Turnout Rates Among All Voting Age and Major Racial and Ethnic Groups Were Higher Than in 2014," U.S. Census Bureau, April 23, 2019, https://www.census.gov/library/stories/2019/04/behind-2018-united-states-midterm-election-turnout.html?utm_campaign=20190423msacos1ccstors&utm_medium=email&utm_source=govdelivery.

CHAPTER 4

1. Ben Nadler, "Voting Rights Become a Flashpoint in Georgia Governor's Race," Associated Press, October 9, 2018, https://apnews.com/fb011f39af3b40518b572c8cce6e906c.

2. "Arrest Rates Higher for Central Ga. Blacks, USA Today Finds," *Jackson Sun*, November 19, 2014, https://www.jacksonsun.com/story/news/local/2014/11/18/central-georgia-arrest-rates/19245875.

3. Michael King, "Why Stacey Abrams Placed an Early Vote," 11Alive, October 22, 2018, https://www.11alive.com/article/news/politics/elections/why-stacey-abrams-placed-an-early-vote/85-606794704.

4. "Voting Outside the Polling Place: Absentee, All-Mail and Other Voting at Home Options," NCSL, http://www.ncsl.org/research/elections-and-campaigns/absentee-and-early-voting.aspx.

5. Tomislav Fotak, Miroslav Bača, and Petra Koruga, "Handwritten Signature Identification Using Basic Concepts of Graph Theory," *WSEAS Transactions on Signal Processing* 7, no. 4 (October 2011): 145–57.

6. Moshe Kam, Kishore Gummadidala, Gabriel Fielding, and Robert Conn, "Signature Authentication by Forensic Document Examiners," *Journal of Forensic Sciences* 46, no. 4 (August 2001): 884–88.

7. *Election Administration and Voting Survey: 2018 Comprehensive Report: A Report to the 116th Congress*, U.S. Election Assistance Commission, June 2019, https://www.eac.gov/sites/default/files/eac_assets/1/6/2018_EAVS_Report.pdf.

8. Voto Latino Incorporated et al. v. Katie Hobbs, complaint for declaratory and injunctive relief, 2019.

9. In March 2020, the state of Georgia reached a settlement regarding rules for curing absentee ballots. While the settlement is legally binding, the state has

not adopted laws to reflect these new rules. Mark Niesse, "Lawsuit Settled, Giving Georgia Voters Time to Fix Rejected Ballots," *Atlanta Journal-Constitution*, March 7, 2020, https://www.ajc.com/news/state—regional-govt—politics/lawsuit-settled-giving-georgia-voters-time-fix-rejected-ballots/oJcZ4eCXf8J197AEdGfsSM/.

10. P. R. Lockhart, "The Lawsuit Challenging Georgia's Entire Elections System, Explained," *Vox*, May 30, 2019, https://www.vox.com/policy-and-politics/2018/11/30/18118264/georgia-election-lawsuit-voter-suppression-abrams-kemp-race.

11. M. Keith Chen, Kareem Haggag, Devin G. Pope, and Ryne Rohla, "Racial Disparities in Voting Wait Times: Evidence from Smartphone Data," NBER working paper no. 26487, November 14, 2019, https://faculty.chicagobooth.edu/devin.pope/assets/files/Racial_Disparities_in_Voting_Wait_Times.pdf.

12. Georgia Muslim Voter Project v. Brian Kemp, 918 F.3d 1262 (11th Cir. 2019).

CHAPTER 5

1. Amy Gardner, "How a Large-Scale Effort to Register Black Voters Led to a Crackdown in Tennessee," *Washington Post*, May 24, 2019, https://www.washingtonpost.com/politics/how-a-large-scale-effort-to-register-black-voters-led-to-a-crackdown-in-tennessee/2019/05/24/9f6cee1e-7284-11e9-8be0-ca575670e91c_story.html.

2. Maya T. Prabhu, "AJC Poll: Strong Support for Roe; Opinion Closer on 'Heartbeat Bill,'" *Atlanta Journal-Constitution*, April 11, 2019, https://www.ajc.com/news/state--regional-govt--politics/ajc-poll-strong-support-for-roe-opinion-closer-heartbeat-bill/jWr5L1S5kooo7akOCkfzGM.

3. Abby Rapoport, "True the Vote's True Agenda," *American Prospect*, October 15, 2012, https://prospect.org/power/true-vote-s-true-agenda.

4. Richard L. Hasen, "Vote Suppressors Unleashed," *Slate*, November 27, 2017, https://slate.com/news-and-politics/2017/11/donald-trump-will-super charge-voter-suppression-if-the-rnc-consent-decree-falls.html.

5. For more information on the link between business and voting rights, see Scholars Strategy Network, "Securing Fair Elections: Challenges to Voting in the United States and Georgia," https://scholars.org/fairelections.

6. "States with Initiative or Referendum," Ballotpedia, accessed January 28, 2020, https://ballotpedia.org/States_with_initiative_or_referendum.

7. "Ballot Measures Toolkit," Bolder Advocacy, https://www.bolderadvocacy.org/resource-library/tools-for-effective-advocacy/toolkits/ballot-measures-toolkit.

CHAPTER 6

1. *National Intimate Partner and Sexual Violence Survey: 2010 Summary Report*, National Center for Injury Prevention and Control, Division of Violence Prevention, Centers for Disease Control and Prevention, November 2011, https://www.cdc.gov/violenceprevention/pdf/nisvs_report2010-a.pdf.

2. Jacquelyn C. Campbell, Daniel Webster, Jane Koziol-McLain, et al., "Risk Factors for Femicide in Abusive Relationships: Results from a Multisite Case Control Study," *American Journal of Public Health* 93, no. 7 (July 2003): 1089–97, https://www.ncbi.nlm.nih.gov/pmc/articles/PMC1447915/.

3. Ibid., 1092.

CHAPTER 7

1. Diana Elliott, Robert Santos, Steven Martin, and Charmaine Runes, "Assessing Miscounts in the 2020 Census," Urban Institute, June 4, 2019, https://www.urban.org/research/publication/assessing-miscounts-2020-census.

2. Antonio Flores, Mark Hugo Lopez, and Jens Manuel Krogstad, "U.S. Hispanic Population Reached New High in 2018, but Growth Has Slowed," Pew Research Center, July 8, 2019, https://www.pewresearch.org/fact-tank /2019/07/08/u-s-hispanic-population-reached-new-high-in-2018-but-growth -has-slowed.

3. Michael Wines, "A Census Whodunit: Why Was the Citizenship Question Added?," *New York Times*, November 30, 2019, updated December 2, 2019, https://www.nytimes.com/2019/11/30/us/census-citizenship-question -hofeller.html.

4. Thomas Hofeller, "The Use of Citizen Voting Age Population in Redistricting," unpublished report, 2015, https://www.documentcloud.org/documents /6077735-May-30-2019-Exhibit.html#document/p55/a504021.

5. "QuickFacts: California," U.S. Census Bureau, https://www.census.gov/quick facts/CA.

6. Ari Shapiro and Alex Padilla, "California Sues Trump Administration over Citizenship Question on 2020 Census," *All Things Considered*, NPR, March 27, 2018, https://www.npr.org/2018/03/27/597390619/california -sues-trump-administration-over-citizenship-question-on-2020-census.

7. "2020 Decennial Census," U.S. Government Accountability Office, https:// www.gao.gov/highrisk/2020_decennial_census/why_did_study.

8. "FY20: Fund the 2020 Census Immediately," Insights Association, October 17, 2019, https://www.insightsassociation.org/sites/default/files/misc _files/ia_issue_paper_census_funding_11-25-19.pdf.

9. *Eighth Broadband Progress Report*, Federal Communications Commission, August 21, 2012, https://www.fcc.gov/reports-research/reports/broadband -progress-reports/eighth-broadband-progress-report.

10. Hansi Lo Wang, "On Census, Facebook and Instagram to Ban Disinformation and False Ads," NPR, December 19, 2019, https://www.npr .org/2019/12/19/789609572/on-census-facebook-and-instagram-to-ban -disinformation-and-false-ads.

11. William S. Custer, "The Economic Impact of Medicaid Expansion in Georgia," Healthcare Georgia Foundation, February 12, 2013, https://www .issuelab.org/resources/14733/14733.pdf.

12. Simon Jackman, "Assessing the Current North Carolina Congressional Districting Plan," Rose Institute, March 1, 2017, http://roseinstitute.org /wp-content/uploads/2016/05/Expert-Report-of-Simon-Jackman.pdf.

13. Hansi Lo Wang and Kumari Devarajan, "'Your Body Being Used': Where Prisoners Who Can't Vote Fill Voting Districts," *Code Switch*, NPR, December 31, 2019, https://www.npr.org/sections/codeswitch/2019/12/31 /761932806/your-body-being-used-where-prisoners-who-can-t-vote-fill -voting-districts.
14. Hofeller, "The Use of Citizen Voting Age Population in Redistricting."
15. Adam Eichen, "The Case Against the Electoral College Is Stronger Than Ever," *New Republic*, August 2, 2019, https://newrepublic.com/article /154598/case-electoral-college-stronger-ever.
16. Wilfred Codrington III, "The Electoral College's Racist Origins," *Atlantic*, November 17, 2019, https://www.theatlantic.com/ideas/archive/2019/11 /electoral-college-racist-origins/601918.
17. Joshua Spivak, "The Electoral College Is a Failure. The Founding Fathers Would Probably Agree," *Washington Post*, April 7, 2019, https://www .washingtonpost.com/opinions/the-electoral-college-is-a-failure-the -founding-fathers-would-probably-agree/2019/04/07/813b706c-56fc-11e9 -8ef3-fbd41a2ce4d5_story.html.

CHAPTER 8

1. "Rising American Electorate" was coined by the Voter Participation Center, and "New American Majority" was popularized by Steve Phillips in his book, *Brown Is the New White: How the Demographic Revolution Has Created a New American Majority* (New York: The New Press, 2018).
2. Page Gardner, "What about the Marriage Gap?," *Politico*, February 4, 2011, https://www.politico.com/story/2011/02/what-about-the-marriage-gap -048788.
3. "2. Changing Composition of the Electorate and Partisan Coalitions," *Wide Gender Gap, Growing Educational Divide in Voters' Party Identification*, Pew Research Center, March 20, 2018, https://www.people-press.org/2018 /03/20/changing-composition-of-the-electorate-and-partisan-coalitions.
4. Ibid.
5. Gardner, "What About the Marriage Gap?"
6. Simon Jackman and Bradley Spahn, "Unlisted in America," Stanford University, August 20, 2015, http://images.politico.com/global/2015/08/20 /jackman_unlisted.pdf.
7. Rafael Bernal, "Hispanic Dems 'Disappointed' with Party's Latino Outreach," *The Hill*, September 24, 2016, https://thehill.com/latino/297515 -hispanic-dems-disappointed-with-partys-latino-outreach.
8. Tung Thanh Nguyen and Viet Thanh Nguyen, "Democrats Ignore Asian American and Pacific Islander Voters at Their Peril," *The Hill*, September 7, 2019, https://thehill.com/opinion/campaign/460357-democrats-ignore-asian -american-and-pacific-islander-voters-at-their-peril.
9. "GOP Makes Big Gains Among White Voters," Pew Research Center, July 22, 2011, https://www.pewresearch.org/wp-content/uploads/sites/4/legacy-pdf /7-22-11-Party-ID-commentary.pdf.
10. Ibid.

CHAPTER 9

1. Not their real names.
2. For example, U.S. senator Sherrod Brown is a self-described progressive populist: John Nichols, "Sherrod Brown Talks About Populism, Work, Health Care, War . . . and 2020," *The Nation*, March 6, 2019, https://www.thenation.com/article/archive/sherrod-brown-2020-populist-progressive.
3. Tamar Hallerman, "A First Trump-Era Bill in Georgia Could Slap Tax on Cash Sent to Foreign Homes," *Political Insider* (blog), *Atlanta Journal-Constitution*, November 15, 2016, https://www.ajc.com/blog/politics/first-trump-era-bill-georgia-could-slap-tax-cash-sent-foreign-homes/ynZ7qIB8JXl8CJ3MB45IVN.
4. Paul Armstrong, "Nigel Farage: Arch-Eurosceptic and Brexit 'Puppet Master,'" CNN, July 15, 2016, https://www.cnn.com/2016/06/24/europe/eu-referendum-nigel-farage/index.html.
5. Jordan Kyle and Limor Gultchin, "Populists in Power Around the World," Tony Blair Institute for Global Change, November 7, 2018, http://institute.global/insight/renewing-centre/populists-power-around-world.
6. "QuickFacts: United States," U.S. Census Bureau, https://www.census.gov/quickfacts/fact/table/US/INC110218.
7. Kate Brannen, "Trump's White, Male Team Is a Bad Look for America and Bad for National Security, Too," *USA Today*, January 13, 2020, https://www.usatoday.com/story/opinion/2020/01/13/women-minorities-missing-from-trump-national-security-team-column/4447800002.
8. "Diversity Statistics, Full-Time Permanent Workforce," State Department Human Resources, American Foreign Service Association, June 30, 2019, http://www.afsa.org/sites/default/files/0619_diversity_data_for_web.pdf.

Acknowledgments

Since November 2018, I have been privileged to found three extraordinary organizations that work tirelessly to ensure that the work of enlarging our democracy continues. *Our Time Is Now* reflects how I think of our obligations in the time to come: do the work—regardless of the title—and build for the now and tomorrow. Because of these fantastic people, I have had a chance to practice what I hope we will accomplish.

At the pinnacle of our efforts is Lauren Groh-Wargo, a dynamic leader, fearless warrior, and my self-described anger translator. She serves as CEO of Fair Fight Action, as chief adviser to Fair Fight PAC, and as conductor of all the trains that zip around our universe. Lauren sees the world in all its parts and conducts change like a maestro, hearing what can be. I can imagine no dearer a friend or more potent an ally.

The Fair Fight teams are composed of an exemplary cohort of women and men who do not wait for a better day. Instead, they create it with ingenuity, a spirit of camaraderie, and a love of humanity that never fail to humble me. And to our extraordinary attorneys and colleagues-in-arms, Allegra Lawrence-Hardy and Dara Lindenbaum, whose creative answers to the challenges we dish up daily remind me of the finest attributes of the law. They seek a renewal of America's drive to be more, and they will hold the powerful accountable until it is done.

Fair Count has built a company of dedicated, fierce, and untiring innovators determined to bring everyone to the table of progress. Together, this team of smart, kind, faithful stewards of an accurate census and long-term civic engagement are defeating the worst instincts of some of our nation's putative leaders. They have devised stratagems that would make Harriet Tubman proud, all in the service of those too often treated as invisible. As they travel the country to tell America's story of diversity, I am honored to be in their company.

The Southern Economic Advancement Project has fulfilled one of my most ardent goals: to translate progressive policy into Southern. It has come together to pursue the righteous initiative of equity and justice for those who share our region but not our national resources. It bridges the gaps between urgency and action, filling in the gaps where it can. SEAP exists to bridge the South between what is and what must be.

Together, this constellation of organizations executes on the best intentions of democracy: we pursue voting to hire leaders, we fight for the census to ensure a fair share of economic access and political power, and we develop policy to make it real.

But the stories in these pages come from others who have long been in this fight with me: Well done to Nse Ufot and Raphael Warnock, who took over the reins of the New Georgia Project and reshaped it for such a time as this. To the donors and advisers who have poured into me and this democracy project for over the past decade, thank you for the investment of time and treasure to bring more to those who need it. To the labor leaders who restore America daily and stand with me at every turn, I am in your debt.

When writing a book that spans time and topics and tries to see around corners, I learned to lean even harder on those whose minds cause me to marvel every time I see them in action. Thank you to Will Dobson, my old and true friend, for showing me a broader world before I knew to look, and for helping me find the words to chart a path forward. I am forever in your debt and in your corner.

Chelsey Hall holds the title of adviser, and she lives her role in full. From reading pages as we jet off to new locations to offering honest critique when a kind lie would be easier, I am a better writer and person for having you by my side.

This book would not exist without the nudging, thoughtful engagement of my agent Linda Loewenthal, who helped bring its thesis into focus. Thank you to my team at Holt, especially the lightning speed and insights of my editor, Serena Jones, and the production magic of Madeline Jones. But no one deserves more credit for *Our Time Is Now* actually being on the pages than Libby Burton, my editor, guide, and friend. You have the patience of Job, wordsmithing of a sorcerer, and the reading speed of a savant. Thank you for never believing my deadlines and always believing in the work.

In the final stretch of writing, I leaned on my family, as I know I can. I offer particular thanks to my sister, Leslie Abrams Gardner, who took time off from meting out justice to pore over my words and make them smarter. I can never be sufficiently grateful. And, again, to my sister Jeanine, I owe you much for how you helped me find ways to bring heavy topics to their most accessible place.

I come from incredible parents, Carolyn and Robert Abrams, and their lessons have shaped the person I am. I am grateful for their fortitude, emboldened by their example and heartened by their persistence to shape a future worthy of us all. And to my siblings, Andrea, Leslie, Richard, Walter, and Jeanine, for the ways you each live lives of grace, redemption and service: thank you.

Index